Regionalism in Global Trade

For my wife Vasanti,
and to a beautiful life lived with her.

Regionalism in Global Trade

Dilip K. Das

Edward Elgar
Cheltenham, UK • Northampton, MA, USA

Published by
Edward Elgar Publishing Limited
Glensanda House
Montpellier Parade
Cheltenham
Glos GL50 1UA
UK

Edward Elgar Publishing, Inc.
136 West Street
Suite 202
Northampton
Massachusetts 01060
USA

A catalogue record for this book
is available from the British Library

Library of Congress Cataloguing in Publication Data

Das, Dilip K., 1945-
    Regionalism in global trade / Dilip K. Das.
        p. cm.
    Includes bibliographical references.
    ISBN 1-84376-817-8
        1. Trade blocs. 2. Regionalism. 3. Free trade. 4. International trade. 5.
Globalization–Economic aspects. I. Title.

    HF1418.7.D37 2004
    382'.9–dc22

                                                                2004048267

Printed and bound in Great Britain by MPG Books Ltd, Bodmin, Cornwall

Contents

Being and non-being create each other.
Difficult and easy support each other.
Long and short define each other.
High and low depend on each other.

Therefore the Master
acts without doing anything;
and teaches without saying anything.
Things arise and she lets them come;
things disappear and she lets them go.
She has but doesn't possess,
acts but doesn't expect.
When her work is done, she forgets it.
That is why it lasts forever.

from *Tao Te Ching*

Abbreviations

AA	Agreement on Agriculture
AC	Andean Community
ACP	African, Caribbean and Pacific
ACU	Asian currency unit
AEMU	African Economic and Monetary Union
AG	Andean Group
AD	anti-dumping
ADMs	anti-dumping measures
AFTA	ASEAN Free-trade area
ANZCERIA	Australia–New Zealand Closer Economic Relations Trade Agreement
APEC	Asia Pacific Economic Co-operation
APT	ASEAN-Plus-Three
APTA	ASEAN Preferential Trading Arrangement
ARFA	Asian Regional Financial Arrangement
ASEAN	Association of South East Asian Nations
ATC	Agreement on Textiles and Clothing
BIT	bilateral investment treaty
CARIBCAN	Caribbean–Canada Trade Agreement
CARICOM	Caribbean Community and Common Market
CACM	Central American Common Market
CATIFTA	Caribbean Free Trade Association
CBI	Caribbean Basin Initiative
CDB	Caribbean Development Bank
CEAO	Communauté Economique de l'Afrique Occidentale
CEEC	Central and East European Countries
CEFTA	Central European Free Trade Area
CEPT	common effective preferential tariff
CEP	Closer Economic Partnership
CER	Closer Economic Relations
CET	common external trade
CETs	common external tariffs
CD	countervailing
CGE	computable general equilibrium
COMESA	Common Market for Eastern and Southern Africa

CPs	contracting parties
CPA	Cotonou Partnership Agreement
CU	customs union
CUSFTA	Canada–United States Free Trade Area
EACM	East African Common Market
ECOWAS	Economic Community of West African States
ECSC	European Coal and Steel Community
EAC	East African Cooperation
EAVG	East Asia Vision Group
EAFTA	East Asia Free-trade area
EEA	European Economic Area
EEC	European Economic Community
EIA	economic integration agreement
EFTA	European Free-Trade Area
EMEAP	Executives' Meeting of East-Asia-Pacific Central Banks
EMPA	Euro-Mediterranean Partnership Agreement
EMS	European Monetary System
EMU	Economic and Monetary Union
EP	export promotion
ERIM	Exchange Rate and Intervention Mechanism
EU	European Union
FDI	foreign direct investment
FSU	former Soviet Union
FTAA	Free Trade Area of the Americas
ETDES	Electronic Trade Documentation Exchange System
GATS	General Agreement on Trade in Services
GATT	General Agreement on Tariffs and Trade
GCC	Gulf Co-operation Council
GDP	gross domestic product
GNP	gross national product
GSP	Generalized System of Preferences
HKMA	Hong Kong Monetary Authority
IAP	individual action plan
ICSID	International Center for Settlement of Investment Disputes
ICT	information communications technology
ICOR	incremental capital output ration
IOR	Indian Ocean rim or region
IORG	Indian Ocean Rim Grouping
IOS	International Organization for Standardization
ITO	International Trade Organization
ITU	International Telecommunications Union
IS	import-substitution

ISI	import-substituting industrialization
JSEPA	Japan–Singapore Economic Partnership Agreement
JSG	Joint Study Group
LAC	Latin American and Caribbean
LDC	least developed country
LAFTA	Latin American Free Trade Area
LAIA	Latin American Integration Agreement
MERCOSUR	Mercado Comun del Sur
MFA	Multifibre Agreement
MFN	most-favored-nation
MRAs	mutual recognition agreements
MTNs	multilateral trade negotiations
NIEs	newly industrialized economies
NIAEs	newly industrialized Asian economies
NTB	non-tariff barrier
NAFTA	North American Free-trade area
OAU	Organization of African Unity
OECD	Organization for Economic Co-operation and Development
OLS	ordinary least square
OPTAD	Organization for Pacific Trade and Development
PAFTA	Pacific Free-Trade Area
PBF	Pacific Business Forum
PECC	Pacific Economic Co-operation Conference
PPP	purchasing power parity
PTA	preferential trade agreement
QRs	quantitative restrictions
R&D	research and development
RIAs	regional integration agreements
ROO	rules of origin
RTA	regional trade agreement
SAARC	South Asian Association for Regional Co-operation
SACU	South African Customs Union
SADC	Southern African Development Community
SAPTA	SMRC Preferential Trade Area
SDT	special and differential treatment
SEACEN	South East Asian Central Banks
SIDS	small island developing state
SMP	Single Market Program
SOEs	state-owned enterprises
SPS	sanitary and phytosanitary
TBT	technical barriers to trade
TFP	total factor productivity

TNCs	transnational corporations
TRIPS	Trade Related Aspects of Intellectual Property Rights
UDEAC	Union Douanière et Économique de l'Afrique Centrale
UEMOA	Union Économique et Monétaire Ouest Africaine
UN	United Nations
UNCTAD	United Nations Conference on Trade and Development
USTR	United States Trade Representative
VER	voluntary export restraint
WAEMU	West African Economic and Monetary Union
WCO	World Customs Organization
WTO	World Trade Organization

Preface

This book addresses one of the most important aspects of international trade, namely, regional trade and regional integration agreements (RIAs). They have become an integral and enduring aspect of the multilateral trading regime. RIAs are groupings of countries formed with the objective of reducing barriers to trade between member countries. They have long historical antecedents. They were also a part of the process of nation building. As noted in Chapter 1, the *Zollverein* in nineteenth-century Germany was responsible for creating the modern German state. RIAs were also a part of the colonial trading arrangements. Over the post-war period the European Economic Community (EEC), presently the European Union (EU), led developments in this area. Over the last decade regional integration became the focus of intense global interest, debate and scrutiny.

To a much greater extent than is often realized and acknowledged, regional and multilateral integration initiatives are complements rather than alternatives in the pursuit of more open global trade. The objective of this book is to evaluate the pattern and gauge the progress of regional integration in the global economy over the post-war, and more specifically during the contemporary, periods. By contemporary period I imply the decade of the 1990s and the early 2000s. Although the essential focus of this book is on trade, it also delves into macroeconomic and investment related issues in regional co-operation and integration.

Although a derogation of the World Trade Organization (WTO) discipline, regional trade and integration is an intellectually challenging phenomenon. RIAs seem to arouse more debate and passion than do most other issues in international economic policy. During the 1990s, this issue led to unseemly spats among academics. The height was when a noted researcher was publicly accused of CIA connections. With virtually all the 146 members of the WTO partners in at least one RIA, and several part of two or more, RIAs have become by far the most important exception to the most-favored-nation (MFN) principle. It is intuitive to assume that with a large number of RIAs of different kinds in force, a great deal of the global trade must be influenced, if not governed, by them. Quantifying trade under various preferential trade agreements is not easy. It faces methodological problems. However, it is believed that at present 'more than half of the world trade' is intra-RIA (World Trade Organization, 2002c).

The RIAs in trade in goods fall under three WTO categories, albeit they are generally treated as falling under the same rubric. The three categories are (1) the Article XXIV arrangements, (2) the Enabling Clause arrangements limited to developing countries and permitting partial preferences under the Generalized System of Preferences (GSP) and (3) the arrangements permitted by the WTO through a grant of an exception of Article I. What is more, regional integration that covers trade in service is governed by Article V of the General Agreement on Trade in Services (GATS). After an RIA is launched, the WTO has to be notified of its date of launch, membership details, legal agreement, coverage and the category under which it has been launched. Since the birth of the WTO in January 1995, on an average 15 RIAs have been notified every year. Compared to this, an average of three RIAs were notified to the GATT annually during its entire lifetime spanning 1948 to 1994. To be sure, the increase in notification reflects in part an increase in the membership of the WTO, and in part, new notification obligations.

RIAs presently have widespread existence in the global economy. As their number multiplies, networks of overlapping agreements may generate intricate webs of discriminatory treatment, which are likely to lead to complex and incoherent regulatory structures for the conduct of a growing share of world trade. Some economists believe that this proliferation of RIAs should be welcomed, while others are less sanguine and emphasize the importance and primacy of multilateral trade liberalization. The latter group warns against the discrimination and fragmentation of the global economy that can accompany the spread of RIAs. References to the EEC and EU have been made repeatedly in this book. The reason is that it is the oldest RIA of the contemporary period, lasting for almost half a century. Progress made by the EEC/EU has a good deal of educational value for the other RIAs.

Interestingly, the present trend of regionalization of the global trading system is progressing in the background of a strong trend toward globalization. Thus, both centripetal and centrifugal forces are working on regional economies simultaneously. There are some who argue that RIAs divert attention from the multilateral efforts to liberalize global trade and expend scarce negotiating resources. Others, however, assert that the negotiating realities require an admixture of regional and multilateral initiatives.

In the early 2000s, several pluri-dimensional and inter-linked issues were the subjects of raging debates among the members of the WTO. Some of them had legal overtones, while other were institutional issues. Some age-old economic chestnuts were also the focus of attention of the members. For instance, Article XXIV of the GATT-1994 was one such issue. Article XXIV has been decried as an antithesis of the spirit of the GATT–WTO system, because it allows members of a trade bloc to discriminate against the non-members. However, the authors of Article XXIV, in their pragmatic desire to accommodate RIAs, were cautious in guarding the interests of the non-RIA members. They also attempted to ensure that RIAs were compatible with a rule-based and progressively more open world trading system. The conventional wisdom in this regard is that Article XXIV ensures that trade bloc formation ensures free trade. However, one view holds that in reality Article XXIV is partly responsible for the difficulties in further multilateral trade liberalization.

There is no presumption in this book that RIAs are benign and welfare enhancing. They can indeed be welfare enhancing, but only under certain conditions. In assessing the appropriate integrative strategy in regionalization for promoting economic growth, it is essential to look at how regionalism in the global economy developed to its current state and what are the most important trends and features during its contemporary phase of development. In this book, we examine *inter alia* the motivating factors and underlying dynamics of the progression towards closer regional and sub-regional cooperation and integration in the global economy. The objective of this book is to address the regionalization of world trade against a background of advancing global integration. In an interesting and scholarly manner, this book attempts to meet the needs of students as well as policy mandarins in this area. This book also attempts to make them understand how the dual forces of regionalism and globalism are impacting upon the world economy, particularly trade in goods and services.

Regional trade is a complex and diffused issue – albeit governed by simple principles – RIAs are even more so. This book covers several important areas germaine to the theme of regionalism in a globalizing world economy. It is divided into six chapters, which cover a large area of contemporary knowledge in regionalism vis-à-vis multilateralism, the RIAs and the recent developments in them. RIA-related economic issues like motivation, rationale and welfare implications are the focus of the second chapter. Regionalism as applied to trade in goods as well as in services is examined. The third chapter focuses on contemporary regionalism, which has been christened the 'new regionalism'. In this context, one can say that what is past is prologue. The characteristics of new regionalism, its impact, evolving landscape and constantly changing RIA kaleidoscope are closely examined. The RIAs and global trading system is the theme of the fourth chapter, along with the idiosyncrasies of Article XXIV of the GATT–WTO system. The post-Uruguay Round developments in regionalism are discussed and so is the progress in the Doha Round of multilateral trade negotiations. Two regional foci of the book are the Asia-Pacific region, the most dynamic regional of the global economy and the Western Hemisphere, where regionalism has had a long history – although the United States and Canada are recent converts. The last two chapters have been devoted to these two regional experiences. They provide a varied perspective on RIAs because their historic and economic features differ radically from each other.

During the 1990s, RIA-related issues grew in significance, both for students of international economics, and academic scholars on the one hand and policy mandarins on the other. In the foreseeable future, they are likely to gain momentum and grow more significant. The agreement for the Free Trade Area of the Americas (FTAA) was signed in 2001. With 34 members, it is potentially the largest free trade area (FTA) ever attempted. Negotiations for the FTAA are progressing rapidly; it is scheduled to come into force in late 2005. The Accession Treaty to include ten more countries in the European Union (EU) was signed in April 2003 and these ten economies are due to become the new members of the EU in May 2004. Save for Cyprus and Malta, these are all Central and East European Countries (CEEC) countries. These eight economies were satellite economies of the Soviet Union until its collapse in 1990–91. Bulgaria, Romania and Turkey, three candidates for future membership, are waiting on the sidelines. The Association of South East Asian Nations (ASEAN) is actively endeavoring to include China – which is fast emerging as a highly successful trading economy accounting for 4.7 percent of global trade in 2002 – and Japan and Korea to complete the ASEAN-Plus-Three grouping. Several 'New Age' initiatives, which entail bilateral free trade agreements, like the one between Japan and Korea, are also underway.

In this book we try to see whether regionalism has a rightful place in a rapidly globalizing world economy in the new century. We try to see what place RIAs have in the global trading system, what their welfare implications are and whether they adversely affect the global trading system.

A unique feature of the book is that it deals with regionalism in a nuanced manner, in the background of on-going globalization. The traditional treatment used to be to analyse regionalism *per se*. Second, it familiarizes the readers with the newest concepts and latest knowledge in this sub-discipline. Regionalism has become a fertile area of academic research. The results of these analyses and research projects need to be presented in a comprehensible manner for the student and policy-making communities.

The book is pitched at the level of masters' level students in International Economics, International Political Economy, Political Science, International Relations as well as MBA students. In business schools courses on 'environment of business' are taught, which would find the book useful. Senior level undergraduate students and researchers in the area of international trade and regionalism can also benefit from it. Decision makers in business and public policy community would find this book germaine to their work. Although analytical, this book is *not* rigorous and is not aimed at academic scholars in the area of international trade. It steers clear of complex modeling exercises, because a great many times they are inaccessible even to bright students.

A recent acknowledgement I read began with the following words: 'This book comes to publishing trailing clouds of the kindness of others.' These gracious sentiments represent what follows in these pages as well. My gratitude is due to my son, Siddharth, for providing efficacious research assistance, so very cheerfully. I thankfully acknowledge the generous assistance of L. Alan Winters, Professor of Economics, School of Social Sciences, University of Sussex; Anthony J. Venables, Yu Kuo-Hwa Professor of International Economics, London School of Economics, London, and Jeffrey A. Frankel, Professor of Economics, Harvard University, for either providing me with drafts of their current research work, or for giving me permission to cite from their work, or both. In particular, Alan kept in touch with me despite his frequent travels and overflowing schedule. He did not make me feel that my e-mail messages were nagging him. Throughout this endeavor my wife, Vasanti, remained a kind friend and wise counselor. She put up with my sixteen-hour long days with a smile and without complaining. I am grateful for her support.

Toronto   Dilip K. Das

September 2003

1. Globalism versus regionalism

1. GLOBALISM VERSUS REGIONALISM

The closing years of the twentieth century are notable for the expansion and deepening of globalization. It essentially refers to the on-going economic, financial, technological, social and political integration of countries around the globe. New technologies, steeply declining transport and communication costs and more liberal trading and financial regimes have led to increased trade volumes, larger investment flows, and creation of increasingly footloose production networks that ignore national boundaries. At this point in time some twenty-five developing economies have successfully joined in the global economic integration process. This new group of economies has been christened the emerging-market economies.[1] Historically, globalization is not known for unidirectional progress. Yet, barring the unforeseen, the contemporary wave of globalization is likely to continue and more countries will try and integrate with the global economy in the foreseeable future (Das, 2003a).

A three-way interaction between globalization, the supra-national institutions and various sub-groups of economies has created a new dynamics in the global economy. All the sub-groups of economies, developing, transition, emerging-market and industrial are feeling the pervasive effects of globalization. Second, these economies are also being affected by, and affecting, institutions like the Bretton Woods twins and the World Trade Organization (WTO).[2] On the one hand, evolution of these supra-national institutions is influencing the policy options in these country groups, and on the other, the ability of these country groups to have an impact on the supra-national institutions has been rising. This dynamic three-way interaction is having a discernible impact on the policy-making process at the national, regional and global levels.

There are several dimensions to the dynamics of the globalization process, including the integration of trade and financial transactions among countries. Powerful economic and political forces have accelerated the globalization of markets. Managed correctly, globalization can turn into a forceful public good. Advancing financial globalization and the resulting contagion effect – which is considered a downside of financial globalization – has added to the problems of individual economies as well as that of regional integration arrangements. On the economic side, globalization is essentially being driven by liberalization, deregulation and technological advancement. The relative costs of air, ocean and land transport have continued to fall, making cross-border merchandise transactions less expensive. The revolution in information communications technology has had an even more dramatic impact on trade in services, particularly financial services. The improved availability of information and declining transaction costs have stimulated international flows of capital, labor and technology – or knowledge in general. To be sure, none of this would have been possible in the absence of political decisions to pursue policies consistent with globalization. The global economic, financial and trade scenarios are fast undergoing a discernible transformation. Scholars like Kenichi Ohmae have pointed out the advent and significance of a 'border-less economy', growth of global federalism, the decline in the significance of the nation state, and the rise of consumer sovereignty (Ohmae, 1985).

After the first oil shock in 1973, a fortiori during the decade of the 1990s until the beginning of the Asian crisis, a good deal of progress was made in economic globalization. Since the mid-1980s, a large number of developing, transition and emerging-market economies undertook unilateral and multilateral liberalization of their economies (Das, 2003b). In the backdrop of rapid globalization during this period, a paradox in the global trading system is easy to see. The reference here is to rising interest in, and number of, regional trading blocs in the global economy. *A la* Peter Drucker, the paradox is that the rapidly integrating global economy is overlain with 'a splintering world polity' (Drucker, 1987). The global economic and trading system has come under dual forces. The economic globalism affecting it was a centripetal force, pulling the global economies together into an integrated, organic whole. As opposed to this, regionalism was a centrifugal force, which exerted pressure in the opposite direction. Although the two forces seemingly pulled the global economy in opposite directions, they reflected complementary dimensions of dynamic capitalist market development. The two opposing forces may well be compatible and may coexist.

The meaning of regional integration must be clarified at the outset, so should the use of the generic term 'regional integration agreement or arrangement' (RIA) used in this book. It basically and traditionally implies discriminatory trade liberalization. Two or more economies, under an RIA, can decide to lower trade barriers against one another vis-à-vis the rest of the global economy. This could be variously described as preferential trade agreement, or reciprocal preferential arrangement, or discriminatory trading arrangement.

It is common to find RIAs between neighboring economies. They are generally regional and contiguous in the geographic sense, although it is no longer a necessary condition. RTAs were formed between: the US and Israel,

Canada and Chile, South Africa and the EU; while Asia Pacific Economic Co-operation (APEC) forum has far-flung members. The use of the term 'regional' continues even when RIAs members do not belong to a particular geographical region. Thus, the use of term 'regional' could be a complete misnomer, and could merely be used for a group of countries that falls short of global.

For an analytical discussion of an RIA, its geographical contiguity, or its being part of a region, is not necessary. In the past, one generally required at least three countries to form an RIA. This condition no longer holds. During the late 1990s, two-economy groups began negotiating RIAs. Regionalism contributes to regional economic integration as well as to creating regional trading blocs. Different kinds and degrees of regionalism will be discussed in this book. Semantics in this regard is important because it can affect the way people think about RIAs. For instance, terms like 'free trade agreement' are not seen as having a protectionist ring around them. To be sure, 'preferential trade agreement' sounds less discriminatory and benign. However, an expression like 'discriminatory trade agreement' sounds offensive, aggressive, something that transgresses and is objectionable (WB, 2000).

That regionalism has been on the rise is a well-accepted fact. The evidence regarding the stock of completed RIAs, and the large number of RIAs planned or under negotiation, is a testimony to the basic attraction of such agreements to virtually all 146 WTO members.[3] As noted above, at the turn of the twenty-first century, both globalism and regionalism have come to coexist in the global trading system. The two trends have been burgeoning together. These developments raise important questions for the global trading system. It is being increasingly assumed that building complementary regional and multilateral institutions is the most pragmatic way of grappling with the complexities of the fast-changing global economic and trade realities. However, in the wake of the debacle at the third Ministerial Conference of the WTO in Seattle,[4] it became necessary to take a good look at this stand and to question this easy assumption. Does regionalism have a direct, effective and systemic link with trade liberalization? The opposite can also be true. Is regionalism fragmenting global trade, and in the process creating a new global disorder characterized by growing rivalries and marginalization (Das, 2001)? How RIAs impact upon the global trading system is another open and moot question. In this book we address these assumptions and queries.

The assumption that regionalism is a short cut to globalization does not always have to be correct. Cogent arguments exist on both the sides of the debate. Growth in regionalism does not necessarily have to lead to expansion of free trade or a liberalized trading regime. It is believed by some that the target of free or liberalized trade is easier to reach in large regional agreements like the Free Trade Area of the Americas (FTAA) and the APEC forum with memberships as large as 34 and 21, respectively. In the European Union (EU), with the signing of treaties of accession with 10 more countries in April 2003, the membership of the EU will extend to 25 in May 2004.[5] None of these qualify as small RIAs. When the FTAA is launched in 2005, it will potentially be the largest, in a geographical sense and in terms of the number of countries, venture in regionalism.

In addition, large RIAs like these three are likely to contain economies as different in size, outlook and level of economic development and industrialization as any in the WTO. Differences and difficulties have bedeviled large RIAs in the past. They are likely to continue to do so. If at all trade frictions are less challenging in a regional grouping than in the WTO, it would only be to a small extent. Also, it is difficult to comprehend how relatively larger trade issues like agricultural liberalization or managing trade disputes, would be any easier in an RIA setting than in the WTO. The difficulties, differences and countries involved in these situations may well be similar, with the same interests and sensitivities as in the WTO.

The flip side of this coin is that regional trade or economic groupings can offer immediate steps to the broader process of integration into the world economy. They can achieve faster and deeper liberalization than is possible at the multilateral level. Some go so far as arguing that regionalization is often a prerequisite to achieving globalization. Some countries, particularly those in Africa, view RIAs as part of a wider economic integration process. There is a possibility that these regional economic groupings can work as a force for creating global public goods. An important illustration in this regard is that of APEC's research on trade facilitation and its leadership on e-commerce, which proved to be of enormous assistance to the WTO.

An amber signal is essential here. Although regionalism is in vogue and it is here to stay, in the ultimate analysis it is neither a substitute for multilateral trade nor for globalism. It is true that the forces of free market do not always govern the global economy; regionalism and globalism can function in a complementary manner. This in turn would open the possibilities of global welfare gains. Regionalism that is not open, and is devoid of globalism, is the antithesis of maximized global output and, therefore, for global economic welfare. As we shall see in Chapter 5, the concept of *open regionalism* was pioneered by Australia and New Zealand and was subsequently adopted by the APEC forum.

In this book we try to see whether regionalism has a rightful place in a rapidly globalizing world economy in the new century. We try to answer queries like what is the place of RIAs in the global trading system, what are their welfare implications and whether they adversely affect the global trading system.

2. THE REGIONALISM AND MULTILATERALISM DEBATE

Of the two, multilateralism is relatively more difficult to define than regionalism. Multilateralism is a characteristic of the global economy that is shaped and defined by the conduct of individual countries or economies. Whether an economy is multilateralist or not is best determined by the degree to which its trading regime is free of vestiges of discrimination and has achieved free trade. As it is an additive process, from the global perspective, multilateralism is a direct function of the degree of multilateralism of individual economies. The sum total of multilateralism of individual economies adds up to global multilateralism. There are periods in which it soars and there are periods in which it sinks, depending upon the rising or falling of multilateralism in individual economies.[6]

Developing a functional multilateral discipline and system is indispensable for the hurdle-free expansion of free trade, as well as for the growth of world GDP. The history of international trade demonstrates that the risk of reversal in market-opening and expanding trade is much higher in the absence of multilateral constraints on national trade policies than in their presence. It is proved by the Cobden–Chevalier Treaty of 1860 between England and France, which contained a most-favored-nation (MFN) clause. Subsequently, the European economies that signed a trade treaty with either England or France, also signed on to the MFN clause. By 1867 a majority of the European economies had signed it with one or other of the two. The result was a network of treaties, which caused a major decline in tariff barriers in Europe, in turn leading to a boom in international trade and output until the eve of World War I. The post-war efforts did not succeed in renewing the network of binding treaties with commitments to market opening based on the MFN principle, and so consequently the global economy did not return to the pre-World War I level of international trade (Anderson, 2001). During the late 1920s, when the Great Depression began, countries adopted beggar-thy-neighbor protection and drove international trade into a nosedive and the world's economy into a prolonged depression. Over the 1929–32 period, international trade shrank by 25 percent in terms of volume and declined 40 percent in value (Anderson, 2001). This demonstrates the pressing need for multilateral discipline in the area of international trade.

A superficial glance at the relationship between multilateralism and regional integration could lead one to believe that they work at cross-purposes. Therefore, the oldest concern in the regional trading blocs and customs union literature is whether regionalism helps or hinders free trade, or whether it underpins or undermines multilateralism.[7] Vigorous debate on this issue continued during the 1990s. The current form of the age-old query is whether regionalism is a 'building block' or 'stepping stone' for advancing towards multilateralism, or a 'stumbling block' on the way to multilateralism or a 'millstone' around the neck of progress towards free trade and multilateralism. While some researchers see regionalism as a potential threat to multilateralism, others believe that it contributes to free trade and multilateralism. Consensus on this issue is yet to emerge.

An oft-cited argument is that RIAs divert attention from multilateralism and expend scarce negotiating resources, but the recent negotiating realities point in a different direction. Before the Doha Ministerial Conference (2001),[8] negotiators from the industrial economies, particularly the EU and the US, built a strong consensus with those developing economies that were in partnership with them in various RIAs, which in turn contributed to the success of the Doha Ministerial Conference. These alliances were also crucial in the launching of the round of multilateral trade negotiations (MTNs), the so-called Doha Development Agenda. Support and cooperation for a new round from the African and Latin American economies was sought by the large industrial economies by making promises of concessions during the MTNs on agriculture, patents and public health related issues (Schott, 2002). Thus, close ties between the developing and industrial economies developed in RIAs resulted in providing an impetus to multilateralism. An admixture of regionalism and multilateralism can potentially coalesce to advance global trade liberalization.

One important reason why a consensus on such an admixture has not emerged is that RIAs differ so much from each other that there is little empirical evidence on their effects, which could be taken for the representative impact of RIAs. Second, there are a number of reasons to believe that RIAs impinge or encroach upon multilateralism. This topic has provoked a good deal of debate among trade economists and concern among policy mandarins – consequently there is a growing body of research addressed to it. Apprehensions regarding proliferation of RIAs undermining the multilateral trade system were frequently raised in the global fora and this concern was partly responsible for the creation of the WTO Committee on Regional Trade Agreements (CRTA) in February 1996.

Using a monopolistically competitive model, Krugman (1991a) demonstrated that regional trade and integration could potentially raise the level of common external tariffs (CET), if the trading bloc is non-cooperative. He also posited that 'countries that join trading blocs will be more protectionist towards countries outside the blocs than they were before, so that the world as a whole will be hurt more than helped by moves that at first seem to be liberalizing in intent'. This analysis was narrow in the sense that it focused only on customs unions, at the exclusion of the FTAs. Yet, it sparked a good many responses and reactions. A group of follow-up studies demonstrated that Krugman's (1991a) results were strongly based on some of his assumptions.[9] Also, those who responded laid far more emphasis on the transport costs than Krugman did in quantifying the impact of the RIA formation. When they introduced transport costs in the model used by Krugman (1991a), they concluded that RIAs resulted in welfare losses if transport costs were low. By relaxing his imperfect substitute assumption, one of these studies found that global welfare rises as the global economy travels between autarky and free trade in the context of a Ricardian trade model (Deardorff and Stern, 1994).

Several studies used the Vinerian logic (see section 6 below) and concluded that there is an overwhelming possibility of a large volume of trade diversion for the RIA members, leading to significant welfare losses, both individually and globally.[10] Krueger (1996), in particular, contended that RIAs constituted a potential threat to the world trading system because they are in general trade diverting. In addition, she posited that RIAs created lobbies and interest groups against multilateral trade liberalization in their member countries.

These results did not go unchallenged. In opposing them, several analysts presented evidence that supported favorable outcomes of RIA creation. Nordstrom (1995) contended that by forming RIAs, small economies received a greater incentive to liberalize multilaterally because by doing so they could deal more effectively with large economies as well as trading blocs. Similar supportive conclusions were arrived at by Perroni and Whally (1996) who argued that as a majority of the recent RIAs have preferred to remain restricted to regional trade agreements, they could choose their common external tariffs freely. Therefore, in contrast to what Krugman (1991a) has contended, regional blocs' monopoly power need not necessarily increase, and forming RIAs has not necessarily resulted in higher tariffs between trade blocs. Therefore, increasing regionalism cannot be taken to necessarily imply an increasing potential threat to multilateralism. Campa and Sorenson (1996) agreed with this inference and argued that the global free trade equilibrium can be sustained if small economies form trading blocs. Their integration can effectively undermine the market power of large trading countries or RIAs.

3. DEFINITION AND TEXTURE OF REGIONALISM

Trade liberalization per se is a complex and diffused issue – although it is governed by simple principles. Regional trade liberalization is even more complex. As set out in section 1, the basic objective of a trading bloc is to bring down tariffs between the members of the bloc and discriminate against trade with other countries. In its most rudimentary form a trading bloc merely removes tariffs on intra-bloc trade in goods. It is appropriate to outline the characteristic structures of RIAs and define them. Functionally, if somewhat loosely, it could be defined as any agreement of preferential trade in which a set of trading partners reciprocally reduce trade barriers. The trading partners may or may not be contiguous or even close to each other. Page (2000) has made a noteworthy attempt and defined an RIA as a group of countries, which have 'created a legal framework of cooperation covering an extensive economic relationship, with the intention that it will be of indefinite duration, and with the possibility foreseen that the region will economically evolve in the future'. The criterion of extensive economic linkage precludes single-issue alliances, while that of permanence is uncontroversial. The criterion of evolution is obvious and reinforces exclusion of groups formed for a limited, or a single, objective. The need for a dynamic evolution over time, *à la* Page, is inevitable because countries' economic structures change constantly, and with that their linkages with the members of their RIA.

Benefiting from the previous literature, Page (2000) took a comprehensive and integrated vision of RIAs. According to this, the economic and regulatory links between trade and the rest of the economic systems of the RIA members are expected to gradually harmonize and strengthen. However, this strengthening process needs to be led by the trading relationship. Conventionally, formation of an RIA entails lowering of the usual trade barriers, which brings to the fore a sequence of other differences in the RIA-forming economies which, if left unharmonized, would necessarily have a negative effect over trade expansion in the RIA.

The typology of RIA (refer to section 8) is not only revealing but it also indicates a linearity of form and the likely process of evolution. It could be called the expansion path of a preferential trade agreement (PTA). The linear movements occur in the following sequence: first, freeing trade in goods and services of all tariff barriers within the RIA; second, freeing capital and labor movements within the RIA, followed by the right of establishment; third, minimizing and subsequently eliminating non-tariff barriers (NTBs) and moving on to the harmonization of taxes as well as monetary and fiscal policies.[11] Finally, a common currency for the RIA is created and economic and financial policies are integrated.

As alluded to in section 1, I employ the acronym RIA in this book, which is used as a generic acronym. It means what it says and sounds benign and businesslike. Although 'regional trade agreement' is the favorite term and acronym of WTO publications, I prefer RIA. Why? Essentially because RTA is narrow in its scope and provides for partners to grant each other merely preferential tariff treatment on a reciprocal basis. Unlike 'RTA', the acronym 'RIA' has broader implications and promotes open trade and cooperation. That is, partners grant each other much more than mere tariff concessions on a reciprocal basis. As revealed by a half century of evolution of the European Economic Community (EEC),[12] the process of evolution of an RIA can have several stages. It may take a myriad of forms and go beyond the RTA stage. Therefore, we consider it a better acronym than RTA for use in a generic sense. It can refer to a variety of preferential agreements that cover liberalization of trade and factor movements. It can also cover bilateral, regional and plurilateral (having three or more members) agreements of a preferential nature. It can also imply deeper integration than a mere trade agreement. Schiff and Winters (2003) also use the acronym RIA to 'first to avoid any unsubstantiated pejorative implication, and second to communicate that arrangements can extend well beyond international trade into areas such as investment, domestic regulation and policies, standards, infrastructure and politics.' Although the primary focus of this book is on free trade areas (FTAs) and customs unions in the area of goods and economic integration agreements (EIAs) in the area of services, partial and non-reciprocal agreements have also been touched upon wherever appropriate. The RIAs that we discuss in this book are those that have been formally notified to the GATT–WTO system.

4.   REGIONAL INTEGRATION AND TRADING AGREEMENTS: THE GENESIS

The current march of regionalism is decisively not the first ever in history. Regional trading arrangements can be traced back to the sixteenth century when proposal for a union between England and Scotland was made in 1547–48. The 1703 Act of Union of England and Scotland established a political and economic union. All the French provinces were united into a customs union by the Revolutionary government of 1789–90.

In the United States, the American colonies maintained separate tariff systems with a moderate number of custom duties, until the Constitution adopted in 1789 barred the individual states from levying any duties on trade with other states. In Germany, the *Zollverein* was formed (1818–34) among eighteen small states. In modern parlance it was a customs union, and preceded the unification of Germany in 1871. Likewise, the Swiss Confederation was established in 1848 as an economic union and Italian states were united as a customs union during 1860–66. A customs union was established between Norway and Sweden in 1874–75. The experiences of the Austro-Hungarian Empire were different as unlike these successful examples, it went down in history as a failed attempt to form a customs union. The Benelux customs union was established between Belgium, Luxembourg and the Netherlands in 1944 (Machlup, 1977).

During the contemporary period, the Treaty of Rome (1957) forming the EEC could be considered the beginning of regional trading blocs, or the first wave of regionalization. The EEC was the precursor to the first wave of regionalism in the 1950s and 1960s. Subsequently, the Stockholm Convention established the European Free Trade Area (EFTA) in 1959, and the Montevideo Treaty established the Latin American Free Trade Area (LAFTA) in 1960. In 1963, the Yaoundé Convention between the EEC and former French, Belgium and Italian colonies in Africa gave these countries preferential access to the EEC markets. This was a non-reciprocal trade agreement. Following the formation of the EEC, there was a proliferation of regional agreements in the developing countries of Africa and Latin America, albeit not Asia. The first wave of regionalism was weak, short-lived and did not go far. With the notable exception of the EEC, the regional initiatives of the 1950s and the 1960s amounted to very little. Thus, the first wave of contemporary regionalism did not flourish outside Europe. Earlier regional initiatives like the Andean Pact had collapsed, although it was reborn in 1988 when Protocol of Quito called for amendment to the Andean Group's (AG's) founding treaty.[13]

The RIAs of this period were neither large in number nor successful. One of the most important reasons was that the US, the largest trading economy, was philosophically committed to multilateralism and opposed to regionalism. The US had a historical bias toward MFN-only liberalization and considered regional initiatives a force which worked against multilateral liberalization, which had the highest priority in its international economic thinking. The US took a polemical stance and relentlessly championed the cause of free trade through the GATT. However, the formation of the EEC received US support because the US saw a united Western Europe as an effective deterrent to the growing Soviet threat.

One important reason why developing countries were initially attracted to the concept of regionalism during this period was their belief that regionalization would help them in industrialization. This was an era when import-substitution (IS) strategy was still popular in the developing economies, in particular in the South Asian and Latin American developing economies. Many developing countries were making serious endeavors to industrialize through domestic and regional import substitution. Policy mandarins believed that infant industries could first learn to export within a protected small regional market – and then face the strong winds of competition in the extra-regional or global markets. However, the story of IS strategy is one of failure. It failed both domestically as well as in regions. By the late 1970s, outward-orientation or export promotion (EP) strategy had begun to capture the admiration of policy makers in the developing economies. Consequently, they considered regionalism as an irrelevant policy instrument and pushed it into the background.

In 1983, the Australia–New Zealand Closer Economic Relations Trade Agreement (or CER) was signed.[14] This was the only major RIA that was negotiated and established during the 1980s. The CER was not a part of the first wave of regionalism. This could be considered a belated reaction to the formation of the EEC and its well-publicized future plan for the Single Market, called the EC-92. The CER is a free trade agreement and supports the trans-Tasman economic relationship. A 1988 Protocol to the CER on the Acceleration of Free Trade in Goods provided for the elimination of all tariffs and quantitative restrictions by July 1990. The Trade in Services Protocol to the CER, signed in 1988, brought services into CER from January 1989. Almost all trans-Tasman trade in services opened up after that. The CER boasts of being the most successful RIA on the globe, both from theoretical and practical viewpoints.

5. STRUCTURAL VARIATIONS AND DIVERSITY

RIAs vary significantly along many dimensions. They come in all sizes and shapes. A glance at the present RIAs reveals that regionalism has varied objectives and can potentially take a myriad of different forms and structures, each with different implications and nuances. For instance, they vary enormously in income levels and the shares of intra-RIA trade. Their structures may vary from loose agreements to facilitate trade of the African Cross-Border Initiative or Asia Pacific Economic Co-operation forum, through to the deep integration of the European Union. They can follow the principle of open or closed regionalism, two fundamentally different varieties. Closed regionalism was rampant in some parts of the global economy in the past, particularly in Latin America and sub-Saharan Africa. An RIA movement can be initiated in a coercive or a benign manner. It can be consensual or hierarchical. It can stop at free trade in goods, emphasize economic integration, or political and strategic ties. It can be a consequence of the decentralized operation of market forces, or a product of determined action of the concerned states. Therefore, one can infer that RIAs are highly dissimilar and each one is *sui generis*.

The extent of liberalization in trade in goods can vary across RIAs. Many do not even cover all trade in goods. Generally services are not included in RIAs, exclusive economic integration agreements are made for regional or preferential trade in services. Cross-border transfer of factors of production only becomes part of an RIA if constituent members move towards deep integration, as does the common external trade policy. It often takes place after an RIA has withstood the test of time and operated in a satisfactory manner for a long enough period, and constituent members feel sanguine about the success of deeper integration. Trade in agricultural products is frequently excluded from the RIAs. It is often dealt with at the multilateral level. Frequently there are loopholes in RIAs that allow for the continued application of contingent protection measures like anti-dumping on intra-RIA trade. Interpretation and application of the rules of origin (ROO) varies enormously across RIAs.[15] It has been observed that even in serious RIAs like EFTA and NAFTA, some exporters prefer to pay MFN tariffs on intra-RIA trade than incur the cost of documenting that their exports fulfill the requirements for the ROO.

The functioning procedures of RIAs also differ considerably. In their operational style, some RIAs are dynamic. They keep moving forward, and work towards eventual deeper integration. Others are consciously stand-alone, static, agreements. Some RIAs are simple in structure and are governed by few regulations. Others are intractably complex and have a large framework of supra-national institution network and intricate regulations. Other than the five formal forms identified in section 8, there are marked differences in substance and form among RIAs. The variety and differences among RIAs reflect differences in the objectives of the countries forming them. Most analytical studies treat them as similar, which is an obvious mistake. Results of many empirical exercises based on this assumption tend to be dubious.

Members of an RIA can and do differ in important economic features. One of the features of economic integration is the level of economic interdependence among the member economies. Large RIAs like APEC forum, the EU and NAFTA provide interesting illustrations. For instance, trade as a proportion of GDP is high for most of the member economies of the EU. This does not apply to the members of APEC and NAFTA. The members of these two RIAs are less interdependent. Furthermore, trade between the member states is lower as a percentage of GDP in APEC and NAFTA. Another interesting difference is that extra-regional trade tends to be more widely spread for APEC and NAFTA than for the EU. The differences among member economies regarding dependence in the areas of trade and investment on the members of the RIA determine the level of symmetry in the economic relationship of the members. As may be anticipated, this relationship can vary between symmetrical and asymmetrical.

An unmistakable fact about RIAs is that they have a political dimension because all countries and regions are political entities in their own right. Therefore, many of their objectives go beyond trade and economic integration and take on political overtones. For instance, the early steps taken by France to create the EEC began with Robert Schuman, the French Minister of Foreign Affairs, suggesting that the coal and steel resources of France and Germany should be pooled, ostensibly for reconstructing the post-War Europe. The celebrated European Coal and Steel Community was created in 1951. This endeavor was largely driven by a strong proclivity to integrate economically to resolve the political and security problems of Western Europe. Franco-German economic integration was meant to tie Germany to France and the other European states, and thereby, reduce its ability to engage in aggression and warfare. The EEC was intended to make a Franco-German war not only 'unthinkable, but materially impossible'. Thus, economic integration was used in an undisguised manner to reduce risks of war and political conflicts (Baun, 1996). Economic agents in the neighboring states can stimulate deeper trade and investment ties and the resulting regional economic interdependence can create a demand for greater political cooperation. This process can potentially work in reverse as well, that is, political integration can become a driving force behind economic integration. The EEC and APEC represent these two kinds of dynamics. The Asia-Pacific region characterizes the first kind of regional integration dynamics, which is the opposite of the top-down process encountered in the EEC. Export-oriented Asian economies have expanded trade and investment in the region without any political agenda. APEC and other region-wide political dialogues have tried to capitalize on the investment and trade ties.

The foregoing exposition brings home the fact that a wide diversity in content and form is commonly to be found between RIAs among both developing and industrial countries. While tariff elimination is common to all of them, differences commonly exist on agreements related to (1) quantitative restrictions, (2) positive or negative list approaches, (3) rules of origin, (4) external tariffs, (5) timetable for liberalization, (6) trade in services, (7) movement of labor and capital, (8) promotion of industrialization, (9) promotion of trade objectives, and (10) payments arrangements (Whalley, 2000). RIAs between industrial economies are generally concerned with and adopt variant approaches in dispute settlement procedures, including dispute settlement in the areas of anti-dumping and countervailing duties, as well as trade provisions relating to environmental standards. Some analysts made a further distinction between unipolar and hierarchical or multipolar and decentralized RIAs (Whalley, 2000; Ikenberry 2000). The former is several small economies entering into an RIA with one large one, while more than one large economy is part of the latter. They are also known to have complex sectoral arrangements in areas like textiles and apparel and vehicles. The EU has extensive sectoral arrangements in agriculture, steel, inter-regional resource transfers and labor mobility provisions. However, these provisions are not to be found in APEC or NAFTA.

Ikenberry (2000) presented the diversity in regionalism along two axes, namely, organizational mode and principal motives behind integration (Figure 1.1). Seen in this manner, APEC will have to be put in the lower left cell of

Principal Motives of Regional Integration

	Economic	Political
Unipolar Hierarchical	NAFTA	Japan's Greater East-Asia CoProsperity Sphere in the 1930s
Multipolar Decentralized	APEC	EU

(row label on left axis: Organizational mode)

Source: Ikenberry (2000).

Figure 1.1   Diversity in regionalism

the matrix, NAFTA in the upper left cell and the EU in the lower right cell. There are not many examples of unipolar, hierarchical and politically driven regionalism during the current period. Japan's concept of Greater East Asia Co-Prosperity Sphere of the 1930s, although it never came about, was the only example of this kind.

Notwithstanding the diversity in the current trend in regionalism, the following characteristics are frequently – albeit not always – to be seen in many of the contemporary RIAs. First, the current RIAs typically involve one or more small countries linking up with one or more large industrial economies. Second, the small economies joining an RIA presently undertake significant economic reforms and restructuring. It is true of the Central and East European Countries (CEEC) and Latin American economies. Third, the trade liberalization that is affected is largely confined to concessions given by the smaller partners of the RIA, generally not by the larger constituent economies. The reason is that the latter group has fairly, if not quite, liberalized economies. Typically the small countries get only small tariff advantage, because the larger partners of the RIAs have low tariffs to begin with (Ethier, 1998a).

6. STAGES OF INTEGRATION AND NOMENCLATURE

There are several possible levels of integration between independent states that apply MFN treatment in trade with each other. Regional integration can potentially have many stages and formal shapes. These stages of integration range from shallow to deep. Corresponding to the stage of integration, an RIA could have a spectrum of institutional frameworks or arrangements varying from preferential trading areas (PTAs), to free trade areas (FTAs), to customs union (CU), to common markets and finally to economic union. These are the five standardized tiers or stages of RIA (Figure 1.2). Combinations of two stages, like a free-trade area and customs union, are also feasible.

PTAs are the first-tier arrangement. In this arrangement, trading partners grant partial non-discriminatory tariff concessions to each other.[16] They leave their other tariffs, non-tariff barriers and quantitative restrictions unchanged. 'Other' in this case means trade barriers towards the non-members or the rest of the world. In a free trade area, which is the second tier, members of a PTA eliminate all tariffs and NTBs among themselves, but each member can set its own tariff rates on imports from non-members or the rest of the world (as with the Association of South East Asian Nations and North American Free Trade Area). The third tier is a customs union in which members go beyond removing tariff barriers and non-tariff barriers among themselves and set a common level of trade barriers vis-à-vis non-members (as with the EU). These three stages of regionalization directly and exclusively affect international trade of the member countries and are considered shallow integration.

Some trade economists take CUs as the beginning of deep integration. The fourth tier is a common market and is considered the first deep integration

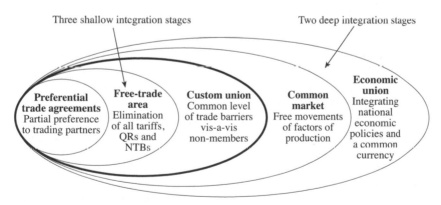

Source: Inspired by Low (2001).

Figure 1.2   Spectrum of formal regional trading arrangements

stage. This stage attempts to harmonize some institutional arrangements and commercial and financial laws. Beyond free exchange of goods and services, a common market entails free movement of factors of production. The fifth stage is the economic union, which goes a step beyond the free movement of goods, services, and factors (Ethier, 1997; Ethier, 1998a, Frankel, 1997).[17] An economic union, the last-tier RIA, involves integrating national economic policies, including taxes and common currency. At its deepest, an RIA may even include construction of shared executive, judicial and legislative institutions (see Figure 1.2).

Given the variety of possible formal shapes and tiers in RIAs, it is easy to find a significant range in them in real life. They vary from simple exchange of preferences on a limited range of products between two or more economies at one end of the spectrum, to agreements that include a large number of trade-related provisions and go beyond traditional tariff reduction or elimination at the other end. Generally, partial-scope agreements are made essentially among the developing economies. In the partial-scope agreements, as the name indicates, economies exchange concessions on a limited range of products. The opposite is true for the industrial economies. RIAs among them are generally deep and far-reaching. This is partly due to decreasing tariffs among them for most non-agricultural products. The recent RIA arrangements among the industrial economies tend to go far beyond the traditional tariff-slashing exercises. They even tend to go beyond the present multilateral discipline. In many RIAs among industrial economies regional regulations include regulations on investment, competition, and standards. In a small number of cases labor and environment are also included.

A CU typically calls for a greater degree of political coordination and integration than PTAs and FTAs. Unlike PTAs and FTAs, CUs need supra-national institutions and a body of common law. These institutions are *inter alia* needed for negotiating common external tariffs and revenue sharing arrangements. Second, the aim in forming a CU generally extends beyond economic objectives. It often includes creation of regional public goods like promoting regional democracy or regional security, as was seen in the cases of the EEC and MERCOSUR. The creators of the idea of the EEC, Robert Schuman and Jean Monnet, were explicit and emphatic about this objective. As regards MERCOSUR, the objectives of international security and strengthening fragile democracies played a significant role. Having a democratic government system was made a pre-condition of membership of MERCOSUR.

Some CUs evolved further into deeper integration and became common markets over time. Common markets entail free movements of factors of production and harmonization of regulations and standards between the constituent members. They need a greater range of supra-national institutions and a body of law to run them than a CU does and a higher degree of political co-ordination between the member states. In the RIAs with deep integration, the integrated markets or economies take precedence over national boundaries and the residency or nationality of the economic agents. The higher levels of economic integration entail the sweeping away of national controls (for customs, fiscal, statistical, health and safety, and security reasons) at the internal frontiers of an RIA. In addition, a common trade policy is agreed upon and established by the constituent members of the RIA. The common trade policy sweeps away technical barriers to trade in goods and services between the members. Also, harmonized policies are established in areas like health and safety, technical and environmental standards, intellectual property rights, competition policy, government procurement, and corporate and labor laws. This is done with an objective of creating a monetary union in the foreseeable future. A historical look at the CUs shows that some of them went further and evolved into nation states over time. For instance there was the unification of Italy in 1861 and the German *Zollverein,* which evolved into the German state in 1871. Romania was created from Wallachia and Moldavia in 1881 (Schiff, 2001).

According to the WTO statistics, in the present population of RIAs the dominant category is that of FTAs, which accounts for 72 percent of all the RIAs currently in force. Partial trading agreements concluded among the developing economies and customs unions account for 19 percent and 9 percent, respectively, of the existing RIAs. The strong penchant for forming FTAs among countries is easy to explain. They do not require prolonged negotiations and are easy to negotiate, although the degree of integration under an FTA is low. Conversely, a customs union promotes greater integration between the member economies, provides for the establishment of common external tariffs and harmonization of trade policies. As the scope of customs unions is wide, they can seldom be negotiated without prolonged negotiations. Their implementation is often also phased over a long period. That is one reason why there are not many customs unions in the global economy (WTO, 2002a).

The membership configuration of RIAs was always diverse and during the second or contemporary wave of regionalism it became complex as well (refer to section 7). During the second wave, RIAs have been concluded between non-contiguous non-regional countries. Cross-regional arrangements have increased in number and the term 'regional' may appear an incongruity. The simplest configuration of an RIA is a bilateral preferential agreement between two economies. Such agreements account for over half of the RIAs in force and almost 60 percent of those negotiated in 2002 (WTO, 2002a).

Such a large number of existing and future bilateral preferential agreements have resulted from the so-called hub-and-spokes strategy of regional integration. This strategy is implemented by each spoke entering into a bilateral preferential agreement with a hub. This strategy was given momentum by the EU. It was a hub to which economies with many spokes tried to link by concluding bilateral PTAs. The spokes, in turn, concluded bilateral preferential agreements among themselves. The EU–Mediterranean agreements under the 'Euro-Mediterranean Partnership' are an example of this kind of bilateral preferential agreement. Numerous agreements following this structure were set up in Latin America during the 1990s. Asian economies started entering into such bilateral PTAs at the end of the 1990s. These bilateral agreements are far simpler than those between the plurilateral RIAs. In this case, on one side of the agreement is an RIA while on the other there can be an individual economy or another RIA. The EU–MERCOSUR agreement is an example of such a complex plurilateral RIA. Such RIAs account for 25 percent of the present RIAs in force (WTO, 2002a).

7.   THE SPAGHETTI BOWL EFFECT

With the passage of time, the RIAs proliferated, so much so that overlapping of RIAs became a common phenomenon. Overlapping RIAs as well as a network of RIAs covering continents at regional and sub-regional levels have managed to create a good deal of complexity in membership configuration. Rapid proliferation raised the level of overlapping so much that a regional map of RIAs began to look like a spaghetti bowl.[18] The networks of overlapping agreements have generated intricate webs of discriminatory treatment, which often lead to complex and incoherent regulatory structures for the conduct of a growing share of world trade. These networks raised several problematic issues. One of them was that one country could now have several sets of rules of origin for different preferential trade partners under different RIAs. This created a confusing maze of ROO, which on occasions were even conflicting. Consequently, the procedural rigmarole and cost of administering such agreements rose considerably, making RIAs an inconvenient means of trading. The other complexity was that one country having membership in a number of RIAs has to maintain tariff schedules for each preferential trade partner with varying phase-out periods.

One negative impact of the spaghetti bowl is that when countries are obliged to spent a great deal of time and resources on the negotiation and maintenance of agreements at regional level, they tend to ignore their responsibility at the multilateral level. When economies feel burdened by membership of different plurilateral RIAs, which often happens, it leads to consolidation of RIAs. The constituent economies rationalize their participation by aligning themselves with one RIA grouping and dropping the other.

As the spaghetti bowl effect intensifies, it results in more criss-crossing tariff concessions and ROO. The level of complexity rises, particularly where each country maintains a distinct preferential regime with the other. An illustration of such rising level of complexity is the RIAs signed by the Central and Eastern European Countries with EFTA. In this case each CEEC has to negotiate preferences with each one of the EFTA members, and vice versa (WTO, 2002a). The complexity level worsens if a country is involved in multiple RIAs covering services. The remedy for this kind of complexity is harmonization of tariff concessions as well as in ROO. It can dramatically reduce the administrative burden associated with membership in plurilateral RIAs. In the early 2000s, the European economies had the largest number of RIA partners. Even countries that participate in a small number of RIAs, do have to negotiate and administer a number of preferential trade relationships. This number of relationships depends upon the composition of the RIAs in which an economy participates. An example of this scenario is the sub-Saharan economies. They participated in a small number of RIAs, all of them plurilateral, making negotiation and administration of RIA relationships an onerous and complex task (WTO, 2002a).

8.   A REPRESENTATIVE RIA IN THE EARLY 2000s

The above exposition has amply demonstrated that RIAs have large variations in their coverage, structures, procedural provisions, general exceptions, and regulations on quantitative restrictions, subsidies, contingency instruments and ROO. However, an attempt can be made to create an imagery of a representative RIA, or one that is something of a statistical 'mode' in terms of essential features of an RIA. To determine its distinctive features, one needs to examine the current RIAs in force. To exemplify the essential characteristics of the entire group, an RIA in the early 2000s should, in terms of broad sectors, cover all industrial products and selected agricultural products. Only a tiny number of RTAs cover all sectors and products, which is atypical of the group. The preferential treatment provided in an RIA applies only to products originating in the constituent member economy. Therefore, the ROO are a significant element in characterizing the scope of an RIA. An RIA has detailed provisions on how origin of an imported product should be determined. If a product comprises inputs from more than one country, the country where the last 'substantial transformation' took place is considered the country of origin. Among the three basic methods for conferring origin, technical tests have gained prominence during the recent period.[19] Occasionally, the ROO are supplemented by a 'cumulative clause', whereby imported inputs from certain countries are treated as domestic.[20]

The institutional structure of RIAs varies in levels and functions, albeit all the RIAs have provisions for coordination between the members' relevant administrative bodies, like customs administration. A representative RIA would have an overarching institution to facilitate the implementation of the agreement and consider whether the members take any initiative towards deeper integration. The overarching institution can be charged with largely procedural functions, or given authority for granting liberalization. In some cases, it was found to have the mandate for further liberalization as well as harmonization. There is a rising trend in endowing the institutional body with a legal personality. As regards settlement of disputes between the constituent members, the institutional process is largely consultative, with a possibility of a formal decision being issued by the institutional body. Elaborate dispute settlement mechanisms are far from common in RIAs, albeit they do exist in some and provide for resorting to an arbitration process, which in turn affords a binding decision. However, the incidence of these elaborate, binding, procedures has been on the increase in the recent period. In RIAs with deeper integration the trend towards having binding procedures for dispute settlements is much higher than in a PTA or FTA. All RIAs with deeper integration contain provisions on harmonization and approximation of economic and trade legislation. To this end, they create necessary institutions.

A representative RIA does not encourage accession of new members without introducing regional or geographical qualification to accession. It also carries provisions regarding accession to other RIAs, and provides for a member country's participation in other RIAs. As noted above, a good number (over 25) of post-1990 RIAs were between one country and a group of countries, which constituted an RIA among them. In acceding to another RIA, the member county is required to ensure that it does not inflict any negative effect on its original RIA membership. What is more, members of the original RIA should be consulted before embarking upon the new membership. This rule is clearly stipulated in the agreement. A representative RIA applies general exceptions (GATT Article XX) and security exceptions (GATT Article XXI) applicable to trade.

Quantitative restrictions (QRs) are considered the most widely trade distorting trade barrier. RIA provisions call for the abolition of QRs on the RIA's date of entry into force, or for their progressive elimination over a stipulated period of time. They apply to all products, or to the subset of industrial products. The current trend is outright abolition of QRs on imports of all goods. With rapid market access liberalization during the 1990s, this trend has gained strength. A rule of thumb in this regard is that the deeper the integration, the faster the elimination of QRs. Specific QRs on agricultural imports are usually dealt with in separate bilateral agreements or protocols, but in the new environment of faster market access they are strongly discouraged.

A representative RTA has well laid out rules on subsidies, with those on agriculture dealt with separately. The reason for dealing with agricultural subsidies differently from subsidies in general is that they are considered a multilateral issue and, therefore, cannot be dealt with on the level of an RIA.[21] Provisions on subsidies are cast in general terms, reminding members that those subsidies that distort or threaten to distort trade are not compatible with obligations under the agreement. Details on subsidies that are expressly permitted are not given. RIAs also provide for the use of safeguard measures, either of a general or a specific nature, to deal with emergency situations. They provide for safeguard actions that are permitted under Article XIX of GATT-1994. Provisions granting the possibility of action when external payment conditions deteriorate are also allowed by an RTA. After 1990, these safeguard measures could also be applied to deal with structural adjustments and for infant industry cases. Increased imports of a product in a member country trigger an emergency safeguard mechanism, which is provided under the RIA regulations. RIA provisions contain the application of anti-dumping (AD) duties.[22] RTA regulations demand compliance with the WTO rules regarding AD duties. Their proportion is higher in PTAs and FTAs than in CUs and deeper integration agreements. Likewise, provisions permitting countervailing (CV) duties are permitted by an RIA in intra-trade. However, consultation with the overarching institutional body is considered necessary before adopting CV measures. Again, CV measures are adopted much more frequently in PTAs and FTAs than in CUs and deeper integration agreements. These are the salient features of a representative RIA during the present period.[23]

9. CONCLUSIONS AND SUMMARY

Over the preceding quarter century, particularly during the 1990s, a good deal of progress has been made in economic globalization. It has markedly expanded and deepened. There are several dimensions to the dynamics of the globalization process, including the integration of trade and financial transactions among countries. A three-way interaction between globalization, supra-national institutions and various sub-groups of global economies has created a new dynamic in the global economy. Against the backdrop of rising globalization, the regionalism trend has been on the rise. All the 146 members of the WTO are members of one or more RIAs. But regionalization is neither a substitute for multilateral trade nor for globalism. An expanding trend of regionalization may or may not underpin the forces of free trade, liberalized trade regimes and globalization.

As it is an additive process, multilateralism is a direct function of the degree of multilateralism of individual economies. For a smooth expansion of free trade and growth of world GDP, developing a functional multilateral discipline and system is indispensable. Formal regionalization of trade is an old phenomenon, dating back to the sixteenth century. A formal preferential trade agreement between England and Scotland was made in 1547–48. Since then, many historic attempts at regionalization have been made, the majority of them successful.

According to one definition, under regionalism, a legal framework of cooperation covering an extensive economic relationship is created, with the intention that it will be of indefinite duration, and with the possibility that the region will economically evolve in the future. The debate over regionalism hindering or helping free trade is an old chestnut. Several empirical studies, particularly those deploying Vinerian logic, have concluded that regionalism can lead to trade diversion. But these results were challenged by other studies. Some analysts believe that global free-trade equilibrium can be sustained if small economies form trading blocs, albeit a consensus in this regard is yet to emerge.

Regional integration between independent states that apply MFN treatment in trade with each other can have several possible levels. It can potentially have many stages and formal shapes. These stages of integration range from shallow to deep. Corresponding to the stage of integration, an RIA could have a spectrum of institutional frameworks or arrangements varying from preferential trading areas, to free trade areas, to customs union, to common markets and finally to economic union. These are the five standardized tiers or stages of RIA. Combinations of two stages, like a free trade area and customs union, are feasible, and do exist.

RIAs vary significantly along many dimensions. They have variegated objectives and can potentially take myriad different forms, each with different implications and nuances. Members of an RIA can and do differ in important economic features. They can follow the principle of open or closed regionalism, two fundamentally different varieties. They can be unipolar and hierarchical or multipolar and decentralized. Their functioning procedures may also differ considerably, as can their operational style. An unmistakable fact about RIAs is that they have a political dimension because all countries and regions are political entities in their own right.

With the brisk proliferation in RIAs, overlapping of RIAs has become a common phenomenon. Overlapping RIAs as well as the network of RIAs covering continents at regional and sub-regional levels have managed to create a good deal of complexity in membership configuration. Rapid proliferation has raised the level of overlapping so much that a regional map of RIAs has begun to look like a spaghetti bowl. This tendency has created a great many operational difficulties and administrative burdens in running contemporary

RIAs. The remedy for this kind of complexity is harmonization of tariff concessions as well as in ROO. It can dramatically reduce the administrative burden associated with membership in plurilateral RIAs.

NOTES

1. An indispensable condition for an emerging-market economy is its sustained ability to attract capital inflows from the global banks and securities markets. Other than the rapid endogenous growth endeavors and extensive macroeconomic and financial liberalization and deregulation, respect of property rights and human rights are considered the basic prerequisites of becoming an emerging-market economy. The national government must offer protection to property and human rights of both the citizens of the country and the non-residents alike. See Das (2003a), Chapter 1 for greater detail.
2. The International Monetary Fund (IMF) and the World Bank were conceived at the Bretton Woods conference, held in July 1944 at Bretton Woods, New Hampshire, USA. The two supra-national organizations became operational in 1946 after a sufficient number of countries had ratified the agreement. The international financial architecture of a post-World War II has largely stayed in place since then, despite major shifts in monetary policy. Since then the IMF and the World Bank are referred to as the Bretton Wood twins.
3. As of July 2003, the WTO had 146 members plus 28 countries with observer status. The Republic of Macedonia became the 146th member on 4 April 2003. With such large membership, it is almost a global institution.
4. Trade Ministers of 135 member countries of the WTO participated in the Third Ministerial Conference, held in Seattle, 30 November–3 December 1999. The Ministerial Conference is the highest-level decision-making body of the WTO. As required by the Marrakesh Agreement, signed on 15 April 1994, the Ministerial Conference is held once every two years.
5. The Treaty of Accession between the European Union and ten countries, namely, the Czech Republic, Estonia, Cyprus, Latvia, Lithuania, Hungary, Malta, Poland, Slovenia, and Slovakia was signed in Athens, Greece on 16 April 2003. These 10 countries are to acquire formal membership status of the EU in May 2004. Save for Cyprus and Malta, they are all Central and East European Countries countries. These eight economies were the satellite economies of the Soviet Union until its collapse in 1990–91. Bulgaria, Romania and Turkey, three candidates for future membership, are waiting on the sidelines.
6. Refer to Winters (2000) for greater detail.
7. For instance, see Viner (1950); Meade (1955); Lipsey (1960) and Arndt (1969).
8. This was the Fourth Ministerial Conference of the WTO, 9–13 November 2001, at Doha, Qatar. The Doha Round of MTNs was launched after it and this is scheduled to end in January 2005.
9. For instance, see Bagwell and Staiger (1993a) and Bagwell and Staiger (1993b), Deardorff and Stern (1994) and Frankel et al. (1996).
10. For instance, see Bhagwati and Panagaria (1996), and Krueger (1996).
11. NTBs include para-tariff measures, price control measures, financial measures, monopolistic measures, and technical measures.
12. The Agreement on a Treaty on European Union was signed in Maastricht on 10 December 1991. It included a timetable for Economic and Monetary Union. On 1 January 1993, the European Single Market was completed. On 1 November 1993, the Maastricht Treaty came into force, and the EEC became the European Union.
13. The Andean Pact was a common market between Bolivia, Colombia, Ecuador, Peru and Venezuela.
14. Although its complete form is Australia–New Zealand Closer Economic Relations Trade Agreement or ANZCERA, CER is used much more often.

15. Rules of origin are the criteria used to define where a product was made. They are an essential part of trade rules because a number of policies discriminate between exporting countries: quotas, preferential tariffs, anti-dumping actions, countervailing duty charged to counter export subsidies, and more. Rules of origin are also used to compile trade statistics, and for 'made in' labels that are attached to products. A great deal of time was spent on the ROO during the Uruguay Round of multilateral trade negotiations. It resulted in an agreement on ROO, which is a part of the GATT-1994. This first-ever agreement on the subject requires WTO members to 'ensure that their rules of origin are transparent; that they do not have restricting, distorting or disruptive effects on international trade; that they are administered in a consistent, uniform, impartial and reasonable manner; and that they are based on a positive standard. That is, they should state what *does* confer origin rather than what does not.' RIAs either conform to the WTO rules in this regard, or formulate their own deviations. These rules vary from RIA to RIA and may be similar, simpler, or more complex than the WTO rules.

16. To be more explicit, if the concessions granted are one-way, it is called a preferential trade arrangement, whereas if the concessions are reciprocal, it is called a preferential trade area.

17. Frankel 1997 and several others of his works have been cited in this work. The author took the initiative in getting express permission from Professor Jeffrey A. Frankel for this purpose.

18. The term 'spaghetti bowl' was first used by Bhagwati and Panagaria (1996).

19. Three principal methods can be used to determine where a substantial transformation occurred: (1) the change-in-tariff classification method, (2) the value-added criteria and (3) technical measurement based on the import content of a product.

20. There are two types of cumulation: (1) bilateral cumulation, where there are inputs from other member countries of the RIA which are considered domestic, and (2) diagonal cumulation, where there are inputs from certain *non*-member countries which are considered domestic. As a generalization, RIAs contain provisions allowing bilateral cumulation.

21. The WTO has two sets of subsidy regulations. The first set of rules relates to industrial subsidies and come under the Agreement on Subsidies and Countervailing Measures. The second set relates to agricultural products and is spelled out in the Agreement on Agriculture.

22. Anti-dumping duties are governed by Article VI of GATT-1994.

23. The sources of this information regarding the RIA are WTO documents published during the recent period.

2. Rationale, motivation and welfare implications

1. THE RATIONALE BEHIND REGIONALISM

Committed free traders among economists turn up their noses at the regional integration agreement (RIA) phenomenon. Whatever the trade expansion properties of RIAs, they can lead to substantial trade diversion, which in turn implies distortion of efficient global allocation of resources, resulting in welfare losses. Preferential reduction in tariffs under an RIA induces purchasers to switch demand towards the RIA partners. This happens at the expense of both domestic producers and imports from non-member countries and the rest of the world. The former is trade creation, while the latter is trade diversion. It needs to be clarified that trade is created only when cheaper and more competitive products from the RIA member economies substitute for more expensive and less competitive domestic products. When intra-bloc imports substitute for cheaper and more competitive imports from the non-RIA-member economies, when both faced tariffs, it is a case of trade diversion. To be sure, the former is beneficial, but the latter can be detrimental. The detrimental effects include loss of tariff revenue. However, the overall effect on national income may well be positive, depending upon the cost of alternative sources of supply and on trade policy towards the non-RIA-member countries.

RIAs can potentially result in the reduction of global trade and welfare. Even if it is not correct, one must know the counterfactual, or more correctly the *anti-monde*. Generally, that is left for one's imagination. Meaning thereby, if an RIA is reducing global welfare, it is doing so in comparison to what. The answer is, in comparison to complete and undistorted global free trade. RIAs are unquestionably the second best compared to global free trade. That being said, in the real-life situation, undistorted global free trade does not exist. But compared to the global trading system in which tariffs and non-tariff barriers abound, the case against RIAs is generally far from clear, and weak if it does occur (WB, 2000). Besides, other than the economic rationale, as we saw in the preceding chapter, multiple non-economic objectives generally lie behind the formation of an RIA. It is widely recognized that most RIA formulations among economies have one or more strong political objectives. An RIA motivated solely on economic objectives is rare. Furthermore, there are both static and dynamic factors that coalesce and encourage the formation of RIAs.

Apparently, trade diversion is one of the realities of an RIA. Notwithstanding the plausibilities of trade diversion, while forming or joining an RIA, countries do not expect trade diversion losses to outweigh the trade creation gains. This assumption strongly drives policy mandarins towards an RIA. In the present global economic *mise-en-scène*, most countries find themselves much more ready to participate in regional rather than in multilateral negotiations because they think that the chances of success of negotiations are maximized when they are undertaken at the regional level. One of the reasons is that negotiations in RIAs generally entail a small number of usually neighboring, like-minded, countries. This general perception is occasionally correct.

2.   MOTIVATION

The commonest and most persuasive motivation behind the formation of an RIA is market expansion in such a manner that all partners of the RIA benefit. Forming an RIA increases the size of the 'home' market for the member country's firms. As the constituent members of RIAs frequently agree to eliminate the possibility of imposing contingent protection measures like anti-dumping (AD) action and countervailing (CV) duties, this improves market access of the member economies in the entire RIA-wide market. In a multilateral context, an agreement to eliminate AD measures and CV duties appears unlikely in the foreseeable future.

The second major objective is to increase bargaining power vis-à-vis third countries by becoming a part of an RIA. This argument applies more to small developing economies as well as small states like the island countries in the Caribbean. In this case, the RIA that can help more is the customs union variety rather than the free-trade kind. This reason is often given as one that spurred the formation of the European Economic Community (EEC).[1] At the time of its formation in the late 1950s, Western European economies believed that individually European countries would have little leverage in negotiations with the United States (US), but if they formed an RIA it would increase their bargaining power. This motive has also been present in some measure in the formation of Mercado Comun del Sur or MERCOSUR. The argument there was that groups of countries would have more leverage in accession to North American Free Trade Area (NAFTA) than individual Latin American economies (Das, 1990; Hamilton and Whalley, 1996).

Third, defensive logic is often resorted to in RIA formation. An RIA may be formed as a reaction to other RIAs, particularly if the other RIAs are perceived as posing a threat of becoming inward-looking, or closed. For instance, if the EU[2] and the NAFTA or FTAA[3] continue to travel down the road with plausible threats of becoming inward-looking blocs, having a 'fortress' mentality, other geographical parts of the globe would surely come up with plans for parallel RIAs. This may be their response to provide a counter-threat to existing RIAs as well as keeping them from turning inward.

Fourth, many developing economies, particularly those in Latin America, treated RIA formation as one of the tools for trade policy reforms. Regional integration initiatives represent a third tier of trade policy reform, which aims to complement and reinforce the unilateral and multilateral liberalization. In addition, a widely agreed achievement of RIAs that motivates countries to participate in them is their ability to lock in economic reforms and liberalization. They are known to have done this better than the WTO. It is partly due to the fact that each RIA covers its own favorite set of policy areas. Some of them are not covered by the WTO at all, or not covered adequately. For instance, investment related issues and factor market policies, although discussed constantly in the WTO forum,[4] are still not covered by it. In spite of the birth of the General Agreement in Trade in Services (GATS), WTO discipline on trade in services is still inadequate. Reforms in these and other areas can be anchored through RIAs in ways that are not available in the WTO forum.

Fifth, even in the traditional domain of the WTO, that is trade in goods and services, the RIA discipline can be made stronger than that of the WTO. An important strand of the systemic credibility of the WTO is its ability to persuade members to 'bind' tariffs.[5] The maximum that can be attained in this respect is to bind tariffs at applied rates. Traditionally, developing economies were slow and reluctant to bind their tariffs because they wanted to save 'bargaining chips' for negotiations. Although during multilateral negotiations, countries are exhorted to reduce differences between bound and applied rates, there is no WTO requirement to bind at applied rates. As their participation in the multilateral trading system increased, developing country governments voluntarily decided to increase the share of bound tariff lines. In an RIA, binding is not voluntary but a requirement. The rate at which the tariffs are bound is zero. Thus, to that extent, RIAs are responsible for spawning greater trade discipline than the WTO. Greater credibility of regional liberalization strategy and trade discipline under an RIA may be associated with higher dynamic growth effects in the member developing economies because they would lead to higher domestic and foreign investment.

Sixth, harmonization of regulatory regimes is another motivation behind the membership of RIAs. Modernization and upgradation of regulatory regimes goes hand in hand with harmonization. In the absence of harmonization, technical barriers to trade and sanitary and phytosanitary measures can be used as protectionist barriers by the importing country. Entering into an RIA provides an economy with a wide variety of opportunities for harmonization and rationalization. For instance, harmonization of product standards, testing and certification procedures and rationalization of documents, particularly in the area of customs clearance, is commonly carried out by RIA members. Constituent members frequently link their computer systems after joining hands in an RIA. Variations in these systems and regulatory regimes work as non-tariff barriers (NTBs). The benefits from the eliminations of these NTBs rise with the rising intra-RIA trade.

Last, the developing economies are motivated to join in RIAs with emerging-market[6] and industrial economies in the expectation of benefiting from capital transfer, receiving foreign direct investment (FDI) and technology transfer from the better-off and more mature partner economies. They tend to see additionality in it. That is, after becoming a member of an RIA with mature economies, the developing economies believe that the financial transfers would rise in volume, although additionality is somewhat difficult to determine. These developing countries may also see such transfers offsetting tariff revenue losses and the cost of trade diversion.[7]

3. MULTILATERAL TRADE LIBERALIZATION AND RIAs

Eight rounds of multilateral trade negotiations (MTNs) have an impressive record for tariff reduction on manufactured products. According to WTO (2001), during the first five rounds of MTNs between 1947–62, weighted tariff reductions of 36 percent took place. In the Kennedy Round (1964–67) tariffs declined further by 37 percent and again in the Tokyo Round (1980–87) by 33 percent. During the Uruguay Round (1986–94) weighted tariff reductions of 38 percent took place. While this was an unmitigated success, the GATT rounds were not as effective in disciplining tariffs on primary products and NTBs, in particular the quantitative restrictions.

At least until the Uruguay Round agreement was signed and the WTO was created, the global trading system was replete with and distracted by voluntary export restraints and administered protection.[8] This made it very difficult to determine whether the liberalization taking place is most-favored nation (MFN) liberalization being done to move towards a free-trade regime, or whether it is merely of an *ad hoc* and discriminatory variety. When the global economy is ridden with protectionist barriers, large welfare gains from regional integration are feasible. Simultaneous regional reductions of tariffs and NTBs will then lead to possible expansion of scale economies for the firms in the member countries. Specialization, plant rationalization and increased product variety will be the other related benefits.

Many large and medium-sized developing economies made significant endeavors to liberalize unilaterally after the mid-1980s. However, they frequently had to stop this after a while because its domestic political unpopularity meant it was not feasible. It is an axiom that at political level, there is a strong mercantilist bias in trade-policy thinking. This bias is not confined to developing economies but is to be found in the industrial economies as well. Bringing down trade barriers is seen as a concession given to the trade partners. Due to this mindset, unilateral trade liberalization has its limits. Liberalization in an RIA context allows liberalization endeavors to go further than this limit (Panagariya, 1998). Under the aegis of an RIA, trade liberalization can be made more acceptable to the electorate than unilateral liberalization. Trade policy is endogenous to any economy and is heavily influenced by domestic politics as well as lobbyists and vested interest groups. In trade policy, they are a disturbing fact of life. RIAs can help the trade policy move towards liberalization. As the lobbying activity tries to influence the level of tariffs and NTBs, an RIA can lower the level of lobbying by making the benefits of lobbying more diffused. They can also make the free-rider problem more acute regionally and force the free-rider to comply with the RIA norms in a short timespan.[9]

Evidence for the decade of the 1990s shows that many developing economies liberalized their economic regimes to be a part of regional economic integration endeavors (Sharer, 1999). Demonstration effect was frequently found to operate. In many of the developing economies, RIAs contributed substantially to structural reforms by creating incentives to eliminate restrictive trade practices and licensing procedures, streamlining customs procedures and regulations, integrating financial markets, and simplifying transfers and payments procedures. A few countries in Africa have gone beyond this, harmonizing investment incentives and tax treatment, as well as standards and technical regulations. In sub-Saharan Africa, many economies took these measures during the late 1990s. It must be noted, however, that most countries in Africa were slow to start liberalization, Egypt and Morocco were two exceptions in this regard.

3.1 Regional Versus Global Liberalization

In a global economy that is full of RIAs, an autarkic economy that is embarking on its path to liberalization is faced with two choices: whether to liberalize its trade regime globally in a non-discriminatory-non-preferential manner or to liberalize preferentially in a limited fashion for its RIA partners. Few empirical or theoretical studies have addressed the issue of whether liberalizing broadly to the global economy is a superior alternative to liberalizing to an RIA. Participation in an RIA does not explain the cross-country GDP growth differentials, although the generalization holds that open economies grow faster and autarkic ones record tepid GDP growth rates, regardless of their RIA participation (Vamvakidis, 1997 and 1998). Comparing the before-and-after scenarios of growth performance of liberalizing economies can be illuminating in this regard. It can reveal the impact of discriminatory and non-discriminatory liberalization on GDP growth performance of the liberalizing economy.

Based on the data set for the 1950-92 period, Vamvakidis (1999) estimated the growth performances of economies that liberalized broadly to join the global economy and those that liberalized preferentially to join an RIA. His study had 109 cases of liberalization aimed at joining an RIA and 51 cases of broad liberalization to join the global economy. His inference was that autarkic economies that want to open their markets to free trade should choose non-preferential non-discriminatory liberalization. On an average, economies were found to grow faster, both in the short and long term, after broad, non-preferential liberalization. Vamvakidis (1999) presented time series evidence to this effect.

The same could not be said about the economies whose liberalization was limited to the preferential variety. In cases where liberalization was limited to the RIA partners, growth was even found to be negative and statistically significant in most empirical specifications. Thus, one can conclude that only non-discriminatory liberalization fosters growth. In terms of short- and long-term growth benefits, a liberalizing economy was found to be better off integrating with the global economy than with an RIA. To test the robustness of these results, Vamvakidis (1999) used two measures of openness. First, the openness index constructed by Sachs and Warner (1995) and second, the trade share, that is, the ratio of total trade to GDP. Both were found to be positive and statistically significant in fixed-effects regressions, when either growth or investment share is the dependent variable.

Although liberalization in the context of an RIA and broad global liberalization are not mutually exclusive theoretically, economies seldom followed them simultaneously. In general, one was taken up at the exclusion of the other. However, in more recent liberalization episodes, there were many cases of two paths of liberalization being followed simultaneously.

3.2   RIAs and Domestic Policy Integration

In international trade, some domestic policies may have an impact identical to that of trade policy measures applied at the border. Reference here is to the domestic policy areas like tax structure, labor market regulations, environmental norms, and competition laws. Although they can be used as trade barriers, often their influence on trade is unintended. Even if policy makers have no intention of discriminating against imports, domestic industries may perceive the differences in regulatory regimes as 'unfair' treatment of foreign firms in the domestic markets. Under an RIA regime if an economy moves towards free trade, some consumer, environmental, and labor interest groups may be apprehensive about erosion of national standards. The reverse is also feasible and often happens. That is, domestic consumer, environmental, and labor interest groups may feel that under the RIA regime, trading partners should be asked to adopt changes in their policy regime. These domestic concerns and external pressures have plagued numerous RIA members, which has led the constituent member economies to negotiate disciplines for domestic regulatory regimes under the RIA.

Domestic policy integration is defined as actions taken by constituent members of an RIA to reduce market segmenting effects of differences in national regulatory regimes through either coordination and harmonization or by way of mutual recognition of national laws, regulations, and enforcement mechanisms (Hoekman et al., 1998). The first objective of policy integration is to ensure a 'level playing field' for the firms from the member countries operating in the RIA. A second objective is to ensure that there is no resurgence in trade barriers through the back door in the member economies. Third, domestic policy integration is also driven by a desire to internalize externalities, reduce waste and redundancy, and increase competition in the domestic markets. A good example of this could be the harmonization of health and safety standards in the industrial sector, or having uniform competition or antitrust regulations for firms, in all the constituent members of the RIA.

One of the strongest benefits of domestic policy integration for the constituent members is enhancement of the contestability of markets. Lowering tariffs is only one way of bringing down barriers that have the effect of insulating markets for similar goods in the member countries, policy integration is another important instrument for attaining the same objective. It can deliver large economic benefits to the constituent members as well as to the non-member economies. All the members of an RIA can benefit from common administrative procedures and unified product standards. The ultimate effect of policy integration is reduction in administrative costs. If that does take place, the attractiveness of an RIA as an instrument of trade and investment policy reforms for the members is enhanced.

Hoekman et al. (1998) contend that where policy integration is being pursued, the optimal domain must be considered properly. In some cases, the optimal domain would be regional while in many cases it would be global. Nation states pursue multilateral efforts all the while to agree on common standards and norms in various areas of trade and other economic activity. In some instance these endeavors succeed in the creation of multilateral institutions like the International Organization for Standardization (IOS), the Basle Committee on Banking Supervision, and the International Telecommunications Union (ITU). These organizations then become the fora where common norms and standards continue to develop. To be sure, regulatory norms are best developed at the global level. When RIAs take initiative to develop them, they need to be conscious of these norms being internationally compatible (Hoekman et al., 1998; Vamvakidis, 1998).

Quantifying the welfare implications of policy integration is not a simple and straightforward exercise, although it should be attempted because policy decisions in this area would necessarily benefit from such an input. Notwithstanding the benefits of policy integration, it is not wise to presume that RIAs incorporating elements of policy integration have better welfare and social implications than those without. This is because the latter may have more far-reaching economic implications than those that do incorporate policy integration. The economic impact of traditional trade liberalization, which is limited to integration of trade policies, can easily dominate the impact of integration of domestic policies.

So far domestic policy integration has been an item low on the agenda of most RIAs and has not played a major role. In RIAs where it does figure, it has remained confined to fiscal and monetary policies. This was noticed in case of Union économique et monétaire de l'Afrique occidentale (UEMAO). Integration of microeconomic policies has only been noticed in RIAs involving industrial economies, like the EU and CER. Some recent RIAs, which have developing, emerging-market and industrial economies as members, do have broad future objectives of economic policy integration. MERCOSUR, Euro-Mediterranean Partnership Agreement (EMPA), the FTAA and APEC come under this category (Hoekman et al., 1998; Vamvakidis, 1998).

4. IMPACT OF RIA CREATION

When tariff barriers are eliminated and an RIA is created, share of imports from partner economies rises. Schiff and Winters (2003) made a before-and-after comparison and found that it is correct in around 80 percent of the RIAs.

> These results look like cause for celebration, for strong international trade performance is now generally accepted as one of the main determinants of economic prosperity. However, before breaking out the champagne we need to ask whether every increase in trade is desirable and whether these increases are actually due to regionalism.

If exports from a constituent member of the RIA displace domestic output in the importing economy because once the tariff is eliminated the exporting partner's product becomes more competitive in the domestic market, the domestic economy benefits from two classical sources of gains from trade. First, real domestic resources are saved and production is diverted in the direction of comparative advantage of the economy. Second, domestic consumers benefit from lower, undistorted prices. This is trade creation and its impact is unambiguously favorable for the domestic economy.

Forming an RIA affects trade flows and their directionality and, therefore, production patterns in the economies that are constituent members of that RIA. Locations of production in the constituent member countries are seriously influenced by RIA formation. As alluded to above, enlargement of national or 'home' market by way of regional integration is another major economic impact of an RIA. Schiff and Winters (2003) noted that:

> A well crafted trade bloc can raise efficiency – and economic welfare – in its member countries by facilitating consumer choice and increasing the competition that producers face. Dropping tariff barriers enlarges markets and gives more efficient producers entry into countries where their prices had been inflated by duties and other trade barriers.

Here the emphasis needs to be on well crafted.

To be sure, the larger regional market provides scale economies to firms, which lead to efficiency gains. A larger market also tends to attract greater investment, including more FDI. This argument applies *a fortiori* to the contemporary wave of new regionalism. Larger manufacturing and services sector projects for which market size matters, become feasible for the first time due to the formation of an RIA. Dismantling of regional trade barriers also forces firms from different member countries into more intense competition with each other than was feasible before the RIA was formed. This induces firms to make efficiency improvements and raise their level of total factor productivity. Thus, the immediate impact of enlarged markets is larger firms and enhanced competition.

Trade theory posited that trade liberalization improves economic welfare by enhancing efficiency in the liberalizing economy. Trade policy liberalization undertaken to join an RIA takes an economy towards this objective, although a better motive would be to liberalize in a non-discriminatory manner, in keeping with the most-favored-nation principle promoted by Article I of the WTO, Article II of the GATS and Article IV of the TRIPS (Trade Related Aspects of Intellectual Property Rights) agreement. The language Article I of GATT-1947 is subsumed in GATT-1994, which unequivocally states that:

> With respect of customs duties and charges of any kind ... any advantage, privilege, favor, or immunity granted by contracting party to any product originating in or

destined for any other country shall be accorded immediately and unconditionally to the like product originating in or destined for the territories of all other contracting parties. (GATT, 1994).[10]

Neo-classical analysis would support this line of logic. As stated above, RIAs are widely considered the second best approach to trade liberalization. It is also well established that RIAs make a valuable contribution by giving early partial delivery of some of the benefits which can be expected from full MFN-consistent liberalization. However, Scollay (2000) has emphasized that this favorable impact of an RIA is subject to the proviso that adequate precaution is taken to ensure that trade diversion effects do not outweigh trade creation ones, and the dynamic gains arising from regional liberalization, which can include productivity gains stimulated by increased competition and exploitation of economies of scale made possible by access to a large market. RIAs also enable developing economies to phase in their integration into global markets.

The favorable impact of an RIA is conditional. The limiting condition is that RIAs are able to achieve a deeper degree of economic integration than the multilateral trading system. This is well within the realm of feasibility because RIAs usually entail neighboring like-minded countries. A smaller forum making negotiations on new trade issues easier than a larger group of countries, has a fighting chance of working. A smaller group of like-minded neighboring countries also makes it possible to establish the necessary centralized institutions or federalizing policy-making and enforcement institutions. Economic theory suggests that RIAs can be so designed as to have favorable impact and be welfare improving, but in a real-life situation 'the required information and the rights to manipulate the trade policy to achieve this result are generally missing'.

Also, politically regions may well be more willing to agree to liberalization than individual economies. The post-war experience with the EEC confirms this observation. The Kennedy Round (1964–67) would not have taken off without EEC support. During that period, individual economies were reluctant to deepen their trade liberalization. France and Italy were resisting the idea of making any trade concession in the 1960s and Germany would not have made concessions in isolation from its close trading partners. However, as a group, the EEC supported the Kennedy Round MTNs.

4.1   Choice of Partners and their Impact

When the constituent members of an RIA are at varying levels of economic development, that is, when RIAs are formed between developing, emerging-market and industrial economies, it is known to promote technology transfers from the high-income, matured, industrialized economies to the lower-income less-developed constituent members. Therefore, the possibility of enhancing such technology transfer motivates developing economies to form RIAs with the emerging-market and industrial economies. Although the mechanisms of technology transfer are neither clear nor fully understood, an important body of literature argues that it is promoted through trade flows.

When members of an RIA are at varying levels of economic development, their knowledge accumulation also varies. Despite the limitations of patents and copyright, knowledge is an international public good and could be transferred to other RIA member economies through trade, FDI and scientific exchanges, affecting their growth, which is at the heart of the development. Coe and Helpman (1995) and Coe et al. (1997) constructed an index of total knowledge capital in each industrial country. They posited that trading partners get access to a country's stock of knowledge in proportion to their imports from that country. They found that access to foreign knowledge is a statistically significant determinant of the rate of total factor productivity across the 30 Organization for Economic Co-operation and Development (OECD) countries and developing countries.[11] Thus, an RIA might work toward promoting technology transfer through trade expansion. Similarly, RIAs are known to promote FDI, which in turn is a well-known source of technology transfer.

Again, when the constituent members of an RIA are at varying levels of economic development, it helps in importing a growth-stimulating environment and institutions of the partner developing economies. Thus, the ultimate benefit to them is that the formation of an RIA is able to enforce a more stable domestic macroeconomic environment (WB, 2000). In the process, it might be able to reform its labor, investment and industrial policies as well as corporate governance. Lejour et al. (2001) examined the economic impact of the enlargement of the European Union (EU) when the eight Central and East European Countries (CEEC) join in 2004.[12] This study focused on the integration process, which *inter alia* involved accession to the internal market, equalization of external tariffs and free movement of labor and capital. They adopted a computable general equilibrium model for the world economy, called WorldScan, to quantify the implication of EU enlargement. Their principal conclusion was that the EU enlargement would result in modest or minuscule gains for the EU economies, but large gains for the newly acceding CEEC economies. Average increase in per capita GDP in the CEEC countries was estimated at 8 percent in the long run (by 2020), with Hungary showing the maximum increase because it is relatively more open than the other nine economies. They suggested that compared to the customs union and free movement of labor and capital, accession to the internal EU market yielded the largest economic benefits. They computed a 0.2 percent expansion of consumption in the EU as a group. This conclusion is in line with the previous model stimulations of EU enlargement by Brown et al. (1997) who estimated real GDP gains for CEECs, ranging from 3.8 percent to 7.3 percent, with consumption gains to the EU of 0.1 percent. Similarly, Breuss (2001) computed gains in real GDP between 4 percent and 9 percent for the CEECs and one tenth of this for the EU.

It is accepted that after joining the EU, Greece, Portugal and Spain clearly benefited from similar gains.[13] However, income convergence between member states was far from uniform or steady. While Ireland, Portugal and Spain are known for rapid catch up, Greece is not. Summary measures of the cross-country dispersion of per capita income were computed for the EU economies by Puga (2002), which indicated significant convergence through the decades of 1960s and 1970s. During the 1980s, no further aggregate change was found. However, convergence resumed across the EU economies in the late 1980s. This was accompanied by divergence at the sub-national level.[14]

Mexico is another example of an emerging-market economy reaping similar benefits by joining large industrial economies in an RIA (see Chapter 6, section 8). Aggregate and micro data on trade between the US, Canada, and Mexico were used by Krueger (1999) to attempt to assess the early effects of Mexican entry into NAFTA. Although the fraction of Mexican trade with the US and Canada has risen sharply, a number of factors have contributed to this result. Mexican reduction of tariffs and quantitative restrictions (QRs) and the alteration of exchange rate policy at the end of 1994 were both important in contributing to the sharp rise in Mexican trade volume.

As a rule of thumb, RIAs between industrial and developing economies are of FTA variety. The NAFTA and Euro-Mediterranean Partnership Agreement (EMPA) are good examples of such RIAs. When developing economies are involved as custom union (CU) partners with industrial economies, as in case of the EU-Turkey CU, the partner developing economy is effectively obliged to adopt the lower tariff rates of the industrial partners, which implies substantial measure of trade liberalization. Such a large liberalization is indeed a source of gains to the member developing economy.

4.2   On Developing Economies

When RIAs are created between developing economies, feasibility of knowledge, technology and capital transfers between the member economies are minimal – even non-existent. Growth inducing effects of such transfers are missing in RIAs between the developing economies. Furthermore, the impact of forming an RIA between the developing economies tends to be problematic in several respects (WB, 2000). Some empirical studies have called into question the economic benefits of such RIAs. Several of them advanced pessimistic conclusions regarding RIAs in Africa.[15] Other than doubtful non-economic benefits, RIAs between developing economies are more likely to spawn trade diversion than trade creation, particularly when common external tariff rates are high. Detailed time series data analysis for sub-Saharan African RIAs revealed that judged by the variance in their trade patterns from that which their comparative advantage would predict, RIAs have negative effects on members and non-members alike. If RIAs succeed in diverting regional imports from low to high cost sources, they would naturally retard the industrialization and real GDP growth endeavors of the member countries (Yeats, 1998).

A lower share of intra-trade was found for RTAs between the developing economies, particularly in Africa, than those between the industrial economies. In an intertemporal analysis, a negative impact of RIAs on trade was not only found for Africa, it was also found and predicted for Latin America (Nagarajan, 1998). The best route to ensure that RIAs among the developing economies result in welfare gains for the members is to liberalize their trade regime with respect to the rest of the world. Also, developing economies should integrate with each other in the areas of regional public goods, which tend to benefit all the partners.

One reason why trade diversion was so commonly found in RIAs in sub-Saharan Africa is that the tariff barriers in Africa before the Uruguay Round (1986–94) were exceedingly high, perhaps higher than any other developing country group. Even in the late-1990s, the average tariff in sub-Saharan Africa was 26.8 percent, more that four times higher than the corresponding average (6.1 percent) for the OECD economies. Such a high level of MFN protection, coupled with the formation of RTAs led, according to customs union theory, to high trade diversion effect in the sub-Saharan RIAs (Cernat, 2001).

There is dissention in views in this respect and the results of studies that concluded that RIAs between developing economies end up diverting trade have been challenged. For instance, Evans (1998) and Lewis et al. (1999) found a positive net effect of RIAs in South Africa. Taking into account the dynamic impact of RIAs, they concluded that economic integration could create threshold scales necessary to trigger the much-needed strategic complementarities within the region.

4.3 On Small Economies

There are several definitions of small economies. A large majority of small economies are covered under the United Nations' (UN) classification of least developed countries (LDCs). In April 2003, the UN classification included 49 countries, of which 30 were members of the WTO and 5 were observers.[16] The World Bank classified 41 countries as small states, while the Commonwealth Secretariat categorized 30 countries as small states. The UN also has another grouping called the small island developing states comprising 28 microeconomies. According to a joint definition of the Commonwealth Secretariat and the World Bank, small states are those that have the population of 1.5 million or less.[17] Here we are only concerned with the low-income small states, not the high-incomes one, like the Bahamas, Bahrain, Cyprus, Malta and Qatar.

Vulnerability of low-income small economies to changes in external environment is far greater than that of other economies. Schiff (2002) examined the various optimal policy responses of small states in the face of on-going globalization and formation of RIAs. A large number of small economies in the Caribbean, South East Asia, and Central, Western and Southern Africa have formed RIAs with other developing economies. As noted earlier, RIAs between developing economies that provide preferential access to the members but do not change their trade policies vis-à-vis the rest of the world, may well end up lowering the welfare of the entire trade bloc (WB, 2000). The case of small economies is no different. RIAs between small and developing economies are more than likely to induce a replacement of cheaper imports from the rest of the world with more expensive imports from the member countries, in effect encouraging the inefficient producers to continue production. The smaller the share of intra-regional trade in total trade of the member countries, the more likely is the possibility of the RIA becoming trade diverting.

It has been observed that larger and more developed members of an RIA benefit at the expense of smaller and less developed ones. This was observed when CARICOM (Caribbean Community and Common Market) finalized its Single Market and Economy initiative in 2002. The smaller and less-developed members were much less enthusiastic about this initiative than the larger and better-off ones. Unless a compensatory mechanism is created, this could cause friction between the RIA members. Another method of mitigating this problem is to lower the CET because this reduces the size of intra-RIA transfer, whether positive or negative.

Small economies integrating with emerging-market or industrial economies are likely to form an RIA which is superior in welfare terms (WB, 2000). It also increases the credibility of the small economy and helps in attracting FDI from the high-income economies in the neighborhood. Visibility and improvement in international negotiations is another benefit that small states can derive from an RIA membership (refer to Chapter 6).

5. THE AGGLOMERATION OR CLUSTERING EFFECT

To be sure, comparative advantage is a force to reckon with in influencing the location and/or relocation decisions in an RIA. These decisions are also significantly driven by the agglomeration or clustering effect. Fujita et al. (1999) posited the concept of 'cumulative causation' which implies that as clusters of manufacturing activity – or, say, economic activity in general – start to develop in a country and/or in an RIA, a spatial clustering or agglomeration of economic activity takes place assisting location-specific development. The advantages of starting at a specific location provide an industry, or economic activity, with a head start.

An age-old dictum is that in all economic activity, spatial clustering is all-pervasive. Why do towns and cities come into existence? It is because economic agents – consumers, producers, workers and capital owners – benefit from being in close proximity. There is a strong symbiotic bond between them. A particular type of economic activity finds an appropriate location and creates a spatial cluster at that location. It has long been the story of industrialization, of which Detroit and Silicon Valley are two good contemporary examples. Banking activity is concentrated in the global financial centers like Wall Street in New York and the City of London for the same reasons. Numerous other industries provide examples of spatial clustering in one, or a few, locations.

Various centripetal forces that pull economic activity towards the spatial cluster are responsible for their creation. One of the most important centripetal forces is the knowledge spillovers and technological externalities which make it logical for firms to locate in the vicinity of each other. Second, the availability of industrial skills and labor market pools encourages firms to be in a location where they are readily available, or where trained human resources are available and their skills can be augmented according to the specific needs of an individual firm at a reasonable cost. Third, the buyer–seller proximity is another important force pulling firms together in a specific location. Some firms produce inputs for the other firms and are vertically integrated with them. If the two sets of firms are close to each other, they both benefit from the proximity. In the theory of unbalanced growth, propounded by Albert O. Hirschman, this phenomenon was explained with the help of the 'backward' or demand linkage and 'forward' or supply linkage.[18] Fujita et al. (1999) formally established that these linkages create a positive interdependence between the location decisions of different firms and industries. This can give rise to the process of cumulative causation creating agglomeration of economic activity. Here the assumption is that the production activity has an increasing return to scale.

The centripetal forces, when they operate at an aggregated level, create backward linkages. That is, aggregate demand created by them strengthens the backward linkages drawing firms from different sectors into locations with large markets. At the aggregate level, agglomeration forces generate the need for a broad class of business activity and create a market demand for basic industrial infrastructure like financial and telecommunication services. There are real efficiency gains from spatial concentration. As opposed to this, centripetal forces can be spatially focused. Need and availability of highly specialized inputs or technologically narrow knowledge spillover operate to create clusters of narrowly defined industries or mere industrial sectors, rather than a broad manufacturing cluster. Silicon Valley is an excellent illustration of this kind of clustering. Conversely, congestion, pollution, rising prices of office space, land or other immobile factors of production pull a cluster in the opposite direction. A rising level of competition is another factor that can deter the spatial clustering process. Usually deterrence strengthens process after the clustering acquires a large size, and seems saturated.

Membership of an RIA affects the creation or expansion of spatial clusters. With such a membership, tariff and non-tariff barriers go down, or are eliminated. This makes forward and backward linkages stronger. A larger number of firms can participate in the creation of spatial clusters after the RIA formation. The opposite also holds, that is, an RIA makes it possible to supply goods to consumers from a small number of spatial clusters. This implies that forming an RIA tips the balance in favor of creation of larger agglomerations, until the centrifugal forces start operating in the opposite direction.

There is a strong possibility that formation of an RIA may generate more spatial concentration of sectors, rather than aggregate level industrial concentrations in the constituent member economies. For instance, industries in the US are far more spatially concentrated than in Europe. This observation holds even after controlling for the distribution of population and manufacturing activity. Therefore, the regional integration process in Europe could well advance agglomeration at the sectoral level. So far there is little evidence of relocation of industries in the EU on these lines, but if or when it happens it would result in considerable short-term adjustment costs for the European industrial sector. The industrial structure of member countries would change with relocation of industries. As there are real efficiency gains from spatial concentration, on balance there would be benefits from such industrial relocation and growth of spatial clusters. Sectoral agglomerations may also contribute to a decrease in intra-RIA inequalities because each member country may attract industrial or services activity of one kind or the other.

One of the impacts of the formation of an RIA could be a smaller number of large industrial agglomerations, which could deindustrialize some of the constituent members of an RIA and mark them as less-favored regions. If this happens, some of the members of the RIA may grow and industrialize at the cost of others. Such an outcome is more plausible if manufacturing and services sectors are relatively small, that is, they account for a smaller share of GDP. If the manufacturing sector is spatially limited to only a few locations, it is less likely to press against the supply constraints. It is also less likely to lead to rising prices of immobile factors like land. This is likely to take place at early stages of economic growth in a group of economies.[19]

5.1 Industrial and Sectoral Specialization in an RIA

As an RIA is created, inter- and intra-industry trade flows expand and with that, it is logical to expect that, each member country's production structure would be reorganized to exploit comparative advantage and possible benefits from spatial clustering of sectors. However, evidence from the EU reveals that regional integration only resulted in modest increase in manufacturing specialization. Midelfart-Knarvik et al. (1999) computed measures of the difference between the industrial structures of the EU economies at the level of 36 different industrial sectors. They concluded that since 1970, all the EU economies except the Netherlands saw their industrial structures become more dissimilar to the other EU economies. That is, industrial structures of the EU economies were not becoming harmonized, if anything they were becoming dis-harmonized and specialized.

The measures computed by Midelfart-Knarvik et al. (1999) were averaged over groups of countries according to the date of their accession to the EU. For the new entrants, it was observed that there was a more or less steady increase in the measures, which indicated that the industrial structure was becoming more dissimilar. Econometric analysis of these changing patterns of industrial and sectoral specialization indicated that it was largely in line with intra-EU comparative advantage. That is, labor-intensive and skilled-labor-intensive industries and sectors tended to relocate towards labor and skilled-labor abundant countries, and knowledge-intensive and R&D-intensive activities tended to relocate towards scientist abundant countries (Midelfart-Knarvik and Overman 2002). It should however be noted that reallocations in line with intra-EU comparative advantage are not necessarily salutary or welfare increasing, as they could result in trade diversion.

However, Venables and Winters (2003) contended that analysis at the level of countries, taking 36 industrial sectors, is likely to understate the degree of specialization that is taking place in the EU economies. At the level of narrow sectors, they believe that there is 'evidence of increasing clustering of activity, and specialization is increasing at the sub-national as well as the national level'. Despite this evidence of progress in clustering and specialization, it has been observed that the EU economies and regions remain very much less specialized than comparable size geographical units in the US. Thus far, integration has not caused 'specialization and clustering of activity to go as far as the US experience suggests would be expected in a single country'.

5.2 Foreign Direct Investment and RIAs

The FDI flows between countries are presently regulated by bilateral investment treaties (BITs). Approaching two thousand of them are in force, linking countries in all continents and at varying levels of development and stages of industrialization.[20] Typically, BITs are agreements with a 'narrow' and specific purpose. Their objective is to remove barriers and uncertainty in the area of foreign investment. They are not made to encourage mutual investment between the two partners. In general, these bilateral treaties cover stipulations regarding admission and general treatment of investment, dispute settlement issues and other specific provisions. BITs defer to the domestic law of the home country and the governments of the recipient country hold discretion to manage the sectors in which FDI is made. However, the US has been more progressive than other investing countries in this regard and in most of its BITs insists on MFN and national treatment on the admission of investment (subject to explicit specific exceptions). Moreover, during the 1990s, when FDI assumed a much more prominent role in development thinking, this approach began to find favor in other investing countries as well.

The BITs essentially call for fair and equitable treatment of FDI, security of ownership, and freedom from unreasonable or discriminatory restrictions on the operation of investments. The MFN treatment in BITs implies that foreign investors should not be treated more favorably than are the partner country's residents, although, as in case of trade, this is subject to exceptions. In the context of RIAs, FDI from the RIA member countries is often treated more favorably. Dispute settlement provisions vary in BITs. However, most define arbitration procedures based on international standards laid down by the organization established by the World Bank Group. It is called the International Center for Settlement of Investment Disputes (ICSID).

For the purpose of RIAs, the BITS have also been made into freestanding multi-country regional treaties. Agreement on Investment and Free Movement of Arab Capital among Arab Countries (of 1970) and the Colonia Protocol on the Promotion and Reciprocal Protection of Investment within MERCOSUR (of 1994) are two such treaties. A BIT can also form a part of an RIA. For example, the Andean Community, the EU, LAIA, NAFTA and Common Market for Eastern and Southern Africa (COMESA) all have elements of a BIT. Of these, the most far-reaching investment provisions are those of the EU. They had to be far-reaching because the EU was aimed at creating a Single Market, which includes movements of factors of production.

The US also took the initiative in the area of making the BIT concept regional, which is reflected in the NAFTA agreement. It contains a well-researched and innovative chapter on investment in NAFTA, notwithstanding the fact that it is only an FTA not a CU. This chapter has been admired and flatteringly imitated by other RIAs, particularly by the APEC and the Group-of-Three. Some of the important features of NAFTA include (1) national treatment in establishment, (2) MFN treatment in establishment and operations, (3) a ban on new performance requirements, (4) phasing out of old performance requirements, and (5) a ban on expropriations except for public policy reasons on a non-discriminatory basis and with full compensation. This is a long list of provisions. Another innovation of NAFTA was to have extensive dispute settlement provisions, which include private action against recalcitrant host governments. Taking their cue from NAFTA, members of APEC agreed on a more extensive set of principles on intra-regional investment in 1994. However, these principles presently exist only on a non-binding basis.

Economies that suffer from low credibility of their policy regimes face aversion by foreign investors. If investors have noticed sudden policy shifts, frequent changes in tariff rates, variations in tax incentives, a history of illiberal trade policy, or instances of nationalization in the past, it is reasonable that they would avoid investing in such an economy. Interest-group-driven governments and kleptocratic regimes also lead to a low image in the global investment markets. In the backdrop of low credibility, when policy reforms are undertaken, their benefits may be slow to arrive because changing an image in the global investment markets is a slow process. In such cases, RIAs can help improve the policy credibility of an economy. For policy reforms and changes to have a positive impact on investment, they must either raise expected returns or lower costs. By anchoring such reforms through a binding commitment to an RIA the economy in question may improve its policy credibility in the global investment marketplace. In this regard, RIAs can set the norms. They can reward a good policy regime and reform measures in a constituent member economy. Conversely, they can punish the bad policy regimes and policy vicissitudes. If the latter target has to be achieved, the RIA partners must have the power, interest and commitment to enforce the necessary reforms. The partners need to be large enough, stable enough and have a sufficiently strong interest in the RIA to make it worth their while to discipline the target country (Fernandez, 1998).

Mexico's membership of NAFTA provided a considerable impetus to its policy reforms, tariff reduction and investment regulation liberalization. Its membership also seriously restrained the ability to raise tariffs and dismantle trade policy and investment reforms. That there was a sea change in its intellectual policy climate became obvious from the manner in which the 1994 financial crisis was handled. Its credibility in the global investment market was enhanced considerably. With southern enlargement of the EU, risk premium on investment in the newly acceding economies declined markedly. Policy commitments by the EU governments reduced future uncertainty and induced additional investment and growth in the newly acceding economies. The same effect is likely to continue in the eight CEECs, Cyprus and Malta that signed the Accession Treaty with the EU in April 2003.[21]

6.   WELFARE IMPLICATIONS

The economics of RIAs has been extensively researched, starting with the seminal contribution of Jacob Viner. The welfare impact of RIA is an issue, which has been the subject of on-going debate since Viner's early analyses over a half century ago. Regional integration, when tariffs are prohibitively high so that economies are autarkic or nearly autarkic, raises the level of welfare of the regional trading blocs because trade diversion cannot take place. The other extreme is when the tariffs are zero or trade with non-partner countries is free. Under these circumstances as well, regional integration among small economies would raise the welfare of the regional trading bloc. However, for any tariffs level between autarkic and zero, regional integration seems to have an ambiguous effect on welfare.[22]

Early research on the welfare impact of RIA was stimulated by the integration experiment taking place in Europe. In the Vinerian analysis, trade creation and trade diversion were the two traditional tools for RIA analysis and were considered marvelous heuristic devises for illustrating the fundamental effects of RIAs. The age-old and well-known *static* Vinerian concept is that the trade creation effect benefits the partners of the RIA, while there is an unambiguous loss from trade diversion (Viner, 1950). These two seminal Vinerian concepts have proved to be central to the subsequent thinking and policy debate on regionalism. Viner's conclusions were that RIAs might predominantly be trade diverting and therefore welfare-reducing for the members. Therefore, the static theory essentially failed to yield universally applicable guidelines for policy application.

The welfare implications of regionalism or preferential trade policies in static economic theory are dependent upon the circumstances surrounding an individual RIA and the member economies. They are consistent with the theory of second-best in which the movements in the direction of Pareto-optimality are not always welfare-improving. Notwithstanding the long-lasting Vinerian concepts, some current researchers (see Winters, 1999) believe that except for the very simple case explored by Viner, the mapping from trade creation and trade diversion to economic welfare is treacherous.

For example, *à la* Winters (1999) 'pure trade diversion can be beneficial if its effect of lowering consumer prices is sufficiently important to welfare. The benefit of trade creation for a single country can be outweighed by the losses of tariff revenues on the pre-RIA volume of imports from the partner countries'. Thus, the results based on the trade creation and trade diversion concepts should be taken as indicative, not definitive. Trade creation for the RIA members indirectly affects the non-members or the rest of the world. Higher income inside the RIA would lead to greater consumption, parts of which will indeed be of goods and services produced outside the RIA. This benefits the non-members.

According to the maxims of the classical trade theory, welfare in the global economy is maximized if the number of RIAs is one, or if the global economy is one large RIA. This amounts to free global trade. By the same token global welfare is also maximized if the membership of RIAs is large. This would stand for zero or near zero optimal tariffs, so that the effect is close to free trade. With the increase in the number of RIAs, economic welfare must first decline, reach a minimum, and then rise again. De Melo and Panagariya (1992) posited that if one starts from one RIA in the world or from a free trade scenario, and divides the world into two RIAs, there is trade diversion due to a positive tariff on extra-bloc imports. This should lead to a decline in global welfare. Next, if the world is divided into three RIAs, the optimal tariff declines, however each bloc becomes smaller. The former leads to trade creation, while the latter to trade diversion. Thus, the net welfare effect would remain somewhat unclear.

Measured static welfare effects of regional integration tend to be ambiguous in sign and small in size. This led many proponents of regional integration to bring in refinement and switch attention from the old stylized static approach to dynamic effects of RIA. They believed that the latter were likely to be positive and large (Hoekman et al., 1998; Cernat, 2001). In the earlier exposition we have seen that RIAs can lead to dynamic benefits through economies of scale for small economies with small markets and also through the effect of enhanced competition. These effects can enhance welfare only if market forces determine which firms expand and which contract and are phased out.

Another source of dynamic benefit in an RIA is the incentive for knowledge and transfer of technology, which may favorably affect the rate of GDP growth. This kind of dynamic benefit may be large in an RIA between developing and industrial economies, and may not exist in one between developing economies. The probabilities of RIAs generating economies of scale and competitive gains under imperfectly competitive market structures are high. This would be another beneficial effect, leading to welfare gains. However, these benefits would potentially double if RIAs also stimulate investment. RIAs can potentially increase FDI flows, both from the more developed members of the RIA and from the rest of the world. In addition, locating (or relocating) of industry among member countries would be logically affected in a manner that enhances growth, and eventually welfare (Hoekman et al., 1998).

RIAs and trade liberalization on a preferential basis does not necessarily have to be benign in itself. Membership of an RIA does not suspend the ordinary laws of economics. That mere membership of an RIA does not necessarily ensure welfare gains is obvious from the EU membership of Greece and Ireland. The latter became a part of the then EEC in 1973, with a per capita GDP level of 62 percent of the EU average, measured in purchasing power parity terms. In 2002, Ireland's per capital GDP was 21 percent above the EU average. In contrast, Greece joined the then EEC in 1981. Between then and 2002, the ratio of per capital GDP to the EU average has risen little. Welfare implications of EU membership for Greece were virtually zero (EIU, 2003).

Numerous studies have empirically examined the welfare effects of RIAs (Laird, 1997; Schiff, 1999; Rutherford and Martinez, 2000). Their conclusions convincingly demonstrated that RIAs could be welfare enhancing *but only* under certain conditions. When they are welfare enhancing, welfare gains are greater (1) the higher the trade barriers being reduced, (2) the higher the share of pre-existing trade between the partners, (3) the larger the trade partner, (4) the more diversified the partner countries' economies are, and (5) the more closely the partners' domestic prices resemble world prices. Riezman (1999) analysed the strategic interactions between trading blocs in a computable general equilibrium model, and concluded that when RIAs are of more or less equal size they are welfare enhancing. If the RIAs are of unequal size, their impact is the opposite.

There are not many studies that provide a comprehensive general equilibrium examination of similarities and dissimilarities across different kinds of RIAs, like customs unions (CUs) and free trade areas (FTAs). Kose and Riezman (1999) tried to fill this gap by constructing a simple model for studying various types of preferential trade agreements. Along with other variables, they analysed the welfare implications of two kinds of RIAs, namely CUs and FTAs. Their results indicated that on welfare grounds, FTAs are better than CUs for the global economy as a whole. However, member economies benefit more in a CU than in an FTA. Decomposition of welfare effects indicated that a major proportion of the welfare gains in both member and non-member countries are explained by the volume of trade effect for the CUs and FTAs. This implies that having free market access is the most significant benefit of participating in RIAs. In the CUs, the terms of trade effects generate relatively large welfare gains because members of a CU determine their common external tariff (CET) rates. Conversely, members of an FTA do not coordinate their trade policies, which diminishes their market power, which in turn results in welfare losses. These losses are also associated with the terms of trade effect in the FTA.

As stated in section 2, the principal objective of an RIA is wider market access. The welfare gains to the members of RIAs also result from the same improved market access. The above-cited empirical studies show that these welfare gains would be greater, the larger the partners' share is in home trade. These studies also concluded that home price effect (the sum of consumer surplus and producer surplus) would also be larger, the greater the market access of the RIA partners. Effect on non-members' welfare is a function of the level of CET of the RIA. At the overall level, taking the rest of the world as a single region, the CET that reflects the minimum tariffs of the RIA would not harm non-members' welfare. However, at the country level the RIA formation with a CET of minimum tariffs would benefit some countries, while harming others. Which effect will be greater for an RIA, trade creation or trade diversion, will depend upon the sizes of the economies (as proxied by their GDPs) forming the RIA and the relative similarities and competitiveness among them. There can be no categorical answer in this regard. These effects will necessarily vary for each RIA (Laird, 1997; Schiff, 1999; Rutherford and Martinez, 2000).

The constituent members of an RIA are the mutual trading partners. The size of the trading partner, generally takes on a great deal of significance in an RIA. A large partner economy, for a given tariff rate, can be a source of several benefits. Foremost, a large partner is more likely to satisfy the home country's import demand at the world prices. Second, the home country is likely to gain more on its exports to the large partner because a large partner would continue to import from the rest of the world even after the formation of the RIA. Since the partner has a tariff on imports from the rest of the world, the home country is more likely to obtain an improvement in its terms of trade by selling to the partner at the higher tariff-inclusive price (Michaely, 1998; Schiff, 1999). Structural complementarity in trade is another important factor affecting welfare. An RIA as an entity would be better off in welfare terms if each country imports what the other exports. This, indeed, is a hypothetical situation. What is feasible is that a large proportion of the imports of one partner are also a large proportion of the exports of the other partner, in turn leading to large welfare gains for both the constituent members.

Which member incurs welfare losses and which one gains from an RIA has been a debatable point. The comparative advantage of member countries, relative to the rest of the world, provides a basis for predicting who gains and who loses. Using two-by-two Ricardian model, Venables (2002) concluded that typically the country in the RIA that has comparative advantage most different from the world average is the most at risk from trade diversion. Thus, if a group of low-income countries form an RIA, there will be a tendency for the lowest income members to suffer real income loss due to trade diversion. As opposed to this, if an RIA includes a high-income country, then lower income members are likely to converge with the high-income partner.[23] That RIAs with higher income countries are likely to lead to convergence of income level is a valuable inference for the policy mandarins.

Following Harris and Cox (1986) and Smith and Venables (1988), a sizable literature has emerged in which the RIAs are treated as operating in an imperfectly competitive world. These empirical studies delved into the changes in the nature of competition due to the creation of RIA. As an economy becomes a member of an RIA, the immediate effect on the domestic firms is that their market enlarges and the special privileges provided by the domestic government decline or disappear. Competition from firms from the member countries reduces the hold of the domestic firms on the domestic market. This generates both gains and losses. The new, post-RIA situation would redistribute rents in the larger market.

There is a distinct possibility of beneficial dynamic effects of an RIA. A good illustration of which is the well-known and widely cited Cecchini Report (1998), which calculated that by 2000 the GDP in the EU economies would rise on the order of 2.5 percent to 6.5 percent as a result of the Single European Market initiative. Higher real income in the EU would raise imports from all trading partners. Assuming elasticity of import demand to be about 2, exports from Asia to EU would go up by at least 5 percent. This positive effect should be netted against the negative effects of trade diversion. However, the dynamic estimates are usually considered uncertain. Yet, it is widely believed in the business community that the 2004 enlargement of the EU will result in spreading financial and macroeconomic 'stability and prosperity across a large swathe of Europe's heartland'.[24]

At the turn of the century, a large number of RIAs and multilateral trading systems coexist. With regard to how RIAs affect the global trading system, it is a difficult proposition to assess. Serious efforts to study this have been made in the past. Opinions on this issue vary widely and researchers and policy makers need to continue examining this issue. One such effort was made by Schill (1996). After synthesizing the conflicting viewpoints, he concluded that the effect on the multilateral system would depend on the structure of the RIA. Whether an RIA facilitates or impedes global free trade essentially depends upon whether procedures for joining it are liberal, whether it satisfies WTO regulations and whether it is accompanied by some degree of trade liberalization of the members' trade regimes. In short, the effect of an RIA on the global trading system would depend upon the terms of the agreement. Clear policy guidelines in this regard are not available because the terms of every RIA and the rationale behind establishing them have differed throughout history (Sager, 1997). RIAs established for different reasons would have varied effects on global trade flows.

Similarly, using both gravity model and simulation using computable general equilibrium model to make welfare estimates, Gilbert et al. (2001) examined the potential welfare effects of RIAs in the Asia-Pacific region. Although both the techniques are quite different, they can offer insight into areas where the other is commonly used. Thus, the CGE model can be used to consider the effect of existing arrangements through backcasting the models. Similarly, the gravity models are often used for predicting the consequences of the proposed agreements by searching for pre-existing trends that might point toward 'natural' trading partners. Gilbert et al. (2001) concluded that both the techniques suggested that there might be 'significant welfare gains' from the RIA proposed in the Asia-Pacific region. The welfare gains were found to be the largest (1) when the RIA had diverse members, and (2) when the RIA is large, having many members. Interestingly, welfare benefits of liberalization within the Asia-Pacific region on an MFN basis were found to be substantially greater than on a preferential basis. The simulation results indicated that even when RIAs had substantial net benefits for the member economies, they managed to impose a substantial cost on non-members, both within the Asia-Pacific region and to the rest of the world.

7.   INCOME CONVERGENCE AND DIVERGENCE

A closely related query to welfare gains is, whether RIAs are a force for income convergence among the member economies or for income divergence. The answer is that it is conditional upon the level of economic development and per capita income of the member economies of the RIA in question. RIA formation can lead to both income convergence and income divergence, although neither can be taken for granted. For instance, labor-intensive production and exports move to those members of the RIA where wages are low. This raises wage levels in that member country. By the same token, RIA formation can lead to income divergence. A good example of this is high technology industries, which may be pulled towards those members of an RIA that have succeeded in making a head start in those industries and have a superior physical and technological infrastructure. The other members of the RIA may be forced to be contented with lower-technology industries.

RIA members can be high-income industrial economies, developing economies and both. As seen in section 4.1, there is evidence that industrial countries that trade heavily with each other in an RTA converge – upward –

in terms of per capital income. An RIA between higher-income, industrial economies is likely to benefit the lower-income members of the RIA, that is, it is likely to lead to convergence in income levels. Lower-income here implies lower than the other members and vis-à-vis the rest of the world. The experiences of the EU are important and enlightening in this regard.

There are economic reasons to believe that RIAs between developing economies may lead to divergence in their income levels, with better-off developing economies benefiting at the expense of the worse-off (refer to section 4.2). An RIA between developing and industrial economies benefits the former by way of transfer of capital, technology as well as creation of trade between the constituent members. In the medium-term, this could result in income convergence. Therefore, there is a case for developing economies forging preferential trade links with industrial economies (WB, 2000; Venables, 2003).

There is a marked contrast between RIAs between developing economies and those between advanced industrial economies having matured institutions. The European economies have historically shown that an RIA led to considerable convergence in per capita income levels of the member economies. One early example in this regard is that of the Benelux union. Created in 1947, it comprised Belgium, Netherlands and Luxembourg. Ben-David (1993) found that per capita income narrowed steadily in this RIA. The same was found for the EEC after it was created in 1957. Tariffs were eliminated between the Benelux members in 1968. Per capita income differences narrowed steadily between the three member economies. They fell by a third between 1957 and 1968, and again by a third between 1968 and 1980 (Ben-David, 1993). A more recent and conspicuous observation is that for Ireland, Portugal and Spain, which have narrowed the income gap with the richer members after joining the EU. In 1985, Ireland, Spain and Portugal had per capita income levels of 61 percent, 49 percent and 27 percent, respectively, of the average income levels of the four large EU economies, namely, France, Germany, Italy and the UK. However, by the end of the 1990s, corresponding numbers had risen to 91 percent, 67 percent and 38 percent, respectively. This income convergence for the lower-income members was nothing short of striking (Venables, 2002).

RIAs between developing economies not only did not demonstrate income convergence tendencies but also provided strong evidence of income divergence among the constituent members. In some cases it became the cause of collapse of RIAs. Several instances of integration, which promoted divergence in per capita income, were identified by Venables (2002). For instance, in the East African Common Market (EACM) two of the partners (Tanzania and Uganda) contended that the benefits from the EACM were being reaped by Kenya because it had succeeded in developing a better industrial infrastructure than the other two members and had a relatively stronger industrial base. Since the 1960s, Kenya had steadily strengthened its position as the industrial center of the EACM. It accounted for 70 percent of the manufactured production of the EACM, which it exported to the relatively less-developed partners. The poorer members were convinced that the EACM was benefiting one member at the expense of the other two. Consequently, the EACM collapsed in 1977. Comparable more recent examples were that of Guatemala City and San Salvador in the Central American Common Market (CACM) where there was a large concentration of industry, commerce and services. These two centers of manufacturing activity in the CACM accounted for 80 percent of the manufacturing value added (MVA) in the CACM in 1997, up from 68 percent in 1980. Abidjan (Côte d'Ivoire) and Dakar (Senegal) in the Economic Community of West African States (ECOWAS) were the two exact parallels of Guatemala City and San Salvador, with the same kind of concentration of industrial activity leading to income divergence among the RIA members. In the ECOWAS, Abidjan and Dakar jointly accounted for 55 percent of MVA in 1972. This proportion soared to 71 percent in 1997. Many more cases exist of this kind of income divergence created by RIAs.

7.1 The Dilemma of 'the Innocent Bystander'

Krugman (1991b) was the first to analyse the problem of 'the innocent bystander', that is, the welfare implications of a developing country that decides not to join an RIA that is being created around it. He concluded that the innocent bystander could suffer from significant welfare losses. This applies all the more if the RIA turns into an inward-looking one, or a closed RIA. Such RIAs while 'doing little damage to themselves or each other, can easily inflict much more harm on economically smaller players that for one reason or another are not part of any big blocs'.

One of the major influences on the welfare of any trading economy is through its terms of trade. Therefore, questions surrounding trade policy should be essentially concerned with this variable. In a seminal paper Mundell (1964) had postulated that in a three-country model in which goods are substitutes, for a single tariff change by one member, the preferred exporting partner's terms of trade unambiguously improve, while the non-member country's terms of trade deteriorate. The net effect of the terms of trade deterioration for the innocent bystander, therefore, leaves it worse off. However, can this response be so categorical?

Formation of an RIA affects traded goods prices of the innocent bystander. Chang and Winters (2000) examined the effect of MERCOSUR on the price of its imports from non-members in an imperfectly competitive setting and with differentiated products. Formation of MERCOSUR had an immediate impact on the pricing of exports of non-members to Brazil, the largest economy in MERCOSUR. The Treaty of Asuncion slashed the MFN tariff rates of the member economies by half at the end of 1991, and the other half was cut to zero in the next four years. The immediate effect of such large tariff cuts for member countries would be to increase their pre-tariff prices, while the non-members would do the reverse, that is, they would benefit from reducing their pre-tariff prices. The broad conclusion of Chang and Winters (2000) was that while an RIA is intended to facilitate trade between the constituent members without raising trade barriers to the non-members, as stipulated by Article XXIV, the non-member or innocent bystander is compelled to reduce its export prices so that it can compete with the firms from within the RIA. This necessarily results in a terms-of-trade loss for the innocent bystander, leading to an unfavorable wealth effect.

With the help of a multi-country, general equilibrium model based on comparative advantages, Kose and Riezman (2000) found that being an innocent bystander could be costly for a developing economy, particularly for a small developing one. However, according to Kose and Riezman (2000), in this case the kind of RIA the developing country is opting out of matters a great deal. The type of RIA significantly affects the size of welfare gains in this model. If the innocent bystander was opting out of a CU, the losses were found to be large, up to 70 percent of GDP. Conversely, if the RIA-forming economies decide to form an FTA, the losses are modest, close to 10 percent of the GDP of the innocent bystander. Thus, the inference for the policy maker is if the RIA is a CU, it is not desirable for a developing economy to be an innocent bystander, but if it is an FTA it does not matter much. The third result of this empirical exercise was that the developing country does best by being part of global free trade, or by liberalizing multilaterally, in other words, by integrating globally.

8.   CONCLUSIONS AND SUMMARY

The concept and phenomenon of RIAs failed to win over committed free traders, who believe that whatever the trade expansion properties of RIAs, they can lead to substantial trade diversion, which in turn implies distortion of efficient global allocation of resources, resulting in welfare losses. Notwithstanding the reality of trade diversion, while opting for the membership of an RIA, countries do not expect trade diversion losses to outweigh the trade creation gains. In the present global economic *mise-en-scène*, most countries find themselves much more ready to participate in a regional negotiation than in a multilateral one because they think that the chances of successful negotiations are maximized when they are undertaken in a regional fora.

For most economies, the most persuasive motivation behind the formulation of an RIA is market expansion in such a manner that all partners of the RIA benefit. Other principal motives include increase in bargaining power vis-à-vis third countries by becoming a part of an RIA, forming an RIA as a defense against other RIAs and for locking in domestic economic reforms and liberalization. Even in the traditional domain of the WTO, that is trade in goods and services, the RIA discipline can be made stronger than that of the WTO. Harmonization of regulatory regimes is another motivation behind the membership of RIAs. Modernization and upgradation of regulatory regimes goes hand in hand with harmonization.

Various rounds of multilateral trade negotiations have an impressive record for tariff reduction, particularly on manufactured products. In addition, many large and medium-sized developing economies made significant endeavors to liberalize unilaterally after the mid-1980s. As it was politically unpopular, they had to stop unilateral liberalization after a while. Evidence for the 1990s shows that many developing economies liberalized their economic regimes to be a part of regional economic integration endeavors. RIAs, thus, contributed to liberalization of trade policy regimes.

On an average, non-preferential-non-discriminatory liberalization was found to be superior to liberalization in the context of an RIA. In the former case, economies were found to grow faster, both in the short and long term. Not the same could be said about the economies whose liberalization was limited to the preferential variety. The constituent members of an RIA also integrate their domestic policies so that market-segmenting effects of differences in national regulatory regimes can be reduced. Domestic policy integration also ensures a 'level playing field' for the firms from the member countries operating in the RIA and ensures that resurgence in trade barriers through the back door in the member economies does not take place.

Forming an RIA affects trade flows and their directionality and, therefore, production patterns in the economies that are constituent members of that RIA. It has several dynamic impacts over the constituent member economies. It changes production patterns in the economies that are constituent members of an RIA. Locations of production in the constituent member countries are seriously influenced. It also enlarges the markets for domestic firms, which provides scale economies to firms, which in turn leads to efficiency gains. Larger market also tends to attract greater investment, including more FDI. Larger manufacturing and services sector projects for which market size matters become feasible for the first time due to the formation of an RIA. Dismantling of regional trade barriers also forces firms from different member countries into more intense competition with each other than was feasible before the RIA was formed. This induces firms to make efficiency improvements and raise their level of total factor productivity. Thus, the immediate impact of enlarged markets is larger firms and enhanced competition.

When the constituent members of an RIA are at varying levels of economic development, it is known to promote technology transfers from the high-income, matured, industrialized economies to the lower-income less-developed constituent members. As opposed to this, the impact of forming an RIA between developing economies tends to be problematic in several respects. Some empirical studies have called into question the economic benefits of such RIAs. RIAs between developing economies that provide preferential access to the members but do not change their trade policies vis-à-vis the rest of the world, may well end up lowering the welfare of the entire trade bloc. It is not different in the case of small economies.

After the formation of an RIA, industries locate and/or relocate based on their comparative advantage. These decisions are also significantly driven by the agglomeration or clustering effect, which implies that as clusters of manufacturing activity – or, say, economic activity in general – start to develop in a country and/or in an RIA, a spatial clustering or agglomeration of economic activity takes place assisting the location-specific development. Membership of an RIA affects the creation or expansion of spatial clusters. With such a membership, tariff and non-tariff barriers go down, or are eliminated. This makes forward and backward linkages stronger. Larger numbers of firms can participate in the creation of spatial clusters after the RIA formation. The opposite also holds, that is, an RIA makes it possible to supply goods to consumers from a small number of spatial clusters.

Welfare implications of an RIA are an extensively researched issue, both from a static and dynamic perspective. Contemporary researchers see several imperfections in the Vinerian concepts and static analysis. RIAs and trade liberalization on a preferential basis do not necessarily have to be benign in themselves, although there are numerous dynamic channels of welfare gains through RIAs. They could be welfare enhancing *but only* under certain conditions. The kinds of economies that are the constituent members of an RIA determine the welfare gains accrued in it.

A closely related query to welfare gains is whether RIAs are a force for income convergence among the member economies or for income divergence. The answer is that it is conditional upon the level of economic development and per capita income of the member economies of the RIA in question. RIA formation can lead to both income convergence and income divergence, although neither can be taken for granted.

Not being part of an RIA when some neighbors are doing so can have its costs, particularly for a small developing economy. The kind of RIA a developing country is opting out of matters a great deal. The type of RIA significantly affects the size of welfare gains. If the innocent bystander was opting out of a CU, the losses were found to be large, but if the RIA forming economies decide to form an FTA, the losses are modest.

NOTES

1. As noted in Chapter 1, note 11, the Agreement on a Treaty on European Union was signed in Maastricht on 10 December 1991. It included a timetable for Economic and Monetary Union. On 1 January 1993, the European Single Market was completed. On 1 November 1993, the Maastricht Treaty came into force, and the EEC became the European Union.
2. The 15-member European Union was expanded when 10 countries signed the Accession Treaties in Athens, Greece, on 16 April 2003, extending its reach to include a broad swath of Europe once allied with the former Soviet Union. The 10 future members – Cyprus, the Czech Republic, Estonia, Hungary, Latvia, Lithuania, Malta, Poland, Slovakia and Slovenia – will formally join in May 2004. This would bring the total membership of the EU to 25.
3. The Free Trade Area of the Americas has 34 members. Countries participating in the negotiations of the FTAA held their Seventh Ministerial Meeting in Quito, Ecuador, on 1 November 2002 with the intent of reviewing progress in the FTAA negotiations so as to establish guidelines for the next phase. The negotiations are scheduled to conclude in January 2005 in accordance with the terms agreed by the Heads of State and Government at the Third Summit of the Americas, held in Quebec in April 2001. The negotiations are to seek the FTAA's entry into force as soon as possible after January 2005, but in any case no later than December 2005. The 34 members of the FTAA are Antigua and Barbuda, Argentina, Bahamas, Barbados, Belize, Bolivia, Brazil, Canada, Chile, Colombia, Costa Rica, Dominica, Dominican Republic, Ecuador, El Salvador, Grenada, Guatemala, Guyana, Haiti, Honduras, Jamaica, Mexico, Nicaragua, Panama, Paraguay, Peru, St. Lucia, St. Kitts and Nevis, St. Vincent and Grenadines, Suriname, Trinidad and Tobago, Uruguay, the United States of America, and Venezuela (see Chapter 6, section 9.4).
4. They were discussed at length during the Fourth Ministerial Conference, in Doha, Qatar, and found an important place in the ministerial communiqué of November 14, 2001.
5. Tariff binding is defined as a commitment not to increase a rate of duty beyond any agreed level. Once a rate of duty is bound, it may not be raised without compensating the affected trading partners. Tariff binding is enshrined in Article II of the GATT-1994.
6. An indispensable condition for an emerging-market economy is its sustained ability to attract capital inflows from the global banks and securities markets. Other than the rapid endogenous growth endeavors and extensive macroeconomic and financial liberalization and deregulation, respect of property rights and human rights are considered the basic prerequisites of becoming an emerging market economy. The national government must offer protection to property and human rights of both the citizens of the country and the non-residents alike. See Das (2003a), Chapter 1 for greater details.
7. See Hoekman and Kostecki (2001) for greater details.
8. After several infringements of the deadlines, the Uruguay Round was successfully completed in 1994 with the signing of the Marrakesh Agreement on 15 April. The WTO was born on 1 January 1995.
9. 'Free-rider' infers that a country does not make any trade concessions, nonetheless profits from tariff cuts and concessions made by other countries in negotiations under the most-favored-nation principle.
10. In trade economics, the two expressions, namely, GATT-1947 and GATT-1994, are frequently used. The latter is the revised version of the original GATT Agreement of 1947. The text of the Agreement was significantly revised and amended during the Uruguay Round and the new version was agreed upon in Marrakesh, Morocco. It is apparent that the GATT-1994 reflected the outcome of the negotiations on issues relating to the

interpretations of specific articles. In its renewed version, GATT-1994 includes specific understandings with respect to GATT Articles, its obligations and provisions, plus the Marrakesh Protocol of GATT-1994.

11. The conclusion has been challenged because these papers assume, rather than test, the idea that imports from industrial countries provide the correct weights with which to combine stocks of foreign knowledge. Keller (1998) has suggested that their results are a little better than would be obtained from relating TPF to a random weighting of foreign knowledge stocks.

12. There are remarkable differences between the CEEC economies and their sectoral structures. For instance, in Hungary agriculture, food-processing, other manufacturing and metals are less important than in Poland and CEEC5 group, which comprises Bulgaria, the Czech Republic, Slovakia, Slovenia and Romania. The characteristics of these sectors are that they are relatively low-skilled and labor-intensive. The services sector is relatively more important in contributing to GDP and value-added in Hungary. In contrast, in the CEEC5, manufacturing contributes a relatively higher proportion to GDP, especially sectors like textiles and apparel and miscellaneous manufactures. The services sector, and therefore trade in services, is much less important in the CEEC5 than in the other economies of this group.

13. Greece joined the EEC in 1981 while Spain and Portugal joined in 1986. This is referred to as the 'Southern enlargement' of the EEC.

14. See, for instance, Puga (2002) and Venables (2003) for greater details.

15. For instance, see Yeats (1998) and Schiff (1997).

16. The total population of these 49 least developed countries was 600 million.

17. The Commonwealth Secretariat/World Bank Joint Task Force Report (2002), *Small States: Meeting Challenges in the Global Economy*.

18. Albert O. Hirschman propounded this theory in his book *The Strategy of Economic Growth*, published in 1958 by the Yale University Press, New Haven, Connecticut. Soon after publication of this book, his theory became exceedingly popular among the academic and policy-making communities.

19. See Venables (2002) for greater details. Also, refer to Midelfart-Knarvik and Overman (2002) for a discussion on the EU experiences in this regard.

20. According to Heydon (2002), the precise number in 2000 was 1941.

21. This section draws on Chapter 4, Schiff and Winters (2003).

22. See, for instance, Viner (1950); Meade (1955); Lipsey (1960) and Arndt (1969).

23. Here a high-income country means one that has relatively higher per capita income relative to other members of the RIA as well as to the world average. Venables (2002) came up with these conclusions.

24. Over 90 percent of the senior European business executives surveyed in July 2003 by the Economic Intelligence unit were of this opinion. See *Europe Enlarged: Understanding the Impact*, July 2003.

3. New regionalism: the evolving landscape

1. THE IMPETUS TO A NEW WAVE OF REGIONALISM

By 1967, the European Communities (EC) had successfully established a Commission, a Council, a Parliament and a Court. These institutions of integration have since evolved and expanded. Progress towards European integration has never been smooth and steady. The early period was characterized by rapid growth and enthusiastic advance towards regional integration followed by periods of doubt and retrenchment. The former seemed to coincide with economic booms and the latter with recessions.

The early 1980s found the European Economic Community (EEC)[1] in a moribund state. The severe anti-inflationary policies at the beginning of the decade helped the US and Japanese economies to recover, but the EEC seemed firmly stuck in the mire. In addition, the growth rate of intra-EC trade was uneven. The rapid increase that had characterized the early stages of integration had lost steam in the mid-1980s. It was around this period that the seeds of the 'second' or 'new' wave of regionalism were sown. Members of the EEC drew up their Single Market Programme (SMP) in 1986. The SMP was to be completed by 1992, and the plan was called the EC-92. The well-publicized EC-92 plans had a great deal of impact on the thinking of the policy mandarins almost all the world over. They began to examine it as their own policy alternative. The rapidity with which regional integration arrangements (RIAs) spread globally after the EC-92 plans were publicized testifies to the fact that policy makers were favorably disposed towards RIAs and their impact on real economic growth and well-being.

On 1 December 1991, agreement was reached in Maastricht on the Treaty on European Union, with a timetable for the Economic and Monetary Union (EMU). The European Single Market was completed on 1 January 1993. On 1 November 1993, the Maastricht Treaty came into force after the Danes voted 'Yes' at the second try, and the EEC became the European Union (EU). The Commission was the prime mover behind the Maastricht Treaty, which formally created the EU and extended the competences of the Union to foreign affairs and justice. The last move turned out to be unpopular among the member economies. However, the success of the SMP encouraged the

Commission to follow it up by further deep integration and centralization, only to find it rejected by governments and electorates. However, rejections did not 'threaten the basic fabric of the common market: tribute to its deep foundation in European perceptions, and to its pragmatic and non-confrontational mode of progress' (Venables and Winters, 2003).

The SMP had a sizable impact on cross-border investment and merger and acquisition (M&A) activity. It was an attempt to move towards deeper economic integration that eventually led to monetary union. The EU had 15 members in 1995 and it moved ahead from a single market stage, so that EMU could be created. A Euro Zone of 12 economies has come into being.[2] The single currency came into being in January 1999, when the Euro was launched.[3] Thus, deeper integration was promoted through various channels. Consequently, the share of intra-Euro area trade has doubled since 1970 and intra-trade flows have risen appreciably. Integration also led to lower dispersion of prices in the EU economies, although it is still fairly high. Progress in integration between countries and markets has been uneven (OECD, 2000; OECD, 2001; de Serres, et al., 2002).

After the EU was created, many policy-imposed barriers to the flow of goods, capital and labor have disappeared. Although some changes, like the launch of the euro, are fairly recent, the bulk of evidence suggests that goods and financial market integration in the EU is sufficiently more advanced than in the 30-country Organization for Economic Co-operation and Development (OECD). This was demonstrated by stronger correlations of consumption and output growth among the EU economies (de Serres, et al., 2002). Also, the euro area's business cycle is far more synchronized than that of other OECD economies. The flip side of the coin is that the degree of market integration is lower in the EU than that observed between regions in individual EU economies. National borders have not lost their significance. Some studies have reported continuance of a large border effect (Wolf, 2000).

In the context of the second global wave of regional initiatives, numerous dynamic developments and a great deal of transformation took place. What was past became the prologue. The 1990s, and the early 2000s, turned out to be prolific in terms of the unprecedented number of RIA agreements that were notified to the GATT and subsequently to the WTO and regionalism returned with a vengeance. Consequently, RIAs proliferated all over the globe. Regional trade data for this period suggests that this trend looks set to continue (WTO, 2002a). There was a strong demand to join or form an RIA on economic as well as political grounds. Analysts studying RIAs never refute the idea that typically there is a strong political motivation, apart from the economic one, behind the creation of RIAs. Bhagwati (1997) aptly quipped that 'no politician is happy unless he put his signature on at least one of them'. The second global wave of regional initiatives is also referred to as the 'new regionalism'. Here, 'new' can be taken as a chronological reference. After the new regionalism started, the possible division of global economy into three trading blocs – never an issue in the first wave of regionalism – was seriously debated by economists and political scientists.

2.   THE ROLE OF TNCs IN THE EXPANSION OF NEW REGIONALISM

Transnational corporations (TNCs) play a large and significant role in world trade. Intra-firm trade among TNCs has been estimated to account for one-third of total world trade and TNC trade with other TNCs and non-affiliates accounts for another one-third of the world trade (Anderson, 2001). The Top 500 TNCs account for nearly 70 percent of worldwide trade and this percentage has steadily increased over the past twenty years (WTO, 2003). Their actions and decisions influence world trade in a significant manner. Those who study the operations of large corporations and TNCs in the large RIAs like the EU, NAFTA and APEC, have inferred that there is not only a great deal of acceptance of regional integration among them but that they also play a proactive role in the RIAs expansion. They are known for establishing horizontal and vertical production linkages in several neighboring countries. Such linkages are common in industries like vehicles, chemicals and pharmaceuticals, machinery, including precision machinery and heavy machinery sectors, and most of all in electronics. In so doing, TNCs increase the ability to exploit scale economies not only in production but also all along the value chain. This enhances efficiency and has led to greater competitiveness. One of the direct impacts of RIAs is creation and expansion of FDI opportunities for the TNCs (Chapter 2, section 5.2). Business associations and chambers of commerce in various regions are known to support RIAs. In some RIAs, like APEC, the role of business has been institutionalized by creating bodies like the Pacific Business Forum.

Global competition has intensified over the last quarter century, which has made market access an important variable. RIAs provide increased market access to corporations and TNCs. With technological advances, product life cycle has become short in many products. This observation applies particularly to the following industries: electronics, precision machinery, chemicals, and pharmaceuticals. Global diffusion of technologies and innovation has become increasingly rapid. The timespan that competitors take to respond to new innovations has shortened dramatically. This has made market access more important for spreading the fixed costs of R&D and innovation. In addition, according to the current customer-friendly business practices in sophisticated products, local presence of the manufacturing firm or services provider is essential. RIAs are also known to facilitate such a presence. Besides, large corporations and TNCs in an RIA can also follow market trends closely and acquire smaller innovative firms, which in turn makes them more competitive (Lawrence, 1996).

As the developing economies began to liberalize and reform their economies, they also sought to attract more foreign direct investment (FDI) and the TNCs. This was the period when they had abandoned import-substitution strategies and their export-led growth phase had just begun. TNCs began to appear more attractive to these developing economies because of their reputation for knowledge spillover. The TNCs bring in knowledge about the newest technologies, management techniques and strategies and ready-made access to markets. Besides, demand for FDI from the developing economies increased *pari passu* with supply from the TNCs.

Most developing economies that shifted towards liberal trade regime also shifted away from statism. It not only lost its attraction but many emerging-market economies also began to equate it with economic decadence. The role of the state was reduced through privatization, which in turn attracted TNCs and foreign investors more towards these developing economies. As international competition intensified, small cost advantages for TNCs began to have large consequences. Large corporations and TNCs found that the complete manufacture of complex products in one country is not the most cost-effective method of production. With advances in information and communications technology and modes of transportation, they found that they could manufacture a range of products in a more cost-effective manner by sourcing from multiple locations in the same contiguous region. The result was development of production networks spread over several economies in a particular geographical region. Sourcing of raw materials, labor-intensive processes, and technologically sophisticated processes began to be done in different countries in the same region. Several Asian economies – particularly the newly industrialized economies (NIEs) and the ASEAN-4 (namely, Indonesia, Malaysia, Philippines, and Thailand) and subsequently China – participated in these pluri-country manufacturing processes. Regionalization of global production has picked up momentum since the mid-1980s, which has aided and abetted regionalism.

Merely dismantling tariffs and non-tariff barriers leads to a relatively shallow form of regional integration. As opposed to this, development of regional production systems and promotion of investment – particularly in services sectors – requires a deeper form of international integration than that formation of regional trading agreements (RTAs). It requires harmonization – albeit initially incomplete – of other policies including competition policies, product standards, regulatory regimes, investment codes and environmental policies. Without harmonization of this kind, multi-country production integration becomes difficult, expensive, or even impossible. In addition, large investing firms and TNCs are not encouraged to invest unless they are sure of credible, stable and capable governments, and unless they are certain about easy access to foreign markets. Harmonized customs procedures help a great deal. They reduce administration and cut down on costs. This brings about a deeper form of international integration, which in turn is easier to achieve at the regional level.

Going by the above exposition, it is easy to believe that large corporations and TNCs can play (and have played) a strong role in promoting regional and multilateral liberalization in the recent past. However, this view has not gone unchallenged. There are those who believe that TNCs are essentially concerned with investment access, and that trade liberalization is low on their priority. Given the emergence of new modes of production operations and regional integration, it seems more likely that TNCs are interested in both, investment and regional integration. Without trade liberalization and the harmonization of standards and regulations, their objective of successful regionalization of their operations is not likely to be met fully. When large corporations and TNCs are a part of the game, RIAs would move members towards economic integration that is deep (Lawrence, 1996). It goes without doubt that intra-TNC trade and investment promotes deep integration.

The downside of this genre of deeper regional integration is that when small and large economies, with unequal bargaining power, negotiate for an RIA, the larger and more matured and industrialized economies may successfully extract concessions of all kinds not just in trade but in non-trade issues from smaller economies. Panagariya (1999) suspected that the agenda for deeper integration is likely to be determined by the larger, more industrialized economies, not by their smaller less-industrialized partners. The expected role of the smaller economies would be to adjust their norms and standards to this agenda. In the process, they may even have to adopt some policy measures that they consider unsuitable to them. A hegemonic power may gain at the expense of the smaller partners of the RIA, if it chooses to bargain sequentially rather than simultaneously.[4]

3.   THE CHANGING KALEIDOSCOPE

In the context of new regionalism, 1988–89 was a watershed point because this is when the US agreed to and implemented the Free Trade Area with Canada[5] (or CUSFTA) and abandoned four decades of opposition to the principle of regional integration. During 1990–92, a new sub-regional customs union was agreed in the eastern half of South America, called MERCOSUR.[6] The North American Free Trade Area (NAFTA) was created in 1994. The deeper integration in the EU and the establishment of NAFTA led to a 'domino effect' of renewed interest in and creation of RIAs. Subsequently, failure to launch the new Round of MTNs in Seattle in 1999 further heightened the popularity of RIAs globally, although few new regional initiatives were designed or launched in the immediate aftermath.

Old preferential trade areas (PTAs) began to be revived. For instance, in Latin America in the early 1990s the Andean Pact[7] (which, like MERCOSUR, was made between a sub-regional group of countries) and the Central American Common Market (CACM) began to be rejuvenated. In Africa, new PTAs were formed on old foundations, and some that had been languishing for a long while were given a new lease of life. For instance, Union Économique et Monétaire Ouest Africaine (UEMOA) was created out of the Communauté Économique de l'Afrique Occidentale (CEAO), and the Common Market of Eastern and Southern Africa (COMESA) was resurrected. The Preferential Trade Area for Eastern and Southern African States was expanded and the Union Douanière et Économique de l'Afrique Centrale (UDEAC) was revamped. There were 13 different RIAs in Africa in 2000. In Asia, the Association of Southeast Asian Nations (ASEAN) countries agreed in principle in 1991 on the ASEAN Free Trade Area (AFTA).[8] Historically, protectionist tendencies in Asia, North America and South America had thwarted proposals for regional integration, creation and rejuvenation of RIAs in these areas was a noteworthy change of attitude of policy mandarins. Thus, in the beginning of the twenty-first century, RIAs are found on every continent and more than half of world trade is being conducted under RIAs.[9]

Many of the discontinued RIAs were superseded by renegotiated agreements among the same signatories. In most cases this reflects the evolution over time of the agreements themselves. The older agreements were superseded by the new, more modern agreements, which adapted to the new dimensions of the members' economies. In some cases the membership was expanded, while in others it remained the same. Generally the new agreements went deeper in terms of integration. Of the RIAs that were concluded in the 1990s, 90 covering goods or services, or both, were notified to the WTO between 1995 and 2000. By March 2002, this number reached 115 (WTO, 2002a).

Since the birth of the WTO in January 1995, an average 15 RIAs were notified every year. Compared to this, an annual average of three RIAs were notified to the GATT during its entire lifetime spanning 1948 and 1994. The increase in notification partly reflects increase in the membership of the WTO, and partly new notification obligations. WTO members are required to notify economic integration agreements (EIAs) in services.[10] This obligation did not exist during the GATT regime. The total number of notified RIAs notified to the GATT–WTO system, by the beginning of the Doha Ministerial of the WTO in November 2001, was 214. I hasten to add that about a quarter of these RIAs are no longer in existence. During 2000, discussions on approximately 20 new ones were in progress. Nine African countries agreed to establish a free trade area, as did the 14 island states of the South Pacific Forum. During 2001, 19 new RIAs were notified to the WTO.[11]

The total number of notified RIAs stood at 250 in March 2002 (WTO, 2002a). According to the WTO 2002 *Annual Report*, 159 agreements were still in force in 2001. It must be clarified that included in this number are notifications made under GATT Article XXIV, GATS Article V, and the Enabling clause. Also, this number does not take into account accession to existing RIAs. Of these 159 notified RIAs, 18 were EIAs in services. Of the remaining 141 notified RIAs in force, 124 were intended as free trade areas (FTAs) and customs unions (CUs). If RIAs not (or not yet) notified are included, the total number of RIAs in force in March 2002 rises to 243, of which 197 have the format of either FTAs or CUs. According to the estimates made by the WTO, if the RIAs currently being planned or negotiated are concluded, a further 87 will be in force by 2007, bringing the total number to 246 (WTO, 2002a).

In its new incarnation, regionalism engulfed all major players of the global economy. Most WTO members were parties to at least one RIA, while many were part of two or more. The only exceptions were the People's Republic of China (hereinafter China), Hong Kong SAR, Macao, Mongolia and Japan which had not notified any agreement by the end of 2001.[12] But these economies are known to be negotiating RTAs at present. Besides, if the APEC forum is counted as a *planned* or *informal* regional trading arrangement, countries on virtually all continents are now members of regional trade agreements.[13] China, Hong Kong SAR, Macao, and Japan are signatories of APEC. The resilience of the trend towards regionalization is likely to intensify further as economies committed to the *multilateral-only* kind of liberalization abandon it and enter into RIAs. In this sense, the option of regional trade liberalization has become an attractive tool for managing their trade policies, alongside multilateral trade liberalization (WTO, 2002a). It needs to be noted that not all the RIAs were negotiated with sincere trade-expansion and economic integration intentions. To be sure, some had mere vague aspirations for moving towards this objective.

Other than the normal RIAs, there are non-reciprocal preferential agreements, involving selected developing and industrial economies. Some of the best-known examples of such agreements are as follows. During mid-2000, the US enacted the Trade and Development Act of 2000, which contained the African Growth and Opportunity Act as well as the United States–Caribbean Basin Trade partnership Act. This legislation reduced tariffs on a publicized list of products, including textiles and apparel, for 48 sub-Saharan African and 25 Caribbean countries. In addition, the Cotonou Partnership Agreement (CPA) between the 71 African, Caribbean and Pacific (ACP) states[14] and the EU was signed in June 2000 (UN, 2001). This agreement replaced the Lomé Convention. It provided for a preparatory period of eight years within which the EU would continue to provide preferential treatment equivalent to the Lomé Convention for projects originating in ACP countries. Following this period, new WTO-compatible trading arrangements would be instituted (see also section 5).

3.1 Distinctive Features of New Regionalism

Trade theorists were not left behind in the rapid growth in new regionalism. In a decade, a large body of theoretical literature shedding light on the political economy of regional trading blocs and integration has developed. Ethier (1998a and 1998b) has identified some characteristics of new regionalism. A crucial feature of new regionalism is reduction of non-discriminatory most-favored-nation tariffs along with reduction in intra-RIA tariffs. Some of the other stylized features are as follows. First, new regionalism entails one or more relatively smaller economies forming a regional or sub-regional bloc with a large emerging-market[15] or industrial economy. Second, it is the smaller country that generally undertakes more significant unilateral liberalization and adopts reform measures. These measures are more or less one-sided. This is a generalization, having several exceptions. Third, dramatic moves to liberalize are not commonly seen in the new regionalism. The degree of liberalization by members is generally modest. Fourth, regional arrangements generally involve 'deep' integration, or plans to move from 'shallow' to 'deep' integration within a stipulated period. The partners do not confine themselves to eliminating barriers to market access but move on to harmonization of codes and adjustment of economic policies.

The new regionalism differs from the old regionalism in several of its characteristics. It is a qualitative departure from the old regionalism in several respects. First, while old regionalism was essentially confined to RIAs between industrial economies or developing economies, the new regionalism is known for cross-alliances between developing, emerging-market and industrial economies. The new bonds forged by developing and industrial economies offer considerable potential for gains from trade. The flip side of this coin is that this new relationship also has a great deal of potential for adjustment problems and trade tensions. Second, while old regionalism was essentially limited to RIA formations by contiguous economies, the new regionalism does not seem to be limited to neighboring economies. In some recent or proposed cases, RIAs are intercontinental. Although there may be coordination related problems, from the gains-from-trade perspective this could be a healthy development.

Third, under the new arrangement RIAs are not exclusive, meaning thereby one country can simultaneously be a member of more than one RIA (refer to Chapter 1, section 7). This may eventually turn out to be an aid to promoting multilateralism through RIAs. Fourth, while old regionalism was limited to shallow integration, the new regionalism is more ambitious. The ambitions of the constituent members' countries are reflected in their initiatives towards deeper integration at an early stage. A number of recent agreements aspire for deep integration, with commitments to harmonization of regulatory measures, freeing factor movements, and other close integrating measures. Implications of RIAs for the global trading system have been extensively debated in the economic literature.

Another respect in which the new regionalism differs from the old one is that during the period of the new regionalism, multilateral liberalization of trade and finance has made a great deal of progress and traveled far. It has also been much more complete in the industrial economies than during the period of old regionalism. Many developing economies, particularly the emerging-market ones, had made a good deal of progress in liberalizing their domestic economies and had become enthusiastic participants in the multilateral trading and financial system. During the period of new regionalism, FDI flows have become much more prominent than they were during the period of old regionalism. A developing or emerging-market economy finds the liberalized regimes in the industrial economies attractive because they see possibilities of FDI flowing their way if they join an RIA with them. Indeed, preferential market access would be an additional advantage for the developing or emerging-market economy. Thus, progress in multilateral trade liberalization has led to new RIAs, which in turn have tended to support the multilateral trading system.

The recent vintage of RIAs and the ones on the anvil, like MERCOSUR, FTAA, APEC, NAFTA and Euro-Mediterranean Partnership Agreement (EMPA), try to use the institution of an RIA to eliminate the market segmenting effects of various regulatory policies. It should, however, be noted that policy integration is not the objective of all RIAs. Only a small, albeit increasing, number of them have included this in their objectives. Proponents of such policy integration point out that that while policy integration can be welfare enhancing, it cannot be taken for granted. Welfare enhancement, or lack of it, would eventually depend upon the initial terms of agreement of an RIA. The content of the agreement and the modalities that are followed to reduce the market segmenting effects of regulatory regimes would impinge upon the welfare enhancement effect in an RIA (Hoekman et al., 1998).

A scrutiny of the current intra-RIA trade statistics reveals that intra-bloc trade share is much larger in RIAs between industrial economies (EEC at 38.6 percent and CUSFTA at 30.2 percent) and RIAs between industrial and emerging-market economies (NAFTA at 42.1 percent) than in RIAs among the developing economies. The largest intra-bloc share in RIAs between developing economies is in ASEAN (at 16.7 percent), followed by MERCOSUR (at 12.9 percent), East African Cooperation (EAC) at 12.8 percent and Central European Free Trade Area (CEFTA) at 10.3 percent. The other developing-country RIAs have much smaller intra-bloc trade shares. For instance, this proportion was 2.3 percent for the Andean Community (AC), 3.3 percent for the Group-of-Three (G-3),[16] 3.2 percent for the South Asian Association for Regional Co-operation (SAARC) and 4.2 percent for the Gulf Co-operation Council (GCC). Similarly, intra-trade was found to be less than 1 percent for the three Sub-Saharan Africa RIAs (namely, Union Douanière et Économique de l'Afrique Centrale (UDEAC), Southern African Development Community (SADC), and Communauté Économique de l'Afrique de l'Ouest (CEAO)), while it was 1 percent for the Central American Common Market (CACM).[17]

The countries that signed FTAs with the EU or the European Economic Area (EEA)[18] were drawn towards the EU by the centripetal force a large market exerts on smaller economies in the vicinity. The EU has fast become the major trading partner of such economies, and a large or significant part of their total trade is with it. There is another fact explaining the viewpoint of the acceding countries in creating an RIA with the EU: as more countries joined it, staying on the outside became ever more expensive and the incentive to join increased. Current intra-trade statistics show that Iceland has 60 percent of its total trade with the EU, Norway 61.3 percent, Morocco 74.4 percent, Tunisia 56.8 percent, Hungary 41.5 percent, Poland 49.4 percent, the Czech Republic 46.7 percent, Estonia 16.7 percent, Lithuania 23.0 percent and Latvia 21.7 percent. These developing and emerging-market economies can be considered well integrated with the EU through trade.[19]

3.2　The Deepening of Integration

During the second wave of regionalism, not only did the number of RIAs being negotiated increased exponentially but also their scope and geographical reach broadened. Greater regional economic integration was frequently taken up as one of the principal objectives of the RIA, which implied deepening of intra-regional trade. Deep integration, as opposed to shallow integration, goes beyond border protection measures, that is, beyond liberalization of tariffs and NTBs. It includes expansion of mutual FDI and harmonization of commercial regulations, standards and practices.

Some RIAs have attempted integration of standards relating to industrial products and safety and health and environmental policies. Some have also tried to integrate policies relating to major sectors like agriculture, industry, transport and corporate law. Presently, under the rubric of deep integration, prospects of integrating corporate and indirect taxation, accounting standards and regulation of financial services are being examined.

The term 'deep integration' also refers to the pace with which scope, coverage and depth of tariff liberalization is adopted by an economy that becomes a member of an RIA. Although a 'big-bang' approach in this regard can be adopted, this happens infrequently. According to this approach tariffs are eliminated on all products on the day of entry into force of the agreement. What is more common is that tariff concessions are introduced in a phased manner, spread over a stipulated transition period. During the brisk expansion of RIAs during the second wave, elimination of existing tariffs on industrial products either took place on the date of entry into force of the agreement, or progressively during the course of the transition period. The goal of free trade in industrial products has become an accepted norm in RIAs, while agricultural goods are treated in a different manner. Generally trade in agricultural products is treated as an exception, with only a small number of RIAs succeeding in instituting free trade in agriculture. They have also failed to remove tariff spikes in agricultural products.

4. NEW REGIONALISM: THE EVOLVING LANDSCAPE

As many countries are members of several agreements – sometimes with very different rules – the contemporary global network of RIAs has become highly complex. As a rule of thumb, one observes that shallow integration is far more common than deep integration. A large majority of existing RIAs fall in the category of FTAs. The only customs unions are the EU, the South African Customs Union (SACU), MERCOSUR in South America, and CARICOM in the Caribbean.[20] The Andean Group (AG) or the Andean Community (AC)[21] and CACM have partial common tariffs, that is, they combine features of an FTA and a CU.

Supported by its economic and political momentum, the EU has been deepening and expanding. As seen earlier, its membership will rise to 25 economies in May 2004. The Maastricht Treaty[22] provided the blueprint for Economic and Monetary Union. Its objective was to further the economic and political integration of the EU. In order to qualify to participate in the EMU, the member states were required to achieve a high degree of sustainable convergence, as laid down in the convergence criteria established by the Treaty. Over the course of the 1990s, the economic policies of the member states were geared towards meeting the convergence criteria. Cyprus, Malta and the eight Central and Eastern European Countries (CEEC) entering the EU automatically become members of the EMU, with a special status. This special status would allow them to participate in the European Monetary System (EMS).[23] Furthermore, there are prospects of increasing EU membership to 28 or even 30 before 2010.[24] When the new members join, it would be much more than a mere change of scale (Vedrine, 2000).

The 2004 wave of EU expansion would increase the Union's population by 20 percent. Most of the accession countries are small, save Poland with nearly 40 million people. The planned enlargement would mark the fifth time the EU has admitted new members.[25] This would dwarf any previous expansion and would almost double the number of official languages within the Union, from 11 to 20. It would increase the land mass by 25 percent.

More importantly, the integration of the EU with the CEEC has significant economic implications. In 1986, when Spain and Portugal joined the EU, their GDP per capita was already 70 percent of the EU average in purchasing power parity (PPP) terms. The 1995 accession countries (Austria, Finland and Sweden) even produced a higher output per capita than the union had had up to then. The ten present candidates post a purchasing-power adjusted GDP per capita of less than 40 percent of the EU average. In euro terms, this ratio is as low as 15 percent. As the accession countries are much poorer, the addition to the EU's GDP (measured at the market exchange rates) would rise by a little less than 5 percent. The per capita GDP of the new EU of 25 members would decline by 14 percent.

Also, CEEC financial sectors are far less developed than those in their EU counterparts (Suppel, 2000). In 2007, the European Council is expected to approve the accession of Bulgaria and Rumania and Croatia would not be far behind (EIU, 2003). With the projected 2010 wave of expansion, the EU is likely to include Albania, Bosnia and Herzegovina, Macedonia, Serbia and Montenegro and Turkey.[26] The concept of bringing them into the fold of the EU in the future has existed for some time. This country group has lower incomes compared to the EU average in PPP terms as well as relatively poor financial infrastructure.

As the expansion was on the cards, the ten new accession economies had started the integration process. It had progressed economically more than politically. The low labor costs in the new accession economies made them attractive destinations for FDI from the older EU member economies. By 2003, trade barriers between the EU and the new accession countries were all but eliminated. Two-thirds of the trade of the ten accession countries was with the EU members in 2003, which was as much as the smallest EU member countries do with each other (EIU, 2003).

During the early 2000s, the majority of RIA initiatives were taken in the Americas and in Asia. Mexico has concluded seven RIAs, four of which are bilateral agreements with other Latin American countries. It is also in the process of negotiating bilateral agreements with Japan and Singapore. The US was involved in at least eight sets of RIA negotiations, mostly with Latin American and Asian nations. It was hoped that the US–Central American RIAs would springboard negotiations for the FTAA. Additionally, the US has extended invitations to all countries in ASEAN to form bilateral agreements, using the Singapore–US RIA as a prototype. ASEAN's larger neighbors have also taken an interest in negotiating trade agreements. For instance, Singapore completed a 'New Age' FTA with Japan (Chapter 5, section 8.1) and is currently working on one with China.

Other recent RIA activity includes EU agreements with South Africa, Croatia, and Macedonia and proposed EU agreements with Chile, the Gulf Cooperative Council, Mediterranean countries, and the African Caribbean Pacific countries. The US has also initiated trade talks for the South Africa Customs Union, and with Australia, and Morocco. Australia has also taken the initiative for a number of FTAs with ASEAN countries like Singapore, and is currently negotiating with the US.[27]

4.1 New Regionalism: A Stimulant to Multilateral Trade?

Some of those who examined the relationship between new regionalism and multilateralism in the current *mise-en-scène* have came to the conclusion that the two trends feed on each other and that they reinforce each other. This perspective on regionalism and multilateralism is something of a reversal of the past relationship between the two trends. Trade economists believed that regionalism and multilateralism had a mixed impact on each other, or that they were the antitheses of each other. The reason was that these trade theorists examined multilateralism and regional integration from an age-old Vinerian perspective. They assumed that regional integration is an exogenous variable and therefore they came up with mixed answers about its impact on multilateralism, multilateral trade liberalization, and its welfare effect in general. However, arguments presented by Ethier (1998b, 1999) in this regard differ radically. His examination was confined to the current wave of regionalism and he posited that the regional integration that began in the latter half of the 1980s, was caused, and strengthened by, multilateralism and/or multilateral trade liberalization. Ethier stressed that the causality goes from multilateral trade liberalization to regional integration. Regionalism in turn benefited from and promoted multilateralism (see Ethier, 1998b, 1999). This is how the causal circle is completed.

As alluded to above, during the current era of regional integration, trade liberalization in the industrial, emerging market and many developing economies has progressed a great deal. Relatively, progress in liberalization in the industrial economies and industrial sector has been more complete. The emerging-market economies, and many developing economies, have abandoned their past preference for anti-trade, anti-market strategy. Instead, many of them are eagerly trying to integrate into the global trading and financial network. With all-round expansion in multilateralism, both cross-border trade and financial flows, including FDI, have expanded considerably in volume.

Several recently created RIAs, where one or more small developing economies have entered into an RIA with a larger emerging-market or industrial economy, demonstrate that multilateralism or multilateral trade liberalization has caused regional integration. A plausible line of logic can be as follows. Production of some industrial products in an emerging market or industrial economy may take place in two stages of manufacturing. The first, or the rudimentary stage of production, may take place in a developing country, while the second one is in the emerging market or the industrial economy, where the product is finally marketed. As the emerging market or industrial economy moves from a non-cooperative Nash tariff equilibrium to a cooperative (or multilateral) one, tariff rates in the industrial economy fall. A greater degree of multilateral liberalization raises the benefit to the developing economy of being a part of the multilateral trading system, and joining the emerging-market or industrial economy in an RIA. Therefore, when developing economies see sufficient gains from reforms and liberalization, they consciously decide to liberalize their domestic regimes, even in the face of intense opposition from domestic lobbying groups. As integration strengthens, these liberalizing developing economies also hope to receive FDI from the partner countries, which invest there to produce and export the final product to their home countries. Furthermore, by adopting reforms, the developing economy obtains access to higher technology and production procedures than available locally. This illustration demonstrates how multilateral liberalization can promote regional integration.

Creation of RIAs also encouraged multilateral trade negotiations (MTNs) to bring down the trade barriers in general. Creation of the EEC, it is believed by many commentators, led to the Dillion Round (1960–61) and Kennedy Round (1964–67) of MTNs. The US thought that MTNs and trade liberalization would mitigate the EEC's potential for diverting trade. This is indeed a likely scenario, but it is difficult to believe that MTNs would not have taken place without the creation of the EEC, especially given the global influence of the US during the 1960s. Similar arguments about regionalism promoting MTNs were made during the Tokyo Round (1973–79) and the Uruguay Round (1986–94) of MTNs. The beginning of the new regionalism coincided with the launch of the Uruguay Round. It is believed that as the Uruguay Round was a highly ambitious round of MTNs. It faced numerous difficulties and progress was halting. At one point it nearly collapsed.[28] Many economies sensed an imminent debacle and reacted by turning away from multilateralism. They saw salvation in regionalism. It is difficult to ascertain whether this stand is correct. It seems plausible that these rounds of MTNs may have been inspired and spurred on by regionalism, but that regionalism was a direct causal factor for the MTNs seems a difficult proposition apart from the Uruguay Round period. Formation of a large RTA could certainly affect the timing, not the incidence, of subsequent MTNs.

In an environment of ongoing multilateral liberalization, many developing economies may see the benefits of liberalization and of joining into the global trading system. Under these circumstances, creating an RIA with the appropriate economy or economies first creates a secure access to the market, second, it locks in reforms, and third it ensures that the emerging-market or industrial economy would feel more safe in investing in the partner developing economy than in other liberalizing non-partner developing economies (refer to Chapter 2, section 5.2). Thus, regional integration results in increased FDI flows. This is obviously different from the usual regional integration scenario, where focus is essentially on trade, not on FDI inflows. Thus viewed, regional integration during the recent past has been spawned by the ongoing multilateralism. In turn, it has strengthened commitment to multilateral trading systems.

4.2 New Regionalism: A Deterrent to Multilateral Trade?

As soon as a new RIA is proposed or formed, the non-member economies that trade with the RIA-forming economies wonder and worry about its 'fortress' aspect. Is it a potential fortress promoting trade only between the constituent members and discouraging that with the non-member economies? Will it create trade between members and in the process divert that from non-members? These have been age-old concerns for the non-constituent economies of any RIA. When the EU was giving final shape to its Single Market initiatives in the late 1980s, these concerns were rampant. The expression 'Fortress Europe' was bandied about frequently in different multilateral fora.

Although some RIAs did raise tariffs and other barriers against the rest of the world, this accusation cannot be generalized. The strategies followed by FTAs and CUs in this regard vary widely. Members of an FTA have a good reason to lower tariffs for the rest of the world because by doing so they reduce trade distortion in the form of trade diversion. This is called 'open regionalism'.[29] By reducing tariff barriers for the non-members, they expand their sources of imports and include the non-members of the RIA in it. Besides, in situations when some imported products from the RIA members are unsettling and squeezing local firms, reducing external tariff barriers in those products would encourage imports from the rest of the world, allowing the governments to generate tariff revenues on the imports without further destabilizing domestic firms.

The objective of minimizing trade diversion is important to the members of CUs as well. Unlike the situation in an FTA, members of the CU set their common external tariffs (CETs) in concert, therefore the option of lowering tariff barriers individually for reducing trade distortion in the form of trade diversion is not open to them. However, membership of the CU increases their market power and they can raise the CETs vis-à-vis the rest of the world. This is, indeed, a theoretical possibility because a CU cannot raise its CETs at will – WTO rules forbid it. The WTO requirement in this regard is that average tariffs are not raised. Non-members can demand compensation if they are adversely affected by a particular increase in CETs vis-à-vis the rest of the world. In a real-life situation, CUs often get away with increasing CETs because WTO rules in this regard are not strictly enforced. In addition, in an ambiance of advancing trade liberalization at the global level, merely slowing down the reduction in protection is equivalent to increasing it. In the late 1990s, the Union Douanière et Économique de l'Afrique Centrale introduced across-the-board increases in CETs vis-à-vis the rest of the world to finance internal trade preference. Such moves indeed go counter to the grain of multilateralism.

In the contemporary period, some RIAs cover areas not yet covered by the WTO system, while others tend to go beyond WTO provisions in several areas of trade regulations. Many have differing regulatory policies which differ from WTO, in areas like anti-dumping, subsidies, intellectual property rights, and technical barriers to trade (TBT) and sanitary and phytosanitary (SPS) measures. These developments again promote the suspicions of the fortress mentality in non-constituent economies.

The fortress RIA concerns particularly relate to the SPS and TBT measures. For instance, as noted above, when the Single Market Programme (SMP) was being debated in the EU, non-EU economies worried whether the SPS, TBT and other measures would be used as protectionist barriers. The WTO agreements on the SPS and TBT measures encourage activities at the international level that reduce barriers to trade resulting from product and product-related regulations. Such activities at the multilateral or WTO level reduce the potential barriers to exports. A new development, encouraged by the TBT Agreement, is the conclusion of mutual recognition agreements (MRAs), on the results of conformity assessment procedures, between trading partners who have established confidence in each other's testing entities and procedures. Until 2001, the trend to conclude such MRAs was, however, confine to the industrial economies.[30]

Harmonization of the SPS and TBT measures for the constituent members of an RIA disadvantages producers and traders from the non-member countries. Conversely, by virtue of harmonization and creating a single market, the insiders come to have an advantage in addressing the single market. Harmonization can have negative effect on the economy. It can diminish welfare by suppression of efficient variation and competition. However, this effect of harmonization may not apply to all economies and all products. It is not incorrect to assume that the impact of harmonization would vary from economy to economy and product to product (Lamy, 2002). Trachtman (2003) believes that Article XXIV, Paragraph 8, does not appear to require harmonization of all the SPS and TBT arrangements among the constituent members of an RIA. If the RIA regulations do require harmonization, the harmonization measures must conform to the WTO – to be more precise GATT-1994 – regulations laid down in the SPS Agreement and TBT Agreement.

In the original Article XXIV of GATT-1947, and its Uruguay Round clarification updated by the Understanding on Interpretation in the GATT-1994, RIA regulations regarding SPS and TBT are still somewhat unclear, in fact fuzzy. The WTO law does require non-discrimination and imposition of national treatment on the constituent members of an RIA. In addition, the WTO system provides an anti-protectionism discipline for the non-constituent economies. The SPS and TBT agreements touch upon the RIAs in a superficial manner. While the TBT leaves compliance with the MFN requirement open, the SPS does have somewhat nuanced requirement in this regard. It stipulates that the SPS measures should not be applied in an 'arbitrary or unjustly discriminatory manner' where 'identical or similar conditions prevail', although it does allow for justifiable discrimination (Trachtman, 2003).

From the perspective of regulatory theory, both SPS and TBT Agreements are protectionist and work as restraints on trade and global competition. Trade authorities who apply these agreements in such a manner that they become barriers to trade, do it after a domestic cost–benefit analysis of these agreements. Being a totally domestic computation, the cost–benefit analysis does not take into account the cost to global trading partners and to producers in the trading economies. RIA provisions in areas like SPS and TBT should be so devised as to reduce the cost to foreign producers, or the domestic rule makers should fairly take into account the cost of these regulations to foreign producers. It is in this sense that RIA provisions should be allied with those of the WTO so that the national regulations do not excessively burden international trade.

An RIA with a fortress mentality, that discriminates against foreign trade with non-member economies may well have its own somewhat unnecessary norms in areas like SPS and TBT. Article I, Article III and SPS Agreement and

TBT Agreement, all prohibit such SPS and TBT regulations. This kind of discrimination can be either *de jure* or *de facto*, the latter being difficult to identify. If the multilateral rules require transparency, such discrimination can be identified and controlled. Also, 'negative integration' rules at the multi-lateral level can also be used to address such discrimination and trade diversion. Negative integration *de jure* applies to standards in the RIA, which eliminate the national standards and regulation to bring the RIA closer (Trachtman, 2003).

4.3   Does New Regionalism Promote Further Regionalism?

Without conscious endeavour, RIAs have been known to inspire creation of other RIAs. During the era of new regionalism one can find several examples of it. When an RIA is formed, it imposes certain costs on the non-members. This cost can be inflicted even without raising CETs. Exporters from the non-member economies are rendered uncompetitive because, unlike the exporters from the member economies, they pay tariffs. Furthermore, in product lines in which scale economies are available, RIAs may help lower the costs of firms from the RIA member countries by increasing the size of their 'home' market. Often the non-member economies respond to this by forming RIAs of their own, or join into an existing one.

During the era of new regionalism, after the Single Market Programme of the EU (or EC-91) and the creation of NAFTA, a good number of RIAs were formed in this manner. This trend was christened the 'domino effect'. Three Scandinavian economies, Finland, Norway and Sweden, sought accession to the EU after the EC-91. As the EU worked towards deeper integration, these Scandinavian economies became concerned about the loss of their export markets. If just one of them had joined, the cost to the other two of remaining outside would have risen. All three tried to join the EU, although Norway eventually backed out.

Creation of the European Free Trade Area (EFTA) may have been in response to the creation of the EEC. Some believe that creation of NAFTA was in response to a 'multilateral system that some countries believed gave the EU too much latitude'. Creation of MERCOSUR is also believed to have been driven by a desire to balance NAFTA. Although a large number of such examples of this kind are not available for the developing economies, there are some. For instance, the same phenomenon contributed to Bolivia and Chile seeking to join MERCOSUR. Another strategy that the non-member countries follow is joining a rival RIA if one exists.

If this process continued, the global economy would be divided into several large and small RIAs. It is a possibility that some large RIAs would take initiative to pursue global free trade. Such cooperation may take place only if there are some evenly matched RIAs with same views regarding attaining global free trade (Winters, 2000).

4.4 New Regionalism and Multilateralism: The Case of MERCOSUR

MERCOSUR is considered one of the most important examples of renewed worldwide interest in regionalism. It is seen as a consolidation of unilateral reforms undertaken in conjunction with major macroeconomic adjustments. The MERCOSUR agreement was brought about by the Treaty of Asuncion signed in 1991 and it came in force in 1995. Although it was launched as a customs union, its ambitions for higher-level integration were clear. MERCOSUR has made some progress towards a common market – albeit not necessarily EU-style.

Wilfred J. Ethier contended that the new regionalism reflects the success of multilateralism, not its failure (Ethier, 1998a, 1998b). MERCOSUR is indeed an important part of the new regionalism in Latin America. In view of its importance, one can take it as a case study and examine first, whether it has the characteristic features of new regionalism *à la* Ethier, and, second, using a simple economic model, look at the likely welfare and trade pattern effects of a MERCOSUR-type trading arrangement on members and non-members vis-à-vis other forms of free-trade area formations. This way it is possible to decide whether or not new regionalism strengthens multilateralism as posited by Ethier.[31]

A noteworthy and crucial characteristic of MERCOSUR is reduction of most-favored-nation (MFN) tariffs concurrently with a reduction of intra-MERCOSUR preferential tariffs. This is one characteristic, which makes MERCOSUR a perfect fit into what Ethier (1998a, 1998b) considered the new regionalism. In several other distinctive features MERCOSUR meets the requirement. For instance, Brazil is the largest country, an important emerging-market economy, while Paraguay and Uruguay are comparatively smaller economies. Second, smaller partners undertook major unilateral reform and liberalization measures. In the case of MERCOSUR, however, even the larger partners did so, albeit to a lesser extent. Third, dramatic internal liberalization by members was not adopted by the member countries. Fourth, MERCOSUR has an on-going agenda for deeper integration. There are plans for creating a comprehensive economic union. Thus viewed, MERCOSUR does incorporate all the distinctive features of the new regionalism.

Between 1985 and 1997, the average MFN tariffs in the MERCOSUR member economies came down from 37.2 percent to 12.3 percent. At the same time the average tariffs imposed on the partner economies declined from 35.2 percent to 4.2 percent. Thus, the MFN tariff reduction was large. The additional preferential tariff reduction for the members of MERCOSUR was modest. Between the signing of the Treaty of Asuncion in 1991 and establishment of common external tariffs in 1995, intra-MERCOSUR trade expanded rapidly. Exports within MERCOSUR had doubled as a share of total exports during the same period, while imports within the group also recorded a strong growth. Not all of this growth in trade can be attributed to the creation of MERCOSUR because trade was expanding rapidly with other countries as well.

Estevadeordal et al. (2002b) developed a Krugman-type trade model based on imperfect competition and product differentiation. They examined the impact of MERCOSUR-type FTA where preferential tariffs decline with the non-discriminatory MFN tariffs, and compared it to the impact of a traditional FTA where only preferential tariffs decline. The results of this rigorous exercise revealed that a MERCOSUR-type FTA leads to trade creation and that the welfare of both members and non-members increases. Thus the new regionalism can be the 'Land of Cockaigne' where everybody is better off than they would be without it. Thus, one can logically conclude that new regionalism does not undercut multilateralism. If anything, it reflects the success of multilateralism and multilateral trading system, not its failure.

5. PARTICIPATION OF THE DEVELOPING ECONOMIES

Virtually all the developing economies are now participants of at least one RIA. Of the RIAs currently in force, approximately 35 percent are agreements concluded between developing economies (WTO, 2002a). These agreements are of various kinds, ranging from customs unions and FTAs to partial scope agreements. The recent trend among the developing economies is to opt for agreements favoring wider trade integration. An example of this is the recently concluded FTA between Chile and Mexico, which was notified to the WTO under the provision of the GATT Article XXIV. The new trend is a break from the past. One of the reasons for it being adopted in the developing economies is that they can lock their domestic liberalization measures and economic restructuring to the schemes of regional integration. Liberalization and restructuring commitments become easier to justify politically, if membership of a regional integration scheme is shown to the electorate as the final target. This process subdues the domestic lobbyists and interest groups, a disturbing reality in trade policy.

Forms of regionalism vary from region to region. For instance, regionalism in Africa is unique and not comparable with that in Asia or Latin America. The final objective of the majority of the regional initiatives on the continent of Africa was establishing customs unions, or common markets. They also tended to have a large number of signatories and long transition periods, of two, even three, decades. In contrast to this, the Asian economies set themselves modest objectives, usually not thinking beyond FTAs. Transition periods were shorter than those in Africa. The developing economies in Latin America were fairly comprehensive in their approach. They tried to establish customs unions, common markets, and plurilateral (having three or more members) regional initiatives, backed up by a network of a large number of bilateral preferential trade agreements PTAs. A large variety of regional initiatives coexisted.

As set out in section 3, the developing economies were also involved in a special variety of RIAs, those that were concluded between them and the industrial economies. These agreements were not the usual RIAs, they were of non-reciprocal as well as preferential in nature. They were provided a waiver from the WTO provisions because of their non-reciprocity and preferential nature. There are three major agreements of this kind in force: (1) US–Caribbean Basin Economic Recovery Act, an agreement between the US and 21 Caribbean and Central American countries, (2) CARIBCAN, an agreement between Canada and 18 Caribbean countries, and (3) the Fourth Lomé convention between the EU and 71 African, Caribbean and Pacific economies. The Cotonou Partnership Agreement was made between African, Caribbean and Pacific states and the EU. This agreement replaced the old Lomé Convention. Over time, this trend underwent a change. There has been a clear shift from non-reciprocal to forming reciprocal RIAs between developing and industrial economies. During the second half of the 1990s, numerous developing economies concluded reciprocal RIAs with the EU, EFTA and Canada. The Euro-Mediterranean Partnership Agreement is a major illustration of the new RIAs between the developing and industrial economies (WTO, 2002a).

6. CONCLUSIONS AND SUMMARY

The Single Market Programme (EC-92) of the EEC was chalked out in 1986, which had a great deal of impact on the minds of the policy makers all the world over, who began to examine their own policy responses. The EC-92 had a sizable impact on cross-border investment and merger and acquisition activity. Evidence is available to show that goods and financial market integration in the EU grew sufficiently more advanced than in the 30-country OECD. This was demonstrated by stronger correlations of consumption and output growth among the EU economies. RIAs have spread rapidly globally since the late 1980s. The past became the prologue for the second global wave of regional initiatives, or the 'new regionalism'. The 1990s, and the early

2000s, turned out to be prolific in this regard. There was a strong demand to join or form an RIA on economic as well as political grounds.

Transnational corporations play a large and significant role in world trade. There is not only acceptance of regional integration among them but they have also played a proactive role in their expansion. They are known for establishing horizontal and vertical production linkages in several neighboring countries. Such linkages are common in industries like vehicles, chemicals and pharmaceuticals, machinery including precision machinery and heavy machinery sectors, and most of all in electronics. In so doing, TNCs increase their ability to exploit scale economies in production. For their part, as the developing economies began to liberalize and reform their economies they also sought to attract more FDI and the TNCs' role in their economies. With advances in information and communications technology and modes of transportation, TNCs found that they could manufacture a range of products in a more cost-effective manner by sourcing from multiple locations in the same contiguous region. The result was development of production networks spread over several economies in a particular geographical region, which in turn supported the second wave of regionalism.

In the context of the second wave of regionalism, 1988-89 was a watershed because this is when the US agreed to and implemented the free-trade areas with Canada and abandoned four decades of opposition to the principle of regional integration. Other major regional initiatives like MERCOSUR and NAFTA followed in the wake of CUSFTA. Several old preferential trade area were revived and many discontinued RIAs were superseded by renegotiated agreements, often among the same signatories. Since the birth of the WTO in January 1995, on an average 15 RIAs were notified every year. Compared to this, an average of three RIAs were notified to the GATT annually during its entire lifetime spanning 1948 and 1994. Total numbers of notified RIAs stood at 250 in March 2002, of these, 159 agreements were still in force. It must be clarified that included in this number are the notifications made under GATT Article XXIV, GATS Article V, and the Enabling clause. This number does not take into account accession to existing RIAs. Of these 159 notified RIAs, 18 were EIAs in services. Of the remaining 141 notified RIAs in force, 124 were intended as free-trade areas and customs unions. The new regionalism engulfed all major players of the global economy.

The characteristics of new regionalism included reduction of non-discriminatory most-favored-nation tariffs along with reduction in intra-RIA tariffs. New regionalism entails one or more relatively smaller economies forming a regional or sub-regional bloc with a large emerging-market or industrial economy. Second, it is the smaller country that generally undertakes more significant unilateral liberalization and adopts reform measures. Third, dramatic moves to liberalize are not commonly seen in the new regionalism.

The degree of liberalization by members is generally modest. Fourth, regional arrangements generally involve 'deep' integration, or plans to move from 'shallow' to 'deep' integration within a stipulated period. Intra-bloc trade share in total trade was found to be much larger in RIAs between industrial economies and RIAs between industrial and emerging-market economies than in those among the developing economies.

During the second wave of regionalism, not only the number of RIAs being negotiated increased exponentially but also their scope and geographical reach broadened. Greater regional economic integration was frequently taken up as one of the principal objectives of the RIA, which implied deepening of intra-regional trade.

As many countries are members of several agreements – sometimes with very different rules – the contemporary global network of RIAs has become highly complex. Some of those who examined the relationship between new regionalism and multilateralism in the current *mise-en-scène* have came to the conclusion that the two trends feed on each other and that they reinforce each other. With all-round expansion in multilateralism, both cross-border trade and financial flows, including FDI, have expanded considerably in volume. FDI is an important part of the current wave of regionalism.

In some ways, the new regionalism works counter to multilateralism. As soon as a new RIA is formed, the non-member economies that trade with the RIA-forming economies wonder and worry about its 'fortress' aspect. Many RIAs have differing regulatory policies in areas like anti-dumping, subsidies, intellectual property rights, and technical barriers to trade and sanitary and phytosanitary measures from those in the WTO regime. These developments again promote the suspicions of non-constituent economies regarding the fortress mentality. In the original Article XXIV of GATT-1947, and its Uruguay Round clarification updated by the Understanding on Interpretation in the GATT-1994, RIA regulations regarding SPS and TBT are still unclear. From the perspective of the regulatory theory, both SPS and TBT Agreements are protectionist and work as restraints on trade and global competition. RIAs have been known to inspire creation of other RIAs, although not quite in a mechanical manner. During the era of new regionalism one can find several examples of it.

Virtually all the developing economies are now participants of at least one RIA. Of the RIAs currently in force, approximately 35 percent are agreements concluded between developing economies. The recent trend among the developing economies is to opt for agreements favoring wider trade integration. The developing economies have also been involved in a special variety of RIAs, those that were concluded between them and the industrial economies. These agreements were non-reciprocal as well as preferential in nature. This trend has undergone a change in recent years. During the second half of the 1990s, numerous developing economies concluded reciprocal RIAs with the EU, EFTA and Canada.

NOTES

1. As noted in Chapter 1, note 11, the Agreement on a Treaty on European Union was signed in Maastricht on 10 December 1991. It included a timetable for Economic and Monetary Union. On 1 January 1993, the European Single Market was completed. On 1 November 1993, the Maastricht Treaty came into force, and the EEC became the European Union (EU).
2. Greece became the twelfth member of the Euro Zone on 1 January 2001.
3. The EU membership reached 15 in 1995, when Austria, Finland and Sweden joined.
4. One example of such hegemonic bargaining power is provided by the formation of NAFTA, when several provisions with respect to intellectual property protection and environment and labor standards were secured by the US from Mexico, while Mexico was unable to obtain similar benefits in return.
5. Its formal name is Canadian–US Free Trade Area or CUSFTA.
6. Its full name is Mercado Común del Sur or the common market of the south. Its membership comprises Argentina, Brazil, Paraguay and Uruguay.
7. The Andean Pact was a common market between Bolivia, Colombia, Ecuador, Peru and Venezuela.
8. The six original members of ASEAN are: Brunei Darussalam, Indonesia, Malaysia, the Philippines, Singapore, and Thailand. The four members who joined later were Vietnam in 1995, Laos and Myanmar in 1998 and Cambodia in 1999. The AFTA agreement was not signed until 1992.
9. Refer to p. 40 of the World Trade Organization's *Annual Report 2002*.
10. By March 2002, 18 EIA agreements in services were notified to the WTO (WTO, 2002b).
11. These statistical data were culled from WTO documents.
12. In April 2003, the membership of the WTO was 146 countries.
13. Unlike the European Union and the North American Free Trade Area, APEC does not have a formal trade treaty to back up its blueprint of trade liberalization.
14. The African, Caribbean and Pacific countries are a group of 71 countries with preferential trading relations with the EU under the former Lomé Treaty, now called the Cotonou Agreement.
15. An indispensable condition for an emerging-market economy is its sustained ability to attract global capital inflows. Other than the rapid endogenous growth endeavors, respect of property rights and human rights are the basic prerequisites of becoming an emerging market economy. The national government should offer protection to property and human rights of both the citizens of the country and the non-residents alike. See Das (2003a), Chapter 1 for greater details.
16. Group of Three (or G-3) Agreement between Columbia, Mexico and Venezuela was signed in 1995.
17. The source of these data is Chapter 3, Table 3.1, Schiff and Winters (2003).
18. The European Economic Area was notified to the GATT in 1994. It included the EU, Iceland, Liechtenstein, Norway.
19. The source of these data is Chapter 3, Table 3.1, Schiff and Winters (2003).
20. CARICOM stands for Caribbean Community and Common Market. During 2001, CARICOM updated its founding treaty in order to establish the legal basis for moving towards a single market. In 2002, CARICOM decided to launch into its Single Market and Economy initiative.
21. The 1988 Protocol of Quito called for amendments to the Andean Group's founding treaty. Its institutional structure was also revised in 1988. In December 1996 its name was changed to the Andean Community.

22. Its formal name was the Treaty on European Union. Its Final Act was signed at Maastricht on 7 February 1992.
23. The European Monetary System is a system of fixed but adjustable exchange rates between the currencies of many EU Member States. It came into being in 1979 and was designed to ensure that currency and exchange rate conditions remain as stable as possible within the EU. EMS comprises a stable currency zone largely free of serious internal fluctuations in exchange rates. It is made up of three elements: (1) an exchange rate and intervention mechanism, (2) a comprehensive financial assistance system, and (3) the European Currency Unit, the ECU, as a reference value and accounting unit. In the EMS the agreed exchange rates of the participating states are not allowed to fluctuate upwards or downwards beyond a margin of 2.25 percent. If a currency comes under pressure and its exchange rate approaches the margin limit the participating central banks intervene: they have to buy up the weak currency and sell the stronger one in order to support the exchange rate. This part of the EMS agreements is known as the Exchange Rate and Intervention Mechanism (ERIM). To prevent the central banks running out of funds when they have to make such interventions they grant each other temporary loans (credit mechanism).

    The goal of stable exchange rates between the participating states was achieved to a large extent in the 1980s. However, in 1992 the British pound and the Italian lira came under pressure to devalue and they withdrew from the EMS. Subsequently, in order to remove the ever-increasing pressure of speculation from the EMS, the margins were increased in 1993 to 15 percent in both directions. Otherwise the EMS remained unchanged. By April 1998, 13 of the 15 Member States of the European Union belonged to the EMS exchange rate mechanism, i.e. all except Sweden and the United Kingdom.

    Twelve of the EU Member States were to join the monetary union or the Euro Zone on 1 January 1999. New agreements had to be made for the relationship between the new single currency, the euro, and the currencies of those EU Member States that did not participate in the monetary union. The EMS II was devised for this group of countries. The aim was to prevent excessive currency fluctuations between the euro and the other non-Euro-Zone currencies. The EU summit in Amsterdam in June 1997 agreed on some basic guidelines for an EMS II. New entrants to the EU would automatically follow EMS II.
24. The principal decision on enlargement was made as early as 1993. Back then, at the Copenhagen summit, the EU members agreed that the associated Central and Eastern European Countries should integrate fully into the Union. At the same time, the European Council established political and economic conditions for accession. These 'Copenhagen criteria' demand of the accession candidates:

    1. stability of institutions guaranteeing democracy, the rule of law, human rights, and protection of minorities;
    2. existence of a functioning market economy with the capacity to withstand the competitive pressures in the EU Single Market; and
    3. adoption of essential EU legislation (*acquis communautaires*) and administrative and judicial structures that ensure its effective implementation.

    In addition, the EU set a reform agenda for its own institutions and a legal framework in the 'Agenda 2000' put forward by the EU Commission in 1997.
25. The previous four expansions of the EEC-EU took place in 1973, 1981, 1986 and 1995.
26. Turkey has been pressing for EU membership since 1987, but the EU has declined to open negotiations because Turkey's democratic credentials were under doubt and it did not meet the so-called 'Copenhagen criteria' mentioned in note 24.
27. The source for information regarding the current developments in RIA initiatives is CID, 2003.
28. In spite of halting progress, the Uruguay Round is credited with a weighted average tariff reduction of 38 percent in industrial countries' tariffs, an agreement on the phase-out of the Multifibre Agreement (MFA), non-tariff barriers on agricultural products being converted to tariffs and lowered, the so-called 'voluntary' export restrictions being abolished and the GATS being created. This was responsible for making progress in the liberalization of

barriers to trade in services. In the end, the Marrakesh Agreement significantly altered the conditions under which international trade is conducted.

29. Open regionalism refers to plurilateral agreements that are non-exclusive and open to new members to join. It requires first that plurilateral initiatives be fully consistent with Article XXIV of the GATT, which prohibits an increase in average external barriers. Beyond that, it requires that plurilateral agreements do not constrain members from pursuing additional liberalization either with non-members on a reciprocal basis or unilaterally. Because member countries are able to choose their external tariffs unilaterally, open agreements are less likely to develop into competing bargaining blocs. Finally, open regionalism implies that plurilateral agreements both allow and encourage non-members to join.

30. For example, by the end of 2001 the EU had concluded MRAs for the results of conformity assessment with Australia, Canada, Japan, New Zealand, Switzerland and the US.

31. A study on these lines was conducted by Estevadeordal et al. (2002b). The case study presented here draws on their work.

4.   RIAs and the global trading system

1.   CHANGING GLOBAL PERSPECTIVES ON RIAs

A group of trade economists follow the logic of regional integration agreements (RIAs) being the 'stepping stones' toward a liberal global trading system, and to that end strongly support regional integration. Expansion of RIAs could have positive effects on the global economy provided the emerging RIAs are 'open' to trade from outside. One key benefit to the global economy comes from the impact of RIAs in stimulating domestic growth, which in turn increases the demand for extra-regional imports, thereby integrating it with the global economy. There are several channels of demand expansion. The principal ones are: (1) demand expansion due to the income effect of gains from trade, (2) increased income induces more investment, (3) increased investor confidence leading to improved ability to attract foreign direct investment (FDI) from the global investing community, and (4) beneficial macroeconomic effects of RIAs.

Open regionalism can certainly promote and facilitate external liberalization, meaning trade with non-member economies outside the RIA. Economies grouped in RIAs can regard them as complementary as well as supplementary to multilateralism. They need not necessarily be the antithesis of multilateralism. By following both regional and multilateral approaches simultaneously, the pace of liberalization of the global trading system can be made brisker. This two-pronged approach to trade liberalization can achieve greater gains for those willing to proceed faster and at the same time put pressure on the multilateral negotiations to perform better and deliver tangible results in a reasonable time. This is essentially the 'building block' argument buttressing the formation of RIAs.

It is noteworthy that after the mid-1980s, developing-country perspective on regionalism differed from that adopted during the first wave of regionalism in the 1950s and 1960s (see Chapter 1). This was partly due to the fact that the economic conditions for the developing countries over the 1990s were markedly different from what they were in the earlier period. Economic and trade reforms – undertaken unilaterally, regionally and multilaterally—since the mid-1980s led to the creation of a liberal trading environment in a good number of developing economies, particularly in the emerging-market economies.[1] The trade policy landscape in the developing economies has undergone a radical transformation since 1985. These extensive trade liberalization endeavors and their outcome have been widely documented and commented upon (Greenaway and Morrissey, 1993; Dean et al., 1994; Dean, 1995). Therefore, at present, additional gains by way of domestic liberalization and deregulation undertaken for joining RIAs would not be as large for the developing economies as they were during the first wave of RIAs.

However, one continuing benefit of commitment to an RIA is the mechanism of 'locking in' or anchoring gains from liberalization and reforms, which result in concrete gains. When a smaller developing economy joins a larger industrial one in an RIA, it ensures that the policy reforms that have been undertaken will not be reversed by a protectionist future government. An RIA takes the legal status of an international treaty. It is harder to repudiate an international treaty than bring in changes through national legislation. This seems to have happened in the agreements between the European Union (EU) and East European economies and in Mexico and the North American Free Trade Area (NAFTA). To be sure, there are exceptions in this regard.[2] Furthermore, it is widely accepted that the domestic policy reforms which go with an RIA are generally helpful in enhancing the credibility of domestic reforms and attracting FDI (refer to Chapter 2, section 2). Mexican experience after joining NAFTA is a good illustration. The NAFTA paid off richly for Mexico even before it was initiated. There was a sudden spurt in FDI in the country. It was over $14 billion in 1991, up 50 percent from 1990. Until 1998, Mexico remained the second largest recipient of FDI in the region, after Brazil, which was a much larger economy. In 1999, FDI inflows into Mexico were $11 billion, which was close to the average of the 1995–98 period (UNCTAD, 2000).

Although the plausibility of the RIA route of a liberal global trading system is clear, it is far from an easy and smooth process. There can be a myriad of problems along the way, and it could well be what Shakespeare called a 'barfull strife'. Not all regional initiatives have progressed smoothly. Indubitably, they have their limits and limitations. For instance, the Bogor initiative of the Asia Pacific Economic Co-operation (APEC) forum, launched enthusiastically in 1994, has not made much progress despite political commitment in the member countries. Its objective of 'free and open trade in Asia-Pacific by 2010 for developed member economies and 2020 for developing ones' through autonomous MFN tariff reductions has not advanced significantly in the recent years. MERCOSUR encountered obstacles following the decision by Argentina, on an emergency basis, to suspend certain regional commitments. In the backdrop of its continuing financial crisis, Argentina applied a surcharge on imports in the autumn of 2000. Several plans to complete free trade agreements (FTAs) and customs unions (CUs) in Africa proved to be difficult to complete, or were inordinately delayed. There were instances when members of one RIA defected towards another RIA. Even when successfully launched, RIAs have their limits. As alluded to in the preceding chapters, typically they do not provide for 100 percent product coverage of free trade. Although not always successful, domestic interest groups and lobbyists often create problems for RIAs as well.

2. PARTICIPATION IN RIAs AND LINKS WITH TRADE POLICY REGIME

To examine whether there is a direct, effective and systemic link between a developing country's participation in an RIA and the restrictiveness or liberalization of its trade policy, one needs to closely examine the trade policy of the members of different RIAs. If this scrutiny reveals that RIAs lead to liberalization then one can infer that RIAs are not the stumbling blocks but the building blocks of a liberal global trading system. Foroutan (1998) took an intertempoal view while defining an effective RIA. According to him, simple before-and-after statistics should be a conclusive test of the impact of an RIA on the global trading system. That is, if data reveal that the share and intensity of intra-RIA trade in the years following the formation of the RIA is significantly larger than in the years before, the RIA has been effective. This is a somewhat crude, albeit useful, criterion. It has been adjudged rough because, first, the very expectation of a positive trade deal may already boost the flow of trade between potential RIA partners even before any formal agreement is signed. Second, it is plausible that an RIA may be important for one or two members of an RIA but not for others. Despite weaknesses, this approach has the advantage of relying on standard trade data that are readily available.

Trade reform can take place at three distinctive levels: unilateral initiatives, multilateral liberalization based on reciprocity, and preferential or discriminatory liberalization. Of these three, unilateral liberalization is the best option for a small country. Here a 'small' country has been defined as one that cannot influence its terms-of-trade. However, if during multilateral trade negotiations other countries reciprocate and liberalize as well, it will indeed increase gains from unilateral liberalization. But small countries cannot possibly plan their reform strategy conditionally upon reciprocity by trading partners. Preferential or discriminatory liberalization, as a part of a RIA, would indeed work for a small country. Starting in the mid-1980s, most of the developing world was moving towards market-oriented economic reforms. In this endeavor, they were followed by the transition economies. Unilateral trade liberalization took place concurrently with the multilateral efforts to liberalize trade in goods and services in Geneva.[3] An extensive analysis of the trade regimes of 75 countries was undertaken by Foroutan (1998). Data collected from various standard sources showed that, excluding countries (such as Hong Kong SAR, Singapore and the Gulf states) which have traditionally had a liberal trade regime, countries that became members of effective RIAs had liberalized their trade regimes during the 1987–97 period. This does establish a direct link between trade liberalization and RIA membership.

The next related query is whether the RIA participation was the causal factor behind trade liberalization. It was not clear because many of the RIA member economies, particularly those in Asia and Latin America, were liberalizing unilaterally and contemporaneously became members of the RIAs. Therefore, it is difficult to determine how much of causality can be attributed to RIA participation. Besides, since the mid-1980s there were some countries that liberalized their trade regimes significantly without being members of any RIA. These countries included Chile, Korea, Mexico and Turkey, to mention a few. Conversely, there were some countries that did not liberalize their trade regimes despite being members of RIAs. The Andean Group (AG) and CACM countries in the early years of their RIA formation provide a good example of this. Their participation in an RIA did not initially lead to overall trade liberalization.

Observing these propensities in trade liberalization and RIA memberships, Foroutan (1998) reasonably concluded that if acceptance of a liberal trade policy regime is a requirement of an RIA membership, it can be said that these kind of RIAs generally succeed in liberalizing the trade regime of the members. With advancing age, RIAs tended to deepen by removing trade barriers, including non-tariff barriers. Therefore, following that deepening process, some member economies may have liberalized their trade regimes. As opposed to these, as noted above, several Asian and other economies fall in the well-informed country group that did not need an RIA to persuade them to see the plausible welfare implications of a liberal trade policy regime. Thus viewed, an RIA may or may not be instrumental in liberalizing the trade regime of a member economy. It would essentially depend upon whether a particular RIA has some degree of liberalization built into its design as a precondition. Thus, the terms of the agreement of an RIA are the answer to the question whether or not the RIA would be one that liberalizes the trade regime of the members. Mere RIA membership cannot be logically equated with liberalizing trade regime and a direct and effective link between them need not exist.

2.1 Quantifying Preferential Trade Among RIA Partners

It is intuitive to assume that with a large number of RIAs of different kinds in force, a great deal of global trade must be influenced, if not governed, by them.

Quantifying trade under various preferential trade agreements is not easy. It faces methodological problems. There are difficulties in defining what, in quantitative terms, could be taken as intra-RIA trade and what could not. Ideally, one should take customs statistics to determine, first, where each import consignment has originated and, second, under which trade regime each import consignment has entered the country. However, this kind of estimate is not only time-consuming but also expensive. These statistics are not readily available. Besides, one cannot ignore the fact that not all trade among the members of an RIA necessarily comes under the preferential trade regime. Sometime economic and administrative costs of meeting all the requirements of the rules of origin (ROO)[4] within an RIA are high. Therefore, traders are forced to ignore the preferential, or free trade treatment, provided by the RIA because the most-favored-nation (MFN) tariffs are less than the cost of complying with the rules of origin and other requirements.

In an attempt to quantify the share of preferential trade between RIAs at the global level, Serra Puche (1998) subtracted the trade of all countries that do not belong to RIAs from the total world trade. The assumption here was that all intra-RIA trade is conducted on preferential terms – an assumption not necessarily correct. With this assumption, 53 percent of the world trade was estimated to be conducted under preferential trade agreements in 1997. This estimate could not be taken seriously because it suffered from biases. First, a substantial proportion of intra-RIA trade is conducted on non-preferential terms, that is, at zero MFN tariffs. Second, not all intra-RIA trade can be pigeon-holed into the preferential trade category because, as noted above, establishing the ROO is an expensive procedure. For these two reasons the estimate made by Serra Puche (1998) had an upward bias. As opposed to these two, the third bias worked in the opposite direction. It was created by preferential trade between the RIA partners that takes place on a non-reciprocal basis, like trade under the Generalized System of Preferences, which was not accounted for in Serra Puche's (1998) study.

The methodology followed by Grether and Olarreaga (1998) improved upon the weaknesses of Serra Puche's (1998) work and also tried to correct the biases. Additionally, they provided comparisons across regions for two different periods, 1988–92 and 1993–97. To this end, they decomposed RIAs into partial RIAs and full RIAs. The former category was defined as those RIAs where trade preferences were only granted either to some specified products or unilaterally to a particular set of RIA members by the more developed member of the RIA. As opposed to this, in a full RIA, as the name indicated, there was full product coverage and all members grant preferential access to other members.

In their methodology they proxy the actual share of trade that entered under preferential treatment by considering only imports within an RIA that took place under tariff rates of higher than 3 percent. The justification was that if the MFN tariff was below 3 percent, the incentive to satisfy ROO requirements and benefit from preferential tariff treatment evaporated. For the preferential trade under GSP, they included imports where there were full preferences, or where there were no tariffs and no quantitative restrictions. Their conclusions were: first, preferential trade represented 40 percent of world trade during the 1988–92 period and 42 percent in 1993–97. Second, preferential trade in agricultural products recorded a large increase over these two periods. Third, the share of trade under GSP in total preferential trade recorded a significant fall, from 7 percent to 3 percent over the two periods. This reflected the general decline of trade under GSP worldwide. Fourth, the regional distribution of preferential trade was found to be highly uneven. As may be expected, at 70 percent in 1993–97, Western Europe had the highest share of preferential trade. Latin America had a low value (27 percent), while Asia and Oceania had a still lower proportion of preferential trade. Lastly, they concluded that countries that have highly open economies also tended to have a larger share of preferential trade.

According to the 2002 *Annual Report* of the WTO, intra-RIA trade could soon 'account for more than half' of world trade.[5] WTO (2002a) also computed the extent to which imports of RIA members are subject to preferential treatment. The same caveats as mentioned above also apply to this set of computations. As mentioned above, these calculations can only provide an indicative picture because not all the imports of members of RIAs from the other members are subject to preferential treatment. It was noted above that only a part of intra-RIA trade could be expected to come under the preferential agreements. The reason is that many tariff lines are MFN-bound at zero. For instance, 25 percent of all Japanese imports fell under the MFN-bound zero tariffs, while for the EU this proportion was more than 40 percent. For these reasons, the proportions of trade that derived from RIA partners computed by the WTO (2002a) study should be taken with a pinch of salt. It is not counter-intuitive that there is a wide variety in the trade, which is derived from the RIA partners. The EU economies are participants in a large number of RIAs. Little wonder that they also derive a significant proportion of their imports from their RIA partners. Their proportion of RIA-controlled trade ranged between 60 percent and 80 percent in 2001. Asian economies were found to be at the other extreme in this regard, while the proportions for economies in Africa and Latin America showed wide variations. The conclusions reached by Grether and Olarreaga (1998) for an earlier period are comparable to those reached by the WTO (2002a) for the contemporary period. They are not only similar but also reinforce each other.

Eighty percent of the total imports of Mexico, Namibia, Lesotho, Malawi, and Uganda came from their RIA partners. In some cases, it was found that countries which did not enter into many RIAs, had a large proportion of their imports coming from their RIA members. In such cases the members were (or a particular member was) also their large trading partners. Canada, for instance, has entered into only five RIAs, but 70 percent of its imports are from its RIA partners. The US is Canada's largest trading partner and a fellow member of NAFTA. Chile provides an illustration of the other kind. It is a member of seven RIAs but these RIA partners only accounted for 34 percent of its total imports. Therefore, number of RIA memberships cannot represent intensity of RIA trade. What is of capital importance is which countries are RIA partners.

Several significant expansions and new initiatives were underway in the early 2000s. For instance, there is the finalization of a 34-member FTAA, potential expansion of the ASEAN to include China – which is fast emerging as a highly successful trading economy – and after that Japan and Korea, and most importantly the expansion of the EU[6] to include ten more Central and East European countries (CEEC) as members in 2004. Given the fact that preferential trade agreements represent the greatest exception to the WTO's fundamental principle of non-discrimination, the future increase and strengthening of RIAs would naturally result in an increase in erosion of trade conducted under the MFN principle (WTO, 2002a).

A word about the rules of origin would not be out of place here. As the trade preferences are assigned only to member countries, the ROO are an important element for trade among the members of any RIA. They are not of any significance for the members of a customs union because in a customs union treatment of imports from third countries is harmonized. For the other kind of RIAs it is important to determine whether the imports are eligible for preferential treatment in the importing country. The justification for the application of the rules of origin is prevention of imports from the non-RIA members, which may try to gain preferential access to the RIA markets through a country that maintains the lowest tariff restrictions. In addition, the MFN tariffs rates vary for the members of the RTA for third-country imports. Besides, each member of an RIA may participate in separate bilateral preferential trade arrangements with third countries.

RIAs have a large diversity in their preferential ROO regimes. As the RIAs frequently overlap, different sets of ROO may exist for any one economy. In fact, it is a frequently found feature of ROO. In a majority of the RIAs in force, preferential ROO requirements tended to be product-specific. They were often supplemented by other provisions, which could either make them more complex and flexible, or less so. As a rule, the preferential ROO were more stringent than MFN rules of origin. The ROO also become progressively more stringent with the increase in margin of preference between the MFN and preferential tariffs.

2.2 Quantifying Preferential Agricultural Trade among RIA Partners

To examine the global and regional trends in agricultural trade, long-term time
series of agricultural trade were constructed for APEC, EU-15, MERCOSUR,
and NAFTA by Diao et al. (1999). Based on statistics for 1970–95, they
inferred that while the average annual growth of world exports in agricultural
products was 3.4 percent over this period, that in APEC was 4.4 percent,
EU-15 was 4.8 percent, MERCOSUR was 4.5 percent and in NAFTA
3.9 percent. Therefore, the share of agricultural exports of these four RIAs in
the world exports expanded from 70 percent in 1970 to 85 percent in 1995.
The four RIAs exhibited considerable diversity among themselves, as
measured by their respective shares in global GDP and agricultural trade. They
also found that the growth rate of intra-RIA trade in agricultural products
exceeded the growth rate of this sector from these RIAs. Total trade is made
up of intra-RIA trade plus trade with the rest of the world. As intra-RIA
agricultural trade accounted for a significant share of each RIA's total of
agricultural trade, rapid expansion in intra-RIA trade contributed to growth in
world agricultural trade.

Owing to considerable diversity in RIAs, their shares of intra-RIA trade in
agriculture in their total agricultural trade also differed considerably. Besides,
these shares should also be expected to vary between periods. Diao et al.
(1999) computed concentration ratios for the entire 1970–95 period and for
various sub-periods, and found that with the exception of MERCOSUR, on an
average over the entire period, a typical member of these RIAs did not appear
to have traded substantially more with another member than with another
trading partner located anywhere on the globe. However, if the entire period is
sub-divided into four equal periods, interesting results emerge. The
concentration ratio of intra-trade steadily rose and reached its highest point in
the 1990s for all the four RIAs. This result implies that the neighborhood
relationship within the RIAs – in terms of adjacency and cultural similarities
– is not likely to be the only explanation for relatively recent appearance of
high concentration ratios in intra-trade in agricultural products. There must be
some other causal factors explaining the rise in intra-RIA trade in the recent
periods. Preferential trade arrangements and rising intra-RIA trade, which is a
relatively recent phenomenon, is one important factor behind rising
concentration of intra-trade in agriculture. Declining transportation costs and
technological changes were also helpful factors in this regard.

To be sure, adjacency and neighborhood characteristics influence trade
between neighbors. This effect is greater if the neighbors change their trade
policy orientation, liberalize and adopt outward-orientation of policy stance.
This would indeed enhance trade dynamism between neighboring economies.
As intra-regional trade grows, neighbors tend to harmonize their trade

policies, customs procedures; technical barriers to trade; and sanitary and phytosanitary barriers are removed, leading to intra-trade expansion. Computing trade concentration ratios for the four large RIAs supports this conclusion.

2.3 RIAs AND REGIONAL ECONOMIC COOPERATION

Even in a situation of few trade barriers in the global markets, there can be goods and services that can only be traded regionally. This amounts to both regional trade and cooperation in regional development endeavors. Larger partners in the RIA generally take initiatives in such collaborative regional endeavors. As noted above, regional trade liberalization of this kind in goods and services can result in welfare gains that accrue from multilateral trade liberalization. An apt example is the increasing trade in electricity between neighboring countries. Likewise, regional development of dams and water resources can broadly be put in the same category. A good example is Singapore and Indonesia signing an agreement (in 1991) to cooperate in the development of water resources in the Indonesian province of Riau in return for a guaranteed water supply for Singapore for half a century. Trade in certain services is also popular regionally. For instance, there are Filipino labor forces in all the Southeast Asian countries and Indian and Pakistani labor forces in Middle Eastern countries employed in sectors like construction, and health, as well as performing mostly blue collar and basic clerical jobs.

A new liberal and optimistic institutionalist approach to the global trading system is possible. Taking this approach, liberal institutionalists justify RIAs on the following grounds (Trebilcock et al., 1990). They view multilateral trade in a decentralized framework of negotiations and maintenance of mutually advantageous bargains among states. They seek ways of designing processes that, by reducing information, transaction, surveillance and verification costs, facilitate Pareto-superior deals[7] between or among states. Trebilcock et al. (1990) believe that performance of these contracts is promoted by both reputation effects and tit-for-tat retaliation strategies that tend to solve the Prisoner's Dilemma problems in multi-period games.

3. BILATERAL, REGIONAL AND CROSS-REGIONAL INITIATIVES

As regards the global spread of RIAs, Western Europe has the densest concentration (WTO, 2002a). Both the EU and EFTA and their constituent member economies have formed a networks of RIAs. Prevalence of RIAs in Europe and neighboring regions is noteworthy. They account for almost half of the total RIAs in the world. This is the result of a half-century-long tradition in using RIAs as an instrument of forging closer ties with neighbors on the part of the European nations.

Numerous small and medium-sized RIAs exist among and between the Baltic States, central Europe, and Turkey. In the late 1990s, RIA formation extended to the Southern and Eastern European economies. The Stability Pact was signed between the countries of former Yugoslavia, under which they started negotiating bilateral preferential agreements with each other in 1999. By 2004, the EU will have 10 more members, 8 of which are CEECs, plus Cyprus and Malta. This would reduce the number of RIAs in Europe because the bilateral preferential agreements of the EU with these ten countries will be void. Concurrently, the participation of these countries would become more intense because they would participate in the EU's network of RIAs directly.

Next to Europe, concentration of RIAs is most dense in Latin America. The Latin American countries were inspired by the example of EU initiative. They launched into serious RIA negotiations earlier than other developing economies. Therefore, the process of forming regional trading blocs is older in this part of the globe than in other areas. During the 1990s and early 2000s, the process of regional integration intensified with the launching of a large number of bilateral and plurilateral (between three or more members) agreements. These initiatives took place both at regional and sub-regional levels. The integration process not only covered the entire continent but also extended to other continents. Chile made a preferential trade agreement with Canada in 1996, while Costa Rica and Canada concluded a similar agreement in 2001. Several Central and Southern Latin American economies are in the process of doing the same. Chile and Mexico developed a network of bilateral preferential agreements in the region. Having completed that, the two economies were looking farther afield to form cross-continental RIAs with European economies and those in East and Southeast Asia. The NAFTA has reached its last stage of implementation. At the plurilateral level, MERCOSUR and EU were engaged in preferential trade negotiations.

In early 2000s, several North African and Middle Eastern economies began strengthening their trade ties with the EU by exchanging reciprocal preferences with it. Their objective was to be a part of a free-trade area with the EU under the Euro-Mediterranean Partnership Agreement (EMPA), which envisaged completing a free-trade area by 2010. This group of economies included Algeria, Tunisia, Morocco, Egypt, Israel, Jordan, Lebanon, the Palestinian Authority, and Syria. During the same period, these countries were trying to enter into similar free-trade area agreements with EFTA, both collectively and with individual member economies. They were also negotiating bilateral preferential trade agreements among themselves. Concurrently, North African and Middle Eastern economies were negotiating for other regional trade initiatives in both the geographical regions. In 2001, the Arab League launched an initiative for an Arab Free Trade Area by 2007. This was expected to include members of the Gulf Co-operation Council (GCC) and Jordan, Tunisia, Egypt, Sudan, Syria, Somalia, Iraq, the Palestinian Authority, Lebanon, Libya, Morocco, and Yemen.[8] The members of the GCC had another initiative afoot. On their own, they were working towards deepening their integration endeavors and having common external tariffs by 2005. They were also engaged in discussions with the EU and EFTA, exploring the possibilities of RIAs. Some progress was made in these negotiations with the EFTA and a Declaration of Cooperation was signed with the EFTA states. All these initiatives by the GCC were still underway in the early 2000s. They were far from reaching their culmination point.

In sub-Saharan Africa, regional integration endeavors have been going on but have not gained momentum. Their progress was unsteady and could not be ascertained because of the complex web of overlapping RIAs and their memberships. To be sure, the intensity of the regionalization process increased in the 1990s. In West Africa, eight regional economies were endeavoring to build the West African Economic and Monetary Union (WAEMU or UEMOA in French).[9] Similarly negotiations were underway for establishing the Central African Economic and Monetary Community (CEMAC in French) between six economies.[10] Another major ongoing endeavor was between the countries of eastern and southern Africa. Members of the Common Market for Eastern and Southern Africa (COMESA) were negotiating in the direction of creating a free trade area grouping of 20 countries. A similar project was underway in South Africa, where the members of South African Development Community (SADC) were working towards their objective of establishing a free trade area by 2004. SADC negotiations were not progressing rapidly and were having a good deal of difficulty due to overlapping membership of the aspiring countries in other African RIAs. The South African Customs Union (SACU) has survived for a long time.[11] South Africa has been active at cross-regional level and completed a free trade agreement with the EU. Having completed that, South Africa was exploring the possibilities for a similar agreement with economies on other continents. An Africa-wide, continental initiative has been on the drawing board. It has been named the African Economic Community (AEC). Efforts to establish an African Economic and Monetary Union (AEMU) by 2028 are gradually advancing. The ultimate goal of establishing the African Union, which is aimed at the economic integration of the continent, was announced in March 2001.[12]

The countries of the former Soviet Union have created several RIAs among themselves since its break up, as well as with their neighbors. Several bilateral preferential agreements were also being negotiated and a customs union has been agreed between the Kyrgyz Republic, the Russian Federation, Belarus,

Kazakhstan, and Tajikistan. In 2001, Georgia notified the formation of an RIA with Armenia, Azerbaijan, Kazakhstan, Turkmenistan, Ukraine, and the Russian Federation. By the early 2000s, a network of bilateral RIAs existed in Central Asia. It is likely to be rationalized and consolidated in the medium term.

Historically, Asian economies were known for their strong bias for MFN-*only* trade liberalization. However, this region has undergone a considerable transformation in this regard. In forming APEC, they moved away from their long-standing historical preference for MFN-only liberalization. Although the APEC adopted 'open regionalism', it began to be counteracted by members' drive towards preferential trade initiatives. Several successful traders in this region (Japan, South Korea and Singapore) took initiatives for entering into bilateral preferential agreements as well as for creating RIAs among themselves. The three countries also took the initiative in entering into cross-regional preferential trade agreements. Negotiations were held between Hong Kong SAR and New Zealand for a closer economic partnership. Japan and Singapore initiated discussions for a similar agreement. Likewise, Australia and New Zealand have been trying to negotiate RIA and bilateral agreements with the dynamic Asian economies. They were also endeavoring to enter into preferential trade agreements with cross-regional partners, particularly those in Latin America. However, the most notable initiative in this regard was the proposed expansion of the Association of South East Asian Nations (ASEAN) to include China.[13] An agreement to this effect was reached. Japan and the Republic of Korea were also endeavoring to follow suit. Negotiations to achieve this objective were under way. In spite of these developments and rising number of RIAs, Asia continues to be the region with the smallest number of RIAs currently in force.

Looked at from a global perspective, the current emerging trend is towards negotiating bilateral preferential agreements and forming cross-regional FTAs. Most of the major regional players are looking for non-regional partners for forming preferential bilateral trade agreements. The pioneers of this new trend are the EU and EFTA. Latin American countries are actively following this trend. Several bilateral agreements were under negotiations during the early 2000s.[14]

4. THE WTO DEBATE ON REGIONALISM

In the early 2000s, several pluri-dimensional and inter-linked issues were the subjects of raging debates among the members of the WTO. Some of them had legal overtones, while other were institutional issues. Some age-old economic chestnuts were also the focus of attention of the members. For instance, as alluded to above, Article XXIV of the WTO has a requirement regarding 'substantially all the trade' between the constituent members of an RIA being covered. Similarly, Article V of the General Agreement on Trade in Services mentions 'substantial sectoral coverage' of trade in services between the constituent members being covered under the RIA. However, members disagree regarding what these wordings imply and interpret them in several different ways.

Second, some institutional issues were also part of the on-going debates. They related to anomalies between rules in RIAs and those in the WTO system. RIAs differ not only in product coverage, but also in areas of trade discipline. That is, some of them cover areas that have not been covered by the WTO system as yet. For instance, investment or competition policies, the so-called 'Singapore issues' are covered by some RIAs, while the WTO debate on these issues is still far from complete. In addition, some RIAs go beyond the WTO provisions in several areas of trade regulations, while others have regulatory policies which differ from WTO in areas like anti-dumping, subsidies, intellectual property rights, and standards. This has caused concern among policy makers and these issues have also been discussed outside the WTO forum. Robert B. Zoellick, the United States Trade Representative, expressed concern in this regard. In one of his depositions he informed the US Senate that, 'Each [RIA] agreement without us [the US] may set the new rules for the intellectual property, emerging high technology sectors, agriculture standards, customs procedures or countless other areas of the modern, integrated global economy rules that will be made without taking account of American interests' (Zoellick, 2002).[15]

Third, several important economic issues continue to generate a good deal of disagreements and debates among WTO members. Although the impact of regional agreements on the constituent members and non-members has been debated since the Vinerian initiative (1950) in this regard, the last word is not yet in, and the raging debate on this issue has not died down. The same observation applies to the impact of regional agreements on the 'shaping and development of world trade itself'. The relationship between regionalism and multilateralism has continued to remain a critical systemic issue (WTO, 2001).

4.1 Multilateral Regulations and RIAs

Article I of the GATT (or GATT-1947) was, as well as Article I of the Marrakesh Agreement (or GATT-1994) is, the cornerstone of the global trading system.[16] It established the central requirement that signatory governments were required to extend unconditionally to all other contracting parties[17] any advantage, favor, privilege or immunity affecting customs duties, charges, rules and procedures, that they give to products originating in or destined for any other country. This is referred to as the much-vaunted MFN principle, which was defined in Chapter 2, section 5.[18]

The superstructure of multilateral trade regulations is squarely based on the classical economic principle of comparative advantage.[19] The MFN principle *inter alia* applies to tariff concessions. The WTO members are rule-bound not to discriminate between imports from different sources. All the WTO members are obliged to treat all the other members equally as 'most-favored' sources. Freedom and equality to import from any origin in the global marketplace is intended to ensure purchase from the lowest-cost producers or sellers, which in turn underpins and reinforces the all-important principle of comparative advantage (WTO, 1995). It promotes competition and minimizes the cost of production, promoting efficiency in the process. This binding stipulation of treating all WTO members as equal in commercial policy is an effective restraint on discrimination against imports from a particular source, for any reason.[20]

The fundamental benefit of the MFN principle is to guard against the extent to which a country can play favorites in its trade relations, and ensure that global trade is conducted on the basis of comparative advantage rather than political advantage. The MFN principle depoliticizes global trade and makes it more efficient. It helps in promoting equal treatment of exports from smaller and larger trading nations. Therefore, non-discrimination or the MFN principle is believed to contribute to the 'regularity, orderliness, and predictability', which is the essence of a rule-based global trading system (WTO, 1995). By taking down the trade barriers and reducing or eliminating distortions in the global economy, the MFN principle works towards helping the price mechanism to work more efficiently at the global level. Due to the MFN principle, the additional trading opportunities created by the GATT rounds of MTNs were automatically extended to all its members. The postwar trading system has served the global economy well. It is credited with facilitating unprecedented expansion of global trade in goods and services. According to WTO statistics, global trade in goods increased 6.5 percent annually in real terms since the creation of the GATT in 1947. There was a twelvefold increase in world trade between 1947 and 2000, versus a sixfold increase in world output. This trade expansion has also led to global economic integration as well as more rational allocation of global productive resources.

The flip side of the coin is that while the MFN principle has had a long history, it has not been controversy-free. Its basic premise and purpose have been called into question. On the one hand, this principle seems to encourage rampant free riding[21] by countries on concessions negotiated between other countries. At one extreme, it might encourage every country to withhold concessions in the hope of being able to free-ride on concessions made by others, thus paralysing the process of trade liberalization. At the other, it might be argued that tariff concessions might be more readily negotiated between two countries, that is if each country is assured that the other country will not subsequently negotiate more generous concessions with third countries, and thus weaken the benefits that would have accrued from the initial exchange of concessions. There is substance in both of these contradictory stands. The negotiating process in the GATT and WTO always presupposed the existence of the free-rider problem, and members have always been concerned about lack of reciprocity.

Any form of regional integration contravenes the MFN principle, the fundamental tenet of the GATT–WTO system. Yet, a provision for RIAs was included in the superstructure of multilateral trade regulations. The GATT and WTO allowed members to conclude RIAs as an exception to the fundamental principle of non-discrimination set out in the MFN clause of Article I. This breach of the regulation has been allowed by the global trading system. This is not as incongruous as it appears on the face of it. One reason to allow this deviation from the MFN principle was to accommodate the reality. RIAs have had a long history (refer to Chapter 1, section 4). Many countries would not have joined the GATT if it had prohibited future RIAs among neighbors and the multilateral trading system would have been much less multilateral. Little wonder that Article I, Paragraph 2, of the GATT-1947 had explicitly exempted from the MFN requirement, all the RIAs in force at the time the GATT came into effect. These included the erstwhile British Imperial Preferences, preferences in force in the French Union, preferences given by the Benelux countries, by the US and the preferences granted by the Lebano-Syrian Customs Union to Palestine and Transjordan. However, these preferences were 'capped' and they could not be raised above the existing (in 1947) levels. This pragmatic move laid the foundation for the future growth of world trade on the basis of the MFN principle (WTO, 1995).

The WTO literature demonstrates that genuine free trade agreements and customs unions were viewed as possibly compatible with the MFN clause in the past. Perhaps this was done to distinguish various forms of ad hoc and partial discrimination that were being formed during the inter-war period (1919–39). By entering into an RIA, economies dismantle trade barriers, which was considered an important step in the direction of liberalizing international trade on the same lines as liberalizing trade between different provinces of the same country. This line of logic apparently persuaded the founders of the GATT. Economic integration between several countries can potentially have an economic effect analogous to the process of integration within a single sovereign state (WTO, 1995). Under these circumstances RIAs were not seen as an inherent threat to the global trading system. A deviation from the MFN principle has, therefore, been allowed since the inception the GATT.

Therefore, RIAs in trade in goods fall under three WTO categories, although they are generally treated as falling under the same rubric. As evident from the foregoing exposition, the three categories are (1) the Article XXIV arrangements, (2) the Enabling Clause arrangements limited to developing countries and permitting partial preferences to these under the Generalized System of Preferences and (3) the arrangements permitted by the WTO through a grant of an exception of Article I. Finally, the conclusion of RIAs in trade in services is governed by Article V of the General Agreement on Trade in Services. After an RIA is launched, the WTO has to be notified of its date of launch, membership details, coverage and the category under which it has been launched.

A word about the Enabling Clause is necessary here. The Tokyo Round (1973–79) led to the creation of an 'Enabling Clause'. Following this Round of MTNs, the contracting parties (CPs) of the GATT allowed this 'derogation' to the MFN clause in favor of developing economies. This derogation provided legal cover for trade concessions granted to developing economies under the GSP initially for a period of ten years. Under the provisions of Part IV, industrial countries were encouraged to allow developing countries to access the industrial country markets on a non-reciprocal basis. It also permitted preferential arrangements among developing countries in trade in goods. Paragraph 2(c) of the Enabling Clause allowed special treatment to regional or global arrangements entered into among developing country CPs for mutual reduction or elimination of tariffs and non-tariff barriers. The authority granted under this Clause to enter into regional arrangements is constrained by several conditions. One of its key requirements is that any such arrangement should be designed to facilitate and promote the trade of developing countries, and not to raise barriers to or create undue difficulties for the trade of other CPs. This requirement is identical to the requirement of Article XXIV, Paragraph 4.

Multilateral regulations of the GATT and WTO on RIAs reflect the founders' desire to accommodate and provide for such agreements. In doing so, they were cautious in guarding the trading interests of the non-RIA members. They ensured that RIAs were compatible with a 'rule-based and progressively more open world trading system' (WTO, 1995). Therefore, the provisions (enumerated below) on RIAs establish numerous conditions, which the RIAs must comply with. Transparency is strictly required so that they can be closely monitored by the multilateral system, which the WTO represents.

The first condition for trade in goods was set out in Article XXIV of GATT-1947. It stated that the purpose of a RIA should be to facilitate trade between the constituent countries and *not* to raise barriers to the trade of other WTO members not parties to the RIA. During the Uruguay Round, Article XXIV was clarified to some extent and updated by the Understanding on

Interpretation. Paragraphs 4 through 10 of Article XXIV of the GATT-1947 (as clarified in the Understanding on the Interpretation of Article XXIV of the GATT-1994) contain the principal provisions of the multilateral trading system related to regional integration agreements.[22] Barriers against non-members cannot be made more restrictive than before the formation of the RIA. Article XXIV, Paragraph 4, stated that closer integration of the member economies must not adversely affect the interests of the non-member countries. Any common external tariff (CET) should be set at a level that is 'on the whole' not higher or more restrictive than was imposed by the RIA members before joining in. If the level of CET of any individual member is higher than before, Paragraph 6 provides a procedure for the withdrawal of previously negotiated tariff commitments.

Second, Part IV of the Articles of Agreement of the GATT comprises Articles XXXVI, XXXVII and XXXVIII. Provisions in this Part relate to non-reciprocity in trade negotiations between industrial and developing economies. They also provide for the former to adopt special measures and plans to promote the expansion of imports from developing countries. The 'Enabling Clause', discussed above, had several provisions permitting the CPs of the GATT to grant differential and more favorable treatment to developing countries, notwithstanding the non-discrimination requirement in Article I. Chapter 3, section 5, provides details regarding these non-reciprocal RIAs.

Third, there is a WTO provision relating to the coverage of trade. When an RIA is created, reduction or removal of trade barriers and NTBs should cover 'substantially all the trade' and/or sectors of trade. Roessler (1993) pointed out that Article XXIV forbids stopping short at partial preferences or excluding major sectors or trade from the RIA. This emphasis on 'substantially all the trade' helps in fending off the inevitable political pressures to avoid or minimize tariff reductions in inefficient import-competing sectors. The substantially-all-the-trade requirement also ensures that RIAs are not abused as a cover for narrow or sectoral discriminatory arrangements. In addition, a wider sectoral coverage enhances the trade-creating effect of RIAs. Thus viewed, this stipulation helps 'differentiate between politically unavoidable and containable deviations from the most-favored-nation principle' by determining 'the point where trade policy is allowed to give way to foreign policy' (Roessler, 1993).

The fourth condition related to the systemic dynamics of the RIA. After the formation, progress towards economic integration should be expeditious. Article XXIV, Paragraph 5 (c), states that an RIA agreement 'shall include a plan and schedule for the formation of such a customs union or of such a free trade area within a reasonable length of time'. The objective is to eliminate or minimize the danger of interim agreements, which are often abused by introducing discriminatory preferences for a long time. In the Uruguay Round this timespan was defined as not exceeding 10 years under normal conditions. Therefore, GATT-1994 in its Understanding on the Interpretation of Article XXIV notes that 'reasonable length of time' 'should exceed 10 years only in exceptional cases. In cases where Member parties to an interim agreement believe that 10 years would be insufficient they shall provide a full explanation to the Council for Trade in Goods of the need for a longer period'.

Fifth, for the purpose of dispute settlement, the provisions of Article XXII and XXIII of GATT-1994, as elaborated and applied by the Dispute Settlement Undertaking may be invoked with respect to any matters arising from the application of those provisions of Article XXIV relating to customs unions, free trade areas or interim agreements leading to the formation of a customs union or free trade area.

4.2   Article XXIV: A Barrier to Free Trade?

Article XXIV of the GATT-1947 has been decried as antithetical to the spirit of the GATT–WTO system, because it allows members of a trade bloc to discriminate against non-members. However, as we saw above, the authors of Article XXIV, in their pragmatic desire to accommodate RIAs, were cautious in guarding the interests of non-RIA members. They attempted to ensure that RIAs were compatible with a disciplined and progressively liberalizing global trading system. The conventional wisdom in this regard is that Article XXIV ensures that trade bloc formation ensures free trade. However, several trade analysts hold the view that in reality Article XXIV is partly responsible for the difficulties in further multilateral trade liberalization.[23]

An RIA can be of the kind where the members drop all the protectionist barriers. It can also be of another kind where they decide the CET strategy together. Such a trade bloc comes to have a power in the world markets, which can be invoked by raising the level of CET. To be sure, as stated above, the provisions of Article XXIV, Paragraph 4, do not allow the RIA to become more protectionistic toward non-members. Some hold the opinion that even under the stipulations of Article XXIV, free trade would not be in equilibrium when groups of economies are allowed to form RIAs. Zissimos and Vines (2000) believed that those who argued against the ability of Article XXIV to support free trade in the global economy did not make a convincing case and did not allow the structure of RIAs to affect free trade in their models. They contended that the RIA structure that emerges under Article XXIV is determined endogenously, and it is not conducive to free trade.

The conventional view was remiss because it neglected the fact that even when RIAs do not (or are not able to) flex their muscles by raising the level of CET, when members become better off, non-members become worse off. This happens when RIAs are perfectly WTO-consistent. The process works through exchange rate and/or terms-of-trade effect. Let us take the case of the EU to illustrate how it works. As the EU Single Market Programme progresses, *ceteris paribus* members will progressively trade more with each other and less with the non-members. Consequently, their currencies would gradually appreciate vis-à-vis the non-European currencies, like the dollar and the yen. The resulting wealth effect would be increased purchasing power of the EU currencies to buy goods from the rest of the world, leaving the EU better off. On the flip side, the same process reduces the purchasing power of the non-European currencies, leaving this group of economies worse off. This has taken place because the trade within the EU has been driven by the Single Market rules, and no measures were taken to make trade with non-members more difficult.

This set of circumstances would discourage expansion of free trade, because if the Single Market framework provides certain concrete benefits to the EU members (while non-members do become worse off), they would be reluctant to let the non-members in and give up their benefits. Consequently, members do not have any incentive to allow non-members into the EU. If the members do allow non-members in, they apparently are not behaving like rational economic agents. There will always be limits to expansion of the EU, and free trade would never be encouraged by the members (Zissimos and Vines, 2000).

4.3   Article XXIV: Evidence of Reciprocity

If non-discrimination is the first pillar of the global trading system, reciprocity is a close second. Whether Article XXIV is in accord with the principle of reciprocity is unclear. Article XXIV emphasizes a 'balance of concessions' among the members and when concessions are withdrawn, the trade partners are permitted to withdraw 'substantially equivalent concessions'. Among RIA partners, literally interpreted, Article XXIV calls for trade barriers 'to be eliminated with respect to substantially all trade between the constituent territories'. RIAs do involve some degree of reciprocity because partners are expected to exchange trade concessions. This reciprocity may not replicate the reciprocity in the multilateral trade negotiations (MTNs). Typically RIAs do not have equivalent concessions because they are formed between economies which differ in terms of size of GDP, and having widely different levels of trade barriers. Yields in terms of gains in market access for such economies cannot possibly be symmetric.

In MTNs, reciprocity has a strong theoretical foundation. Motivated by possibilities of improvements in terms of trade, countries try to maintain positive tariffs, creating a 'prisoner's dilemma', whereby all countries would be better off if they cooperate and reciprocate in lowering tariffs (Bagwell and Staiger, 2000). In MTNs, the benefit of reciprocal tariff concessions is to help governments undo inefficient trade barriers of all kinds that generate terms-of-trade externality. Reciprocal trade negotiations provide an opportunity for negotiations among the trading partners to credibly commit to lower tariffs and, thereby, reach a higher welfare level.[24]

In RIA negotiations, unlike those for MTNs, the utility of reciprocity is not so clear because it furthers discriminatory tariff reductions. If an RIA is being negotiated between a developing and industrial economy, reciprocity can be detrimental to the interests of the developing economy. Asymmetries in size of the economies would make it necessary for the smaller developing economy to make large-scale concessions to achieve an agreement with the high-income industrial economy. A corollary of this line of logic is that an RIA between a small developing economy, having low tariff barriers, and a large industrial economy may just not be possible. The gains from trade for the potential partner industrial economy would be so puny that it would not be worth its while to form an RIA with the small developing economy. Taking this line of logic one step further, in such an RIA negotiation the principle of reciprocity provides incentives for the small developing economy to keep its tariff levels as high as it can so that it can obtain concessions from the large industrial economy, and in the process generate greater trade diversion.

Using trade, tariffs and income data of 91 RIAs negotiated between 1980 and 2001, Freund (2003) tested for reciprocity in RIAs. The results offered strong support to the existence of reciprocity in RIAs between industrial economies as well as those between developing economies. After controlling for the determinants of trade preferences, the results suggested that 'a one percent increase in preferences offered leads to about one-and-a-half percent increase in preferences received' in both industrial country RIAs and developing country RIAs. However, there was little evidence of reciprocity in RIAs between industrial and developing economies. Results also supported the hypothesis that 'large countries extracted greater trade concessions from smaller countries. This led to a modified form of reciprocity in North–South agreements: a large increase in access to a developing-country market leads to only a small increase in access to a rich-country market'.

Using a repeated game model, Freund (2003) examined the kind of RIAs that are sustainable. She concluded that 'trade preferences granted are increasing in trade preferences received'. That is, a country can extract higher concessions from an RIA partner if it has managed to keep higher trade barriers. However, if the developing economy does maintain its trade barriers high so that they can work at the appropriate time as a bargaining chip, this may not always produce desired outcome because in an RIA negotiation the value of tariff concessions of a small developing economy for an industrial economy is very small in terms of gains from trade. Another important conclusion was that 'reciprocity is more likely to be observed in North–North and South–South agreements', while in the case of agreements between developing and industrial economies, its place is dubious.

4.4 WTO Committee on Regional Trade Agreements

Under the GATT regime, the multilateral examination of RIAs was conducted in individual working groups set up in an ad hoc manner for performing this task. The WTO attempted to bring consistency and uniformity to the examination of RIAs. To this end, in February 1996, the WTO General Council[25] established a single committee named the Committee on Regional Trade Agreements (CRTA) to examine individual regional agreements and consider the systemic implications of the agreements for the multilateral trading system and the relationship between them. The Committee is mandated to develop procedures to facilitate and improve the examination process and to ensure that the reporting on the operations of the regional agreements is adequately carried out by the parties to the agreements.

The CRTA also studied how to correctly interpret expressions like 'substantially all the trade', 'on the whole' and 'other regulations of commerce' which are found in Article XXIV (WTO, 1998). To this end, the WTO Secretariat and delegations of several large trading countries made written contributions.[26] CRTA proposed that 'substantially all the trade' requirement should be measured in terms of tariff lines and trade flows. The debate on economic and legal perspectives of the term on 'other regulations of commerce' continued to rage. However, the issue is far from settled and the Secretariat has been asked to conduct further analysis on these issues by the General Council. In addition, the CRTA was assessing whether RIAs and EIAs are consistent with WTO discipline. At the time of the Doha Ministerial Conference in November 2001, over 100 regional agreements were under examination in the CRTA (WTO, 2001). Since its inception, the CRTA has accomplished several of its objectives, although due to lack of consensus on legal yardsticks a large and increasing backlog of unexamined RIA reports existed in the early 2000s. The accomplishments of the CRTAs includes:

- Restructuring and improving the RIA examination process;
- Standardizing the information requirements for RIAs' examination;
- Determining a streamlined method of evaluating each RIA in terms of its consistency with WTO provisions.

RIAs are examined to analyse whether the system of rights and obligations under the WTO, related to the RIAs, should be modified and clarified further.

So far WTO members have not reached a common ground regarding RIAs' contribution to the multilateral trading system. Whether they strengthen or go against the growth of multilateral trading system is still beyond agreement. Some WTO members believe that RIAs, by moving faster than the multilateral trading system, represent a way of strengthening the global trading system. The impact of RIAs on integrating the developing economies into the global trading system is cited as a favorable effect. Other members disagree regarding the systemic implications of RIAs. Many WTO members also believe that in the contemporary period, a redefinition of relationship between RIAs and the multilateral trading system is badly needed, so that a better synergy is developed between the two vitally important institutional arrangements. They feel that a mere modification or reinterpretation of rules formulated half a century ago would not suffice to take into account the fundamental changes observed in the nature and scope of RIAs during the present period.

5. LAUNCHING THE DOHA ROUND OF MTNs AND RIAs

The Fourth Ministerial Conference of the WTO was held in Doha, Qatar, 9–13 November 2001, with 142 members participating.[27] The Ministerial Conference is the highest-level decision-making body of the WTO. It meets 'at least once every two years', as required by the Marrakesh Agreement establishing the WTO. As the Third Ministerial Conference, in Seattle, was a spectacular failure, the preparations for the fourth one started in earnest in January 2000 (Das, 2000c). One of the many reasons for the collapse of the third Ministerial Conference was the breakdown of the Green Room consultation process.[28] With 135 WTO members participating in the Third Ministerial Conference, it was not possible for the Green Room consultation process to be functional. While the Green Room process could not work no alternative to it was devised or in sight in Seattle. Being left out of the information sharing and consultation process, many developing economies felt marginalized.

Although theoretically the WTO – and its predecessor, the GATT – operated by consensus, the reality was generally different.[29] The members of the Quadrilateral Group, the so-called Quad, namely Canada, the European Union, Japan and the US, had traditionally functioned as an informal steering committee for the WTO system.[30] They continued to function in a non-transparent manner and held important meetings on crucial issues in small groups to which many of the developing countries' ambassadors were not invited. It must, however, be stated that the principal trading developing countries were frequently invited for consultations along with the members of the Quad. These Green Room consultative meetings were criticized by many developing member countries of the WTO for their lack of transparency.

After the breakdown of the Green Room consultation process, a system of frequent, open-ended and informal head-of-delegations meetings was devised. The objective of this system was regular meetings, for consultation and exchange of information with all the WTO members. All the continuing activities across a broad spectrum were taken up for discussion in the meetings. Before the fourth Ministerial Conference was launched in Doha, the Chairman of the General Council and the Director-General of the WTO held hundreds of consultations with the delegations of member countries in a variety of formats, ranging from heads-of-delegations meetings to one-on-one discussions. Regular meetings of the Director-General with the trade minister provided further strength to the consultation process. This approach supplanted the Green Room process of yore and won praise from the developing-country members for being open, transparent and efficient (Das, 2002).

Serious disagreements over the agenda items were the other major reason for the collapse of the third Ministerial Conference. Notwithstanding the preparations by the WTO secretariat and the general perception of a strong performance by the global economy in 1999, seeds of discord existed well before. There were deep divisions of opinions, beliefs and expectations, which could be divided into both North–South and East–West axes. Further divisions existed which were more complex and could not be divided along these traditional axes. The difference of opinion and expectations between the US, the EU and Japan on the one hand, and among the industrial and developing economies on the other, were too large to bridge in a short space of time. Numerous contentious issues existed between countries and country groups.

Before the Doha Ministerial Conference, the WTO secretariat adopted a bottom-up approach to the process by encouraging a proponent driven system, where those member countries that are in favor of including a certain topic on the agenda would meet in an effort to raise support for their positions. The member countries met outside the formal General Council process to test the level of support on a range of issues, which included non-agricultural market access, investment, competition, the environment, fisheries subsidies, and reform of the Dispute Settlement Understanding. The trade ministers' meetings, noted above, helped in bridging differences between positions.

Certain adjustments in the global trading system were needed for it to be a better reflection of the social, economic and financial realities of the rapidly transforming global economy. The system still remains fairly vague on precisely how existing rules should be changed and what form the new regulations should take. At Doha the WTO achieved what many skeptics believed was beyond the reach of the organization, namely, the launch of a new round of MTNs. The 142 WTO members agreed upon the Doha Development Agenda.[31] It offered the prospects of a stable trade framework, against the background of a sharp slowdown in global economic growth and trade. In 2001, global GDP and trade recorded their weakest performance in more than a decade. The early 2000s have been a problem-ridden period for the global economy.

Paragraph 4 of the Doha Ministerial communiqué of 14 November 2001 stressed the commitment of the WTO members to regional trade agreements and the Conference Declaration highlighted the importance of regionalism:

- through its recognition that regional trade agreements can play an important role in promoting the liberalization and expansion of trade and in fostering development;
- through agreement to negotiations aimed at clarifying and improving disciplines and procedures under the existing WTO provisions applying to regional trade agreements;
- through agreement that in the work of the WTO Working Group on the Relationship between Trade and Investment account should be taken, as appropriate, of existing bilateral and regional arrangements on investment.

Following the Doha Ministerial Conference, the multilateral round of trade negotiations was launched, scheduled to end in January 2005. Despite its successful launch, the developing country members were not enthusiastic. Many of them were opposed to it because they felt that they got a raw deal from the Uruguay Round and were not convinced that they had much to gain from a new round. In addition, many developing economies were having difficulties implementing the recommendations of the Uruguay Round. They were persuaded to go along with the Doha round of MTNs because the industrial countries held out the prospect of significant concessions in several areas, including agriculture. In early 2003, it appeared that the developing countries' initial skepticism was justified (*The Economist*, 2003a). The promised changes to existing trade agreements, aimed at helping developing countries, were yet to materialize – even though the deadline was the end of 2002. A deal to improve poor countries' access to cheap medicines was also due to have been concluded by the end of 2002. American refusal to go along with the deal agreed by everyone else scuppered the long drawn out negotiations. In addition, there was the usual impasse in negotiations on agricultural trade. On the whole, at the end of the first quarter of 2003, the progress in the Doha round was inadequate and it was being felt that the schedules were likely to be delayed. Real possibilities of the round collapsing began to appear (*The Economist*, 2003a).

A work program was designed for the MTNs, which included RIA related issues. In Paragraph 29 of the work program it says that: 'WTO rules say regional trade agreements have to meet certain conditions'. But interpreting the wording of these rules has proved controversial, and has been a central element in the work of the Regional Trade Agreements Committee. As a result, since 1996 the committee has failed to complete its assessments of whether individual trade agreements conform to WTO provisions. This is now an important challenge, particularly when nearly all member governments are parties to regional agreements, are negotiating them, or are considering negotiating them. In the Doha Declaration, members agreed to negotiate a solution, giving due regard to the role that these agreements can play in fostering development. The declaration mandates negotiations aimed at 'clarifying and improving disciplines and procedures under the existing WTO provisions applying to regional trade agreements. The negotiations shall take into account the developmental aspects of regional trade agreements.' These negotiations fall into the general timetable established for virtually all negotiations under the Doha Declaration ... 'The 2003 fifth Ministerial Conference in Mexico is to take stock of progress, provide any necessary political guidance, and take decisions as necessary.'

6.   TRADE IN SERVICES AND REGIONAL INTEGRATION

Although numerous empirical analyses are available on the costs and benefits of forming RIAs in goods, those in services have been ignored. Theoretical research is almost non-existent in the area of impact of unilateral, regional and multilateral liberalization in trade in services and the relationship between them. As the formal models deal only with border measures, they fail to capture the reality of a large part of trade in services. This is, for sure, unusual. Of the large number of the RIAs that were negotiated during the second wave of regionalism in the 1990s, a large proportion had a services dimension. Intellectual curiosity in this regard has been low so far. Although attracting FDI is considered one of the crucial motives behind the entry into RIAs, there is little theoretical work that develops a link between FDI inflows and RIA creation. It is also possible that most analysts think that we really do not need a new trade theory or analytical approach to grapple with trade in services-related issues, particularly costs and benefits from RIAs in services. However, conventional trade theories that deal with trade in goods are not totally inapplicable to trade in services.

The analysis of RIAs in services does require an extension of conventional theory for two reasons. Mattoo and Fick (2003) have pointed out that trade in services 'require proximity between supplier and consumer, we need to consider preferences extended not only to cross border trade, but also to foreign direct investment and foreign individual service providers'. Second, the basic requirement of creating an RIA is to provide preferential treatment to members. In the case of trade in services it could be granted not through tariffs (which are infrequent, if not rare, in services trade), but through repealing of restrictions on the movement of labor and capital (in terms of quantity or share of foreign ownership), and a variety of domestic regulations such as technical standards, licensing and qualification requirement. Thus the preferences in trade in services are given to RIA members through different instruments from those used in trade in goods. This has an impact over both product and factor mobility (Mattoo and Fick, 2003).

The implications of repealing restrictions on factor mobility in a preferential manner and providing preferential treatment (or liberalization) to the constituent members of the RIA depends on whether this preferential treatment is for the short term, for meeting a particular trade-in-services requirement, or relatively permanent. In the former case, where the preferential treatment to the services providers (consultants or construction companies) is on a temporary basis, the arrangement resembles that for preferential treatment in trade in goods. That is, the services were carried to the importer as if they were goods. Having delivered the services, the supplier of services withdraws from the scene.

The other extreme is the scenario where the RIA is the kind that entails complete integration of product and factor markets, as in case of the EU and the Caribbean Community and Common Market (CARICOM). Several intermediate scenarios are also feasible, for instance, limited permanent movements of individual suppliers of services through immigration and permanent movement of capital by way of FDI. Such movements directly affect the factor endowments of the members of the RIA. In such cases 'the positive impact will depend on the specificity of the factors that move and the normative impact on the extent to which incomes are repatriated' (Mattoo and Fick, 2003). In an RIA arrangement, the manner in which privileged market access can be granted by one constituent member to another will depend upon the instruments of protection that are being employed for a particular kind of trade in services. The examples given below clarify how different instruments of protection determine the mode of RIA integration in services:

1. When an economy imposed quantitative restrictions on trade in services or on the number of services providers, its preferred treatment for the members of the RIA would entail allocating higher quotas. In the case of transport services (air, road and maritime) many economies allocate freight and passenger quotas on a preferential basis. Similarly, in

audiovisual services, preferential quotas of airtime are allocated to pre-identified foreign programs.

2. A member of the RIA can also lower restrictions on foreign ownership, type of legal entity, and branching rights for the other members on a preferential basis. For instance, when the NAFTA was formed, Mexico removed ownership restrictions on financial institutions from the other two member countries of NAFTA (Canada and the US). Typically, foreigners are given percentage limits on ownership of financial institutions. The financial institutions based on other countries are not given this privilege. Interestingly, European banks benefited indirectly from this preferential treatment of the members of NAFTA because many of them had a presence in the US.

3. Domestic taxes and subsidies are another mode of executing discrimination policies in trade in commercial services. Many countries assure the other members of the RIA national treatment in this regard. The other foreign providers of services are not given this preferential treatment. They are subject to different tax rates and do not have access to domestic subsidies.

4. Preferential treatment to members of the RIA can also be granted through licensing and qualifications requirements, domestic regulations pertaining to technical regulations, and general TBT measures. In many countries licensing and qualifications requirements are imposed on foreign services providers. However, these requirements are waived for those foreign providers who are part of the RIA. This amounts to de facto preferential treatment of services firms from the RIA. Regulatory practices and norms in sectors like transport, insurance and financial services can also be waived for the services firms from the member countries. Requirements like proofs of solvency and utilization of chartered accountants trained in a particular country come under this category.

With regard to welfare gains from regional trade liberalization in services, the implications of gains from liberalization in trade in goods cannot be directly extended to those in services. Non-preferential liberalization, *ceteris paribus*, is sure to produce larger gains than regional trade liberalization, which entails preferential liberalization for the constituent members of the RIA (Mattoo and Fick, 2003). Non-discriminatory liberalization neither limits nor biases consumer choices. It allows the least-cost, or most competitive, producer of services to be the most successful exporter. In a hypothetical situation where all the exporters of services are the least-cost producers, the welfare gains for the global economy are enormous. Furthermore, non-discriminatory liberalization leads to a less complex policy regime than the one based on preferential discrimination for the members of the RIA. By the same token, the former regime has lower administration costs for the government agencies and lower transaction costs for the firms than the one based on preferential discrimination.

If liberalization measures were initially aimed at RIA formation, with a future plan for their expansion to the global economy, the benefits of eventual multilateral liberalization would be lower than those achieved by non-discriminatory liberalization from the start. The reason is that in the case of many services, the location-specific 'sunk costs of production' are high for many services firms. Therefore, even after the privilege of being a regional member dissipates, the less competitive or inferior producer, continues to supply to the regional market. The inferior producer, who was established in the regional market, also hinders the market entry of the more efficient services providers outside the region, unless their competitive advantage is so large that it offsets the advantage of the incumbent services provider (Mattoo and Fick, 2003).

6.1   GATS and Economic Integration Agreements

Economic integration agreements (EIAs) are the preferential trade agreements in the area of commercial services.[32] By March 2002, 18 EIAs were notified to the WTO under the GATS Article V (WTO, 2002b). Article V of the General Agreement on Trade in Services (GATS) is equivalent to the Article XXIV of the GATT and lays down the regulations. Article V provides liberty to the signatories of the GATS to enter into an agreement liberalizing trade in services. Country groups are not prevented from forming RIAs, again *provided* such an agreement has 'substantial sectoral coverage' and *provided* such an agreement provides for the absence or elimination of 'substantially all discrimination' in the sense of Article XVII between or among the parties, in the sectors covered. This can be achieved through elimination of existing discriminatory measures. In addition new discriminatory measures can be prohibited after the entry into force of an agreement or 'on the basis of a reasonable time-frame'.

Article V of the GATS also lays down that where developing economies are constituent members of an EIA, flexibility should be provided in meeting the conditions set out in Article 1, Paragraph 1, which relate to elimination of all discriminatory measures. Before elimination of discriminatory measures the level of development of the member country should be taken into consideration as well as the level of development of the services sectors and sub-sectors. If all the members of an EIA are developing economies, 'more favorable treatment may be granted to juridical persons owned or controlled by natural persons of the parties to such an agreement'.

Article XXV of the GATS, which is on waivers, provided the GATT basis for several GATS agreements (Das, 2000a; WTO, 1995, 1998). Furthermore, Article V, Paragraph 4, of the GATS sets out detailed parameters of services trade liberalization for integration agreements. These requirements have been thoughtfully laid down to keep control over the effect of an EIA on the non-member economies. Accordingly, the new set of trade barriers, which came into being after the formation of the EIA, cannot be higher or more restrictive than before the EIA was formed.

6.2 Expansion of Trade in Services and the GATS

The services sector not only dominates the industrial economies, it also accounts for more than 50 percent of GDP in countries like Argentina, Colombia, Peru, the Philippines, and Poland. For some years, commercial services have accounted of some 20 percent of the world trade on the balance-of-payment basis. According to the 2002 *Annual Report* of the World Trade Organization, merchandise exports worldwide were \$6162 billion in 2001, while exports of services amounted to \$1440 billion, which was 18.99 percent of the total world trade in 2001, even though that was a bleak year for trade in commercial services and there was little rise in the value of trade in services compared to the previous year. The decrease in the value of transportation and travel services was not fully compensated by the rise in the value of other commercial services, comprising *inter alia*, communication, insurance, and financial services as well as royalties, licenses and fees.

Until the Uruguay Round, commercial services were not seriously considered for inclusion in a round of MTNs. Discussions and information exchanges between the contracting parties of the GATT in this regard were highly informal. However, exports of commercial services went on expanding rapidly. Their value was \$62.9 billion in 1970, \$362.8 billion in 1980, and \$751.6 billion in 1990. The value of exports of commercial services soared to \$1435 billion in 2000, falling to \$1440 billion in 2001. Since 1990, services have been the fastest growing segment of world trade. The value of exports of commercial services almost doubled between 1990 and 2000.[33] This was despite contraction (of 1.5 percent) in world trade in merchandise in 1998.

By creating the GATS, the Uruguay Round brought services into the fold of the multilateral trading system. Since the launching of the Uruguay Round, numerous developing economies have initiated liberalization movements that covered their commercial services sectors as well. This trend was a natural extension of a broader reform movement focusing on trade in goods. By the early 1990s, developing economies were liberalizing their services transactions faster than the industrial economies (Das, 2001).

As a group, the industrial countries have been the largest traders in commercial services.[34] This does not imply that developing countries do not have a significant stake in the performance of international trade in services. Importance of the services sector in the developing economies in terms of GDP, employment and trade has been gradually rising. China was the largest services exporter among developing countries in 2001, accounting for 2.2 percent of world services exports. Over the last three decades, developing countries as a group have recorded faster growth of trade in commercial services than industrial economies. Among the developing economies, the dynamic East and Southeast Asian economies have been posting the most rapid expansion in trade in commercial services.

Establishment of the GATS was a first step towards creating a comprehensive framework to liberalize and regulate trade in commercial services. The obligations of individual countries under the GATS were specified in their 'schedule of specific commitments' to market access, which also provided a list of exceptions. These schedules are an integral part of the agreement. The GATS operations have a long way to go. The degree of liberalization of global trade in services has been relatively meager, with many GATS schedules involving simple standstill commitments. Interestingly, informal liberalization progressed further than the commitments in the GATS. There is still considerable scope of further global liberalization of trade in commercial services. As the Uruguay Round was not able to conclude negotiations in all the services sectors and it was felt that there is enormous room for improvement, it was decided to continue negotiations immediately after the entry into force of the GATS.

In March 1997, 40 countries agreed to eliminate customs duties on trade in information technology products beginning 1 July 1997, and eliminating tariffs altogether by 2000. International trade in these products amounted to $600 billion in 1997. Negotiations on basic telecommunications services were successfully concluded in February 1998. Sixty-nine countries agreed to wideranging liberalization measures. Financial services negotiations were concluded in December 1998. Seventy countries agreed to open their financial services sector covering more than 95 percent of trade in banking, insurance, securities, and financial information. The agreement on financial services entered into force in March 1999.

6.3   The Doha Ministerial Conference and the GATS

Many key obligations in the GATS apply only to those services for which the countries concerned have made liberalization commitments in its 'schedule of specific commitments'. During the Uruguay Round, it was hoped that the next round of MTN negotiations in trade in services would focus attention on improvements in rules, but their primary emphasis would be on extending the reach of the rules by adding to the coverage of WTO members' services schedule (Das, 1998a). In January 2000, under Article XIX of the GATS, negotiations were initiated on the proposals submitted by the members. The proposals covered a wide range of services sectors as well as horizontal issues, and included issues related to movement of natural persons.

A set of Guidelines and Procedures for the Negotiations was adopted by the Council of Trade in Services in March 2001 as a basis for continuing future negotiations. The Doha Ministerial Conference, held in November 2001, subsequently reaffirmed them. The Doha Communiqué (World Trade Organization, 2001a) reconfirmed the commitment of the GATS to furthering negotiations in trade in services, repeating the objective of 'promoting the economic growth of all trading partners and the development of the least developed countries'. It also reaffirmed the objectives of the GATS as stipulated in the Preamble, Article IV and Article XIX of the GATS. The participants to the Doha Ministerial Conference were given the time limit of 30 June 2002 to submit initial requests for specific commitments under the GATS.

Strengthening Article VI of the GATS, which provided the basic framework for minimizing trade distortions created by domestic regulations, should be one of the important objectives of the Doha Round of MTNs. This Article stated, 'In sectors where specific commitments are undertaken each member shall ensure that all measures of general application affecting trade in services are administered in a reasonable, objective and impartial manner'. A strengthened version of this Article, and a clearer interpretation, could go a long way in facilitating market access liberalization by committing member countries to the reform of regulations that impede trade and competition in the services sectors. Under the amended version of Article VI, member countries can be asked in the Doha Round to establish procedures for the review of regulations at the request of the exporters of services. The Doha Round negotiations need to ensure that the amended version of Article VI is based on transparent criteria, which are not more burdensome than necessary to ensure the quality of services that are exported.

7. DUAL-PRONGED DEVELOPMENTS IN SINGAPORE ISSUES

While there have been concerns regarding the incompatibility between the rule-based multilateral trading system and preferential regional agreements, there can also be complementarity between them. This can be found in the area of international trade known as the Singapore issues, which include investment, competition and trade facilitation-related issues.[35] FDI was an important issue in the context of economic development. In the 1980s it became an important issue in the context of financial globalization as well. FDI began to be perceived as one of the new modes of global integration. FDI statistics show that it outpaced both growth rate of global trade and GDP in the 1980s and 1990s. These developments and perceptions made it imperative to have an international framework of rules in this important area, although many CPs were not in favor of including FDI-related issues in the MTNs and the GATT during the decade of 1980s. After a great deal of resistance from some contracting parties, the Uruguay Round succeeded in placing investment issues on the multilateral trade agenda. Around the same period, several large RIAs began focusing on the negotiations on rules on regional investment. These negotiations picked up momentum during the 1990s.

In making regulatory provisions, bilateral investment treaties dominated the FDI scenario. In 2000, close to 2000 BITs were in operation.[36] FDI-related issues at the bilateral or regional level could also be addressed through RIAs and other plurilateral (having three or more members) arrangements. A typical RIA was not the principal vehicle for negotiating investment-related rules in the past, although a small and growing minority of them began to deal with them in the 1990s. They now represent one of several important institutional settings in which FDI-related rule-making is taking place.

Competition is the second important Singapore issue and RIAs are known to play a significant regulatory role in this area. Competition-related regulatory provisions exist in almost all RIAs, which includes RIAs between and among industrial and developing economies. A gradual consensus regarding the appropriateness of competitions-related provisions emerged among the members of RIAs, although it is still an issue for debate at the global level. It should, however, be emphasized that RIAs are only one of the many fora where competition-related regulations and policies are dealt with. The United Nations and OECD are also actively involved in this area. The former is involved through the United Nations Set of Multilaterally Agreed Principles and Rules for Control of Restrictive Business practices. Numerous OECD Recommendations are also put out from time to time.

Similarly, in the area of trade facilitation, RIAs have remained active. The WTO defines trade facilitation as the 'simplification and harmonization of international trade procedures'. It entails 'activities, practices and formalities involved in collecting, presenting, communicating and processing data required for the movement of goods in international trade'. The regional initiatives in trade facilitation have ranged from mandatory to voluntary. International bodies like the World Customs Organization (WCO), United Nations Conference on Trade and Development (UNCTAD), and United Nations Economic Commission (UN-ECE), in turn influenced them for Europe. As the RIAs have started dealing with these issues only recently, comprehensive regulatory provisions in this area are at an early stage of development. The older RIAs concentrated on tariffs and excluded simplification and harmonization of trade procedures. Only a small number of RIAs have started addressing import, export and border-crossing procedures in sufficient detail. Awareness of cumbersome procedural intracacies unduly increasing costs and reducing efficiency is promoting increasing attention to trade facilitation. An interesting illustration is the efforts initiated by the Asia Pacific Economic Cooperation (APEC) forum, in which members have devised a set of voluntary principles to be used by regional firms for reducing procedural burdens in mutual trade. The newly born bilateral trade agreements or the economic partnership agreements have assigned a great deal of importance to trade facilitation. The Japan–Singapore Economic Partnership Agreement (JSEPA) and the Free Trade Area of the Americas (FTAA) testify to this new approach (Heydon, 2002).

While RIAs have played a complementary role in developing policies and making regulatory provisions in the area of three Singapore issues, they have also gone beyond the provisions of the WTO. How far they went beyond the multilaterally agreed regulatory provisions could not be generalized because it varied from one RIA to another and from one issue to another. Various instances and their extent of 'going beyond' have been documented in detail by Heydon (2002).

8. CONTINGENT PROTECTION MEASURES IN RIAs

During the 1990s, a surge was noticed in contingent protection measures, in particular anti-dumping measures (ADMs). Although they are considered the most divisive instrument of protection, they are used as a substitute for countervailing duties, which are often more difficult to apply. Although the Uruguay Round agreement on ADMs, as set out in GATT-1994 Article VI, was expected to scale ADMs back, expectations of improvement on this count were belied. Between 1988–90 and 1991–94, the use of ADMs by the CPs nearly doubled from 384 to 730. This number dropped to 508 during 1994–97 and it was believed for a short time that the Uruguay Round agreement on ADMs was making the difference, but this optimism turned out to be ephemeral. In the three years ending June 2001, use of ADMs leapt to 825, the highest ever three-year level. Although it has been a highly controversial issue in the past, it has been included in the agenda for the Doha Round.[37]

Based on the WTO data, a study examined 29 RIAs and APEC over the 1989–2001 period for initiating internal and external ADM against the constituent members of the RIAs as well as non-members (WTO, 2002b; Spinanger, 2002). This study calculated the degree to which RIAs directed their contingent protection activities at other members and at the third countries. For NAFTA, the share of ADMs against the members steadily declined over time. Conversely, MERCOSUR and APEC were found to apply ADMs to non-members more easily. This study did not provide any conclusive evidence of members of RIAs initiating more ADMs against non-members because some of them provided evidence to the contrary.

9. CONCLUSIONS AND SUMMARY

Some trade economists believe that RIAs contribute to a liberal global trading system and, to that end, strongly support regional integration. Expansion of RIAs could have positive effects on the global economy provided the emerging RIAs are 'open' to trade from outside. Open regionalism can promote and facilitate external liberalization, meaning trade with non-member economies outside the RIA. Thus viewed, RIAs are complementary as well as supplementary to multilateralism. Not all concur. Besides, the RIA route of a liberal global trading system is far from an easy and smooth process. There can be myriad of problems along the way. The developing economies, which were largely antithetical towards RIAs in the past, have had a change of mind. Presently, developing-country perspective on regionalism is radically different from the one that prevailed during the first wave of regionalism in the 1950s and 1960s.

It is believed by the trade economists that accession to RIAs liberalized the trade regimes of developing economies. To examine whether there is direct link between liberalization and RIA accession, an intertemporal study of 75 RIAs was undertaken (Foroutan, 1998). The inference was that economies that became members of effective RIAs had liberalized their trade regimes. This did establish a direct link between trade liberalization and RIA membership. However, it was difficult to determine how much of causality can be attributed to RIA participation. Since the mid-1980s there have been many countries that liberalized their trade regimes significantly without being members of any RIA. But if acceptance of a liberal trade policy regime is a requirement of an RIA membership, it can be said that this kind of RIA generally succeed in causing liberalization of the trade regime of the members. With advancing age, RIAs tended to deepen by way of removing trade barriers, including non-tariff barriers.

With such a large number of RIAs in operation, a great deal of global trade is influenced by RIAs. Quantifying trade under various preferential trade agreements is not easy. It faces methodological problems. Besides, one cannot ignore the fact that not all trade among the members of an RIA necessarily comes under a preferential trade regime. Sometimes economic and adminis-trative costs of meeting all the requirements of the rules of origin (ROO) within an RIA are high. It is, however, agreed by the trade economists that intra-RIA trade has gone on increasing over the preceding two decades and could soon 'account for more than half' of the world trade. Preferential trade in agricultural products recorded a large increase. The share of trade under the Generalized System of Preferences in total preferential trade recorded a significant fall, from 7 percent to 3 percent over the last two decades. This reflected the general decline of trade under GSP worldwide. The regional distribution of preferential trade was found to be highly uneven. Western Europe had the highest share of preferential trade. Latin America had much lower value, while Asia and Oceania had a still lower proportion of preferential trade. Finally, it was noted that countries that have highly open economies also tended to have a lager share of preferential trade. Trade under various preferential agreements is expected to grow in the foreseeable future because several significant expansions and new initiatives were underway in the early 2000s.

Western Europe has the densest concentration of RIAs in the global economy. The network of RIAs, particularly FTAs, between the EU and neighboring regions is noteworthy. They account for almost half of the total RIAs in the world. In May 2004, the EU will have 10 more members. Next to Europe, concentration of RIAs is most dense in Latin America. In sub-Saharan Africa, regional integration endeavors have been going on but they have not gained momentum. Their progress was unsteady and could not be ascertained because of the complex web of overlapping RIAs and their memberships. As pointed out in section 3, the former Soviet Union economies have formed several RIAs among themselves. In some RIAs they included their neighbors as well. In addition, some bilateral trade agreements have been entered into and they have agreed to working towards formation of a CU at some time in the future. Historically, Asian economies were known for their strong bias for MFN-*only* trade liberalization. However, Asia has undergone a considerable transformation in this regard. In forming APEC, they moved away from their long-standing historical preference for MFN-only liberalization. Although APEC adopted 'open regionalism', it began to be counteracted by members' drive towards preferential trade initiatives. Several successful traders in this region (Japan, South Korea and Singapore) took initiatives for entering into bilateral preferential agreements as well as for creating RIAs among themselves.

During the early 2000s, several pluri-dimensional and inter-linked issues were the subjects of raging debates among the members of the WTO. Some age-old economic chestnuts were the focus of attention of the members. For instance, Article XXIV of the WTO has a requirement regarding 'substantially all the trade' between the constituent members of an RIA being covered. Wordings and their interpretation have long been discussed. Second, some institutional issues were also part of the ongoing debates. They related to anomalies between rules in RIAs and those in the WTO system. Third, several important economic issues continue to generate a good deal of disagreement and debate among the WTO members. The impact of regional agreements on the constituent members and non-members has been debated since the Vinerian initiative.

The superstructure of multilateral trade regulations is squarely based on the classical economic principle of comparative advantage, enshrined in the MFN principle. Any form of regional integration contravenes the MFN principle. And yet a provision for RIAs was included in the superstructure of multilateral trade regulations. The GATT and WTO allowed members to conclude RIAs as an exception to the fundamental principle of non-discrimination set out in the MFN clause of Article I. One reason for allowing this deviation from the MFN principle was accommodating reality. The WTO literature demonstrates that genuine free trade agreements and customs unions were viewed as possibly compatible with the MFN clause in the past. Little wonder that Article I, Paragraph 2, of the GATT-1947 had explicitly exempted from the MFN requirement, all the RIAs in force at the time the GATT came into effect. Multilateral regulations of the GATT and WTO on RIAs reflect the founders' desire to accommodate and provide for such agreements. In doing so, they were cautious in guarding the trading interests of the non-RIA members. They ensured that RIAs were compatible with a 'rule-based and progressively more open world trading system'.

Several trade analysts hold the view that in reality Article XXIV is the one which is partly responsible for the difficulties in further multilateral trade liberalization. They believe that those who argued against the ability of Article XXIV to support free trade in the global economy did not make a convincing case and did not allow the structure of RIAs to affect free trade in their models.[38] It is also unclear whether Article XXIV is in accord with the principle of reciprocity.

Under the GATT regime, the multilateral examination of RIAs was conducted in individual working groups set up in an ad hoc manner for performing this task. The WTO attempted to bring consistency and uniformity to this examination. Therefore, the WTO General Council established a single committee named the Committee on Regional Trade Agreements (CRTA) to examine individual regional agreements and consider the systemic implications of the agreements for the multilateral trading system and the relationship between them.

The ministerial communiqué of 14 November 2001 from Doha, in Paragraph 4, stressed the commitment of the WTO members to regional trade agreements. The Doha Declaration highlights the importance of regionalism as well as its place in the multilateral trading system. However, despite a successful launching, the progress in MTNs by mid-2003 was poor and several deadlines could not be met.

Few empirical analyses of costs and benefits of RIAs in the area of trade and services are available. Econometrists have so far ignored this increasingly important area of research. Theoretical research is almost non-existent in the area of impact of unilateral, regional and multilateral liberalization in trade in services and the relationship between them. The analysis of RIAs in services does require an extension of conventional theory. The instruments which give preferences in trade in services to RIA members are different to those used in trade in goods. This has an impact over both product and factor mobility.

Article V of the GATS lays down that where developing economies are constituent members of an EIA, flexibility should be provided in meeting the conditions set out in Article 1, Paragraph 1, which relate to elimination of all discriminatory measures. Before this happens the level of development of the member country should be taken into consideration as well as the level of development of the services sectors and sub-sectors. If all the members of an EIA are developing economies, 'more favorable treatment may be granted to juridical persons owned or controlled by natural persons of the parties to such an agreement'. The Doha Communiqué reconfirmed the commitment of the GATS to furthering negotiations in trade in services, repeating the objective of 'promoting the economic growth of all trading partners and the development of the least developed countries'. It also reaffirmed the objectives of the GATS as stipulated in the Preamble, Article IV and Article XIX of the GATS.

The Singapore issues, which include investment, competition and trade facilitation-related issues, were in general addressed at the bilateral, regional and multilateral levels. As regards anti-dumping measures, no pattern has emerged so far and they have varied from RIA to RIA. It cannot be said that RIAs initiated more ADMs against non-members because some of them provided evidence to the contrary.

NOTES

1. An indispensable condition for an emerging market economy is its sustained ability to attract capital inflows from the global banks and securities markets. Other than the rapid endogenous growth endeavors and extensive macroeconomic and financial liberalization and deregulation, respect of property rights and human rights are considered the basic prerequisites of becoming an emerging market economy. The national government must offer protection to property and human rights of both the citizens of the country and the non-residents alike. See Das (2003a), Chapter 1 for greater details.
2. The most notable one being Greece, which has been a member of the EU since 1981 and yet subject to serious macroeconomic shortcomings. This shows that RIAs are not sufficient for sound policy and hence presumably not particularly good sources of credibility in themselves. This outcome of an RIA has not attracted the attention of the developing economies so far.

3. The Uruguay Round, the most ambitious round of multilateral trade negotiations, was launched in September 1986 in Punta des Este, Uruguay.
4. Rules of origin are the criteria used to define where a product was made. They are an essential part of trade rules because a number of policies discriminate between exporting countries: quotas, preferential tariffs, anti-dumping actions, countervailing duty charged to counter export subsidies, and so on. Rules of origin are also used to compile trade statistics, and for 'made in' labels that are attached to products. A great deal of time was spent on the ROO during the Uruguay Round of multilateral trade negotiations. It resulted in an agreement on them which is a part of the GATT-1994. This first ever agreement on the subject requires WTO members to 'ensure that their rules of origin are transparent; that they do not have restricting, distorting or disruptive effects on international trade; that they are administered in a consistent, uniform, impartial and reasonable manner; and that they are based on a positive standard. That is, they should state what *does* confer origin rather than what does not'. RIAs either conform to the WTO rules in this regard, or formulate their own deviations. These rules vary from RIA to RIA and may be similar, simpler, or more complex than the WTO rules.
5. Estimated by the WTO. Refer to Chapter 3, Section 5, p. 40 of the *Annual Report 2002*.
6. As noted in Chapter 1, note 11, the Agreement on a Treaty on European Union was signed in Maastricht on 10 December 1991. It included a timetable for Economic and Monetary Union. On 1 January 1993, the European Single Market was completed. On 1 November 1993, the Maastricht Treaty came into force, and the EEC became the European Union.
7. A situation in which it is impossible to make someone better off without at the same time making someone else worse off is called Pareto optimal. However, if someone can be made better off without making someone else worse off then the situation is called Pareto superior.
8. The membership of the Gulf Co-operation Council includes Bahrain, Kuwait, Oman, Qatar, Saudi Arabia, and the United Arab Emirates.
9. These eight West African economies were Benin, Burkina Faso, Côte d'Ivoire, Guinea-Bissau, Mali, Niger, Senegal, and Togo.
10. These six countries comprised Cameroon, Central African Republic, Congo, Equatorial Guinea, Gabon and Chad.
11. The membership of the SACU comprised Botswana, Lesotho, Namibia, Swaziland, and South Africa.
12. The objective was announced at the Fifth Extraordinary Summit of the Organization of African Unity (OAU) in March 2001.
13. The membership of ASEAN comprised the following 10 countries in 2003: Brunei Darussalam, Cambodia, Indonesia, Laos, Malaysia, Myanmar, the Philippines, Singapore, Thailand, and Vietnam. Cambodia was the last to join ASEAN (in 1999).
14. The source of historical information and data in this section is WTO, particularly WTO (2002a), Section C.
15. Robert B. Zoellick made these remarks to the US Senate urging them to approve the 'fast track' authority.
16. In economics of international trade, the two expressions, namely, the 'GATT-1947' and the 'GATT 1994', are frequently used. It is essential to be clear about the distinction between the two. The latter is the revised version of the original GATT Agreement of 1947. The text of the GATT Agreement was significantly revised and amended during the Uruguay Round and the new version was agreed upon in Marrakesh, Morocco. The GATT 1994 reflected the outcome of the negotiations on issues relating to the interpretations of specific articles. In its renewed version, the GATT 1994 includes specific understandings with respect to GATT Articles, its obligations and provisions, plus the Marrakesh Protocol of GATT 1994.
17. As the GATT was an accord, not an organization, its signatory governments were called the contracting parties. The WTO is a treaty and an international organization, therefore, the signatory governments are called members.
18. The history of discrimination in tariff policy began in the nineteenth century. Although commercial treaties since the sixteenth century had contained the most-favored-nation (MFN) pledge, it was not until the second half of the nineteenth century that its general use became the basis of international tariff policies.

19. Paul A. Samuelson, noted economist and Nobel Laureate, was once challenged by mathematician Stanislaw Ulam to name one proposal in all Social Sciences that is both true and non-trivial. It is said that Samuelson struggled for an answer for years. Eventually, he came upon 'comparative advantage' as the answer to the challenge. That it was logically true was not needed to be argued before a mathematician. That it is non-trivial is testified by thousands of important and intelligent men and women who have never been able to grasp the doctrine for themselves, or to believe it after it was explained to them.

20. A detailed account of the multilateral framework vis-à-vis RIAs is available in WTO (1995). Seekers of greater details are referred to it. This section draws on this and various other WTO documents.

21. A term used to infer that a country that does not make any trade concessions, nonetheless profits from tariff cuts and concessions made by other countries in negotiations under the most-favored-nation principle.

22. Although there were numerous changes in the Articles of Agreement, the noteworthy ones included those in Article II regarding tariff schedules, in Article XVII regarding state trading enterprises, in Article XXIV regarding regional trade agreements, in Article XXVIII regarding modifications of tariff schedule, and in the area of balance of payments provisions covered by Articles XII and XVIII. The GATT-1994 has superseded the GATT-1947. While GATT-1994 was a natural progression of multilateral trade regulations, it also enabled the CPs to bypass the need to formally amend the original GATT-1947. By creating a GATT-1994 they agreed to create a Single Undertaking, applicable to all. This was a pragmatic plan. All the members of the WTO only had to sign the GATT-1994, in lieu of GATT-1947 together with all of its subsequent amendments (Milner and Read, 2002).

23. See, for instance, McMillan (1993); Yi (1997); Bagwell and Staiger (1999) and Zissimos and Vines (2000).

24. Bagwell and Staiger (2000) provide a survey of this literature.

25. The General Council is the WTO's day-to-day governing body.

26. Delegations from Australia, Hong Kong SAR, Japan and Korea made the written contributions.

27. The first three Ministerial Conferences of the WTO were: (1) in Singapore, held 9–13 December 1996, (2) Geneva, held 18–20 May 1998 and (3) Seattle, held 30 November–3 December 1999.

28. These meetings took place in a 'Green Room' next to the office of the Director-General of the WTO at the Centre William Rappard in Geneva, and were therefore referred to as 'Green Room meetings'.

29. Technically voting is possible but in practice it is limited solely to the times of new accessions.

30. The four members of the Quad comprise some of the largest trading economies of the world. Historically, they wielded enormous influence over the formation of multilateral trade policy. Together they accounted for 47.8 percent of the world merchandise exports in 2002. (See Appendix Table II.2, *Annual Report 2002*, World Trade Organization, p. 23).

31. The General Council of the WTO had drawn lessons from the failure in Seattle and prepared an agenda that did not contain empty spaces with parentheses that are conventionally substituted for disagreeing on an agenda framework. An ambitious and comprehensive agenda was prepared for the next round of MTNs, at Doha, Qatar. It contained some items that could not have been on a risk-loving punter's betting chit. Yet, the Fourth Ministerial Conference was a success and it was followed by the launching of a new round of MTNs.

32. It is appropriate to define the term 'commercial services'. In the fifth edition of the *Balance of Payments Manual* of the WTO the definition of the commercial services category includes: transport, travel, communications, construction, insurance, financial services, computer and information services, royalties and license fees, trade-related services, and personal, cultural and recreational services.

33. Data compiled from UN and the WTO sources by Das (2001).

34. According to the latest available data (2001), the US topped the WTO league table of services exports, accounting for 18.3 percent of the world's total. It was followed by the UK

(7.5 percent), Germany (5.5 percent), France (5.5 percent), Japan (4.4 percent), and Italy (4.1 percent).

35. The Singapore issues are (i) trade and foreign investment, (ii) trade and competition, (iii) transparency in government procurement, and (iv) trade facilitation. They are referred to as the Singapore issues because they were raised for the first time by the industrial economies during the Singapore Ministerial Conference in 1996. These issues were never a part of the international trading system in the past. On the insistence of the industrial economies, particularly the EU, the US and Japan, the Doha Round of MINs included them for negotiations, but the members had diverse positions on them and disagreed. They are widely considered one of the principal reasons behind the failure of the Fifth Ministerial Conference of the World Trade Organization (WTO) held in Cancún, Mexico during 10–14 September 2003.

36. According to Heydon (2002), the precise number in 2000 was 1941.

37. See Paragraphs 28 and 29 of the Ministerial Declaration of the Fourth Ministerial Conference or the so-called Doha Ministerial Communiqué of 14 November 2001.

38. Article XXIV of the GATT-1947 and the understanding on the interpretation of Article XXIV of the GATT-1994 relate to free trade areas and customs unions. They recognize the contribution that RIAs may make to the expansion of world trade through 'closer integration' between the parties to such agreements.

5. Regionalism in Asia-Pacific

1. STRUCTURAL TRANSFORMATION OF THE ASIA-PACIFIC REGION

Although approximately half of the trade is at present intra-regional, institutionalized regionalism was slow to put down its roots in Asia.[1] Relative to other regions, the Asia-Pacific region was slow and late in catching on to the concept and phenomenon of regionalism. Asian policy makers ignored the institutional form of the concept for a long time. Economic growth in Asia has a certain characteristic pattern to it. Following a brief flirtation with the import-substituting industrialization strategy, over the preceding three-and-a-half decades, the high performing Asian economies adopted outward-oriented strategies, promoting trade and foreign investment. This led to brisk expansion of intra-regional trade and investment. Asia-Pacific regionalism was essentially market-led and uninstitutionalized. Regional production networks were the consequence of market-led economic dynamics of the region. Large corporations, including transnationals, contributed to the growth of the pan-Asian industrialization process (Chapter 3, section 3).

Some institutional arrangements followed market initiatives, albeit with a substantial time lag. Some regional institutional initiatives were taken, which are presently operating with varying degrees of success. We shall see that empirical exercises, using a gravity model, concluded that East and Southeast Asian economies clearly show certain inward bias among themselves. Although this does apply to all, the dynamic economies of the Asia-Pacific region do seem to be natural trading partners.[2] These regional initiatives not only coexist with globalism but also serve as stepping stones to multi-lateralism.

A large body of research is available proving that trade and outward economic orientation were the principal forces behind rapid economic growth in Asia. This literature is too well known to be referred to here. Several empirical studies have concluded that with rapid growth, the economic structure of the newly industrialized Asian economies (NIAEs)[3], the four Southeast Asian economies in the Association of Southeast Asian Nations (ASEAN-4),[4] and the People's Republic of China (hereinafter China) underwent substantial structural transformation, which had a direct bearing on factor endowments. Growth, structural transformation and changing factor endowments naturally ushered in transformation in the manufacturing sector, followed by that in the services sector. The Heckscher–Ohlin theory supports and provides an explanation for the resulting transformation in the comparative advantage of different Asian economies and/or country groups (Das, 1998b). However, Asian economies did not record high (or low) trade in relative and absolute terms only in certain product lines or sectors. Similarly, trade in these economies was not concentrated in just a few select sectors (Das, 2000a). Another noteworthy observation in this regard is that there was no characteristic Asian export path or Asian export route and few generalizations could be made in this regard for the region.

2.   HIGH-PERFORMING ECONOMIC SUB-GROUPS

The successful sub-groups among Asian economies and their performance can be divided in the following manner. Following Japan, the NIAEs were the first and the most successful in export-led or trade-induced growth, followed by the ASEAN-4 and subsequently China. By 2000, China had become the largest developing-country exporter, accounting for 3.5 percent of global merchandise exports. Although global GDP growth rate decelerated from 4.7 percent in 2000 to 2.3 percent in 2001 and then recovered marginally in 2002 (3.0 percent),[5] China continued its rapid emergence as a highly successful trading economy, and accounted for 4.7 percent of global merchandise exports in 2002.[6]

The long-term GDP growth rate of the South Asian economies was not only slow but they were also the last and the slowest to embark on export-led or trade-induced growth path. An admixture of bilateral trade ties, neo-mercantilism policy stance, and liberalized and diversified multilateral trade regimes were the driving forces behind the emerging trade patterns in the region. Market forces played a notable role in the developments of these trends. As the economies grew and the supply-side synergy gained momentum, Asian trade not only expanded rapidly, it also advanced ahead of regional conventions like the ASEAN Free Trade Area (AFTA) and the Asia Pacific Economic Co-operation (APEC) forum. There was a steady growth in the internal Asian markets and, therefore, intra-regional trade. The WTO league tables of leading exporters for 2001 included China (6th), Hong Kong SAR (10th), Korea (13th), Taiwan (14th), Singapore (15th), Malaysia (18th), Thailand (24th), and Indonesia (27th).[7]

When the Asian crisis broke out in mid-1997, most successful Asian economies were carrying on as much as 50 percent of their total trade with the other regional economies (refer to section 3). The only exception in this regard was Indonesia. Apart from this, only China saw the proportion of its intra-regional trade share decline during the 1990s, essentially because its trade share with the United States (US) expanded. Over the recent period, most of the successful exporters in Asia held or reduced their share of trade with Japan, the dominant regional trader which accounted for 6.6 percent of global exports in 2001. Although Japan's significance as a regional trade partner has declined over the years, in absolute terms it has expanded its exports to the region. During the last decade and a half, the most rapid growth in trade opportunities came instead from the four NIAEs, as well as the ASEAN-4.

Lee and Roland-Holst (1998) showed that the market expansion that took place in Asia was both vertical and horizontal. First the NIAEs and then the other emerging-market economies of Asia fit into the lower tiers of complex trade hierarchies. This tendency was conspicuous in association with the large flows of FDI into China and Southeast Asia. Over the preceding quarter century, Japan, Taiwan and Korea have provided massive amounts of foreign direct investment (FDI) to China and Southeast Asian economies, increasing their commitments in these markets in the process. Firms in these countries have built subsidiaries or partnerships in China and the Southeast Asian economies, which in turn export intermediate goods to the investor firms' home countries. These intermediate goods can be exported to the subsidiaries of the investing firms in other parts of the world. This kind of trade expansion is usually supported by complex commercial alliances in which the new partners enjoy many growth externalities (Lee and Roland-Holst, 1998). Trade between China, Hong Kong SAR and Taiwan[8] – together referred to as Greater China – is large and increasingly closely linked. China trades much more directly both intra-regionally and outside the region. Its trade dependence on Hong Kong SAR has declined considerably since 1990, because its capability to trade directly has increased.

3. TRENDS IN INTRA-REGIONAL TRADE AND INVESTMENT

Historically, intra-trade in Asia was well developed in the early decades of the twentieth century. The share of intra-trade in total trade in Asia was 45.5 percent in 1928 (WTO, 1995). In the late 1930s, during the Japanese imperial domination, intra-regional trade in Asia was high. After 1931, the Japanese colonial pattern of economic relations – which was nothing more than exchanging raw materials for manufactured goods – gave way to building independent industrial capacity outside Japan, essentially in China, Korea and Taiwan. This kind of economic relationship between Japan and Asian economies led to significant intra-regional investment as well as development of regional transportation and communications infrastructure networks. Development of production networks supported mutually reinforcing trade and investment in Asia.[9] Both Beasley (1987) and Sakakibara and Yamakawa (2003) have provided a graphic account of how a sophisticated set of economic linkages between Japan and other Asian economies grew during this period. Economic complementaries within the region underpinned a rapid expansion of intra-regional trade and a decline of trade between Asia and the rest of the world.

When World War II ended, trade and investment patterns in Asia, particularly East Asia, were redirected toward the US. Economic linkages and intra-trade ties between Japan, Korea, China, and Taiwan were weakened considerably in the aftermath of the war. Besides, the Chinese civil war had a devastating impact on the country's trade which virtually collapsed. Japan also experienced an abrupt redirection in its trade ties at the end of the war. Its trade with Asia, both East and Southeast, fell from 73 percent of total trade in 1940 to 31 percent in 1951 (Petri, 1994). Thus, the war broke down the old trading pattern between Japan and Asia and a new, diversified pattern emerged. Its concentration on East Asia declined.

American economic policy in Asia after the World War II worked counter to this trend and sought to reestablish and strengthen Japanese trade ties with the regional economies so that the synergy could stimulate the regional economies. The expectation was that a steady trade expansion would also contribute to political stability in the region. The legacies of pre-war economic relationships in Asia and the post-war endeavors ensured that in the period immediately after the war – notwithstanding its ravages – intra-regional trade was not seriously reduced. Although a sharp fall was to be expected, on average, intra-regional trade stabilized around 41 percent of all Asian trade between 1951 and 1958. It is noteworthy that this happened without any institutional support.[10]

3.1   Market-Driven Regional Economic Integration

As set out above, East and Southeast Asian economies traditionally used to export industrial raw materials to Japan and import intermediate and capital goods. Owing to remarkable supply-side developments in the Asian economies, there was a complete reversal in this trend during the contemporary period. By the early 1990s, more than 60 percent of their exports to Japan were manufactured goods. NIAEs' exports to their ASEAN neighbors also expanded. Exports among the NIAEs jumped to $22.4 billion or 10 percent of their total exports in 1988 from $5.9 billion or 5 percent of their total exports in 1986. NIAE exports to ASEAN countries rose from

$6.4 billion in 1986 to $14.5 billion in 1998, or from 5 percent of the total to 7 percent (Das, 1993).

Likewise, ASEAN exports to NIAEs also rose from $8.2 billion or 21 percent of the total to $15.5 billion or 24 percent over the 1986–88 period. Intra-ASEAN exports rose only in terms of value, from $1.5 billion to $2.3 billion during this period. The share of exports of individual ASEAN economies in the internal market of the ASEAN remained constant and low at 4 percent. Intra-trade started rising again in the late 1980s and early 1990s, reaching 49.7 percent in 1993 and 50.7 percent in 1997. In 1998, intra-trade declined to 44.6 percent of the total Asian trade (Das, 1993; WTO, 1995, 1999). This decline was to be expected as regional economies were languishing due to the 1997-98 Asian crisis. In 1999, the five crisis-affected Asian economies made a sharp V-shaped recovery and the regional growth rate improved from 1.0 percent in 1998 to 6.1 percent in 1999.[11] The recovery led to the return of intra-regional trade. Growing exports stimulated demands for each other's imports and in turn stimulated GDP growth. During 2000, regional GDP growth rate was estimated at 6.9 percent (ADB, 2000). Thus intra-trade was a cause – and effect – of rapid growth in the region (*The Economist*, 2000a).

Towards the end of the 1990s, when China was making concerted efforts to join the WTO, previously closed sectors for FDI were liberalized under WTO requirements. This led to a surge in FDI in high-technology industries like semiconductors and electronics from the other Asian economies that had strong high-technology bases. During the latter half of 2000, prices of semiconductor chips were on a downward trajectory. Severe competitive pressure was pushing Asian chipmakers to relocate to cheaper production bases and areas with marketing potential. China seemed to meet both the conditions. Thus the pan-Asian wave of industrialization in high-technology areas is continuing. Until 2000 the electronics industry in China met 86 percent of its semiconductor needs by imports from Malaysia, the Philippines, Singapore and Thailand. In the latter half of 2000, China was attracting Taiwanese investment in new semiconductor capacity and building up its electronic production facilities. Taiwanese venture capitalists launched several initiatives involving billions of dollars in building high-end wafer plants in China, which in turn helped China in upgrading its industrial mix. In 2000, it was projected that by 2003, China would have capacity to export semiconductors, which would put pressure on all current Asian semiconductor exporters to move up the value chain and be more competitive (CSFB, 2000).

Asian economies were also endeavoring to provide mutual support for exchange rate stability. They put in place a variety of inter-governmental mechanisms designed to provide cooperative support for exchange rate stability in the region. As early as 1972, ten Southeast Asian nations established the South East Asian Central Banks (SEACEN) Research and Training Center, at Kuala Lumpur, Malaysia. Since then, the SEACEN has been organizing training programs and hosting an annual meeting of the ten central bank governors. Current membership of SEACEN is eleven.[12] In 1991, these eleven Asian central banks established the Executives' Meeting of East-Asia-Pacific Central Banks (EMEAP), which organized high-level meetings and hosted working groups on financial markets, central bank operations, and prudential supervision.[13] In 1995, the Hong Kong Monetary Authority (HKMA) and the central banks of Indonesia, Malaysia, and Thailand announced repurchase agreements designed to provide mutual exchange rate support. Singapore, the Philippines and Japan subsequently joined this network. At the April 2000 meeting of the Asian Development Bank, in Chiang Mai, Thailand, the ASEAN-Plus-Three[14] countries agreed to establish a pan-Asian liquidity backstop – a so-called Asian Regional Financial Arrangement (ARFA) – to prevent future speculative crises in the region. Under the AFRA, the old $200 million network of repurchase agreements, where reserves were provided only against valuable collaterals, were replaced by a new network of swap agreements where central banks were simply going to swap currencies. Under the ARFA, the Asian economies have freer access to one another's support (refer to section 7.5 also).

3.2   Intra-Regional Trade

Intra-regional trade increased to 47.0 percent of local trade in 1963, but again declined to around 41 percent all through the 1970s (WTO, 1995). The reason behind this decline was that the brisk real GDP growth in the NIAEs, and subsequently in the Southeast Asian economies and *pari passu* rapid growth in export volume. Together these factors coalesced and these economies began to establish strong trade linkages outside their region, particularly with the US market. More importantly, all these economies had adopted similar economic development paradigms and sought to achieve growth through the movement toward higher value-added manufacturing production geared towards export expansion. This made is necessary for them to look for markets outside the region. For many of these economies it increasingly meant the large US market.

During the 1970s, a triangular production relationship developed between Japan, the NIAEs and the US, bringing the former two sets of economies closer together. Japan supplied the necessary components and technology to the NIAEs, which in turn produced and competitively marketed industrial products to the US market. After the Plaza Accord[15] in September 1985, the currency value configuration changed. The dollar had reached a high against the yen in early 1985, which intensified imports from East and Southeast Asia into the US market, and Japan was able to maintain its exports even as its production costs were rising vis-à-vis its Asian rivals (Bernard and Ravenhill, 1995). The post-Plaza Accord appreciation of the yen was not initially matched by the appreciation of the other Asian currencies.

Between 1985 and 1987, the yen appreciated by 40 percent (Das, 1996). Consequently, Asian exports to the US continued to expand, and *pari passu* Japanese exports to Asian markets also grew. The structure of regional trade underwent a radical transformation. The Plaza Accord contributed to a new division of labor in Asia as well as a greater shift of the regional production locus towards production networks[16] (Bernard and Ravenhill, 1995; Das, 1996). The regional economic dynamism was such that the division of labor in the region enlarged to include the ASEAN-4 economies and China more than ever in the past. A wave of pan-Asian industrialization in high-technology industries expanded into the ASEAN-4 and China. These economies had depreciated their currencies during this period. Consequently, not only did their exports to the US became more competitive but they also attracted more investments from Japan and the NIAEs. The ASEAN-4 economies and China soon started developing as export platforms of their own into the industrial-country markets. Closely related with the spatial enlargement of the triangular relations has been the shift from the firm to networks as the locus of production and innovative activities.

As regards the recent trends in intra-regional trade, since 1985 it has grown at a rate roughly double that of world trade. The growth rate of intra-regional trade was much higher than that in the EU and NAFTA. Evidence based on intra-industry trade in the region demonstrated that economic linkages or interdependence in the region have strengthened considerably since the mid-1980s (Ng and Yeats, 2003). The 2001 value of intra-regional trade in Asia was $722 billion, or 48.2 percent of total Asian merchandises trade.[17]

The general direction of Asian economic regionalism and intra-regional trade over the preceding two decades is clear from the foregoing discussion, if we ignore the 1997-98 Asian crisis. NIAEs, followed by ASEAN-4, China and most recently Vietnam, have pursued outward-oriented economic development strategies, while stimulating inward flows of FDI. This included FDI from more industrialized Asian economies to the less industrialized ones. Together, they have created complex regional economic ties among these economies as well as trade dependencies. The increasing trade dependence of Asia is clearly shown by a simple measure, namely, intra-regional trade as a share of total trade of the region (Frankel, 1997).[18] Intra-regional trade as a share of total trade of the region, as well as various sub-groups in the region has a rising trend. Frankel (1997) also concluded that the entire growth of Asian trade regionalization could be explained in terms of economic growth among the countries in the region and the general increase in trade dependence of the regional economies. The rising intensity of intra-regional trade is a reality that cannot be ignored. In spite of this trend, Japan and the US are still the overwhelmingly dominant economies for this region, consequently their importance as markets and as sources of investment continues to be large.

3.3 Intra-Regional Production Networks

The exposition in the preceding sections shows that the trend towards becoming natural trading partners took several decades of intensive intra-regional trade and investment among the Asia-Pacific economies. Changes in currency value configuration and economic complementarities buttressed this trend. Gradually the focus of production shifted from the firms to mutually supporting networks of regional production. Asian economies were pioneers in this respect.[19] Production networks soon became a significant force driving the process of economic integration in East and Southeast Asia as well as of globalization. They went far beyond the horizontal and vertical integration of production in the past in Asia. The integration of Malaysia, Thailand and the Pearl River basin of China with Northeastern Asian production has been one of the most marked changes in the spatial organization of the Asian economy since the Plaza Accord.

Although superficially this trend lent credence to Akamatsu's (1961, pp. 42–76) age-old flying geese hypothesis, emerging organizational and spatial changes in production actually undermined many of its key assumptions.[20] The regionalization of production networks in Asia came to be organized in ways that made the avian analogy neat, logical and orderly. Akamatsu's hypothesis, somewhat simplistically, had failed to grasp the complexities of technological changes and technology transfer. The product life-cycle theory explains regionalization of production much more convincingly than the avian analogy. It takes individual products as 'disembodiments' from larger industrial structures, whereby the life cycle of any given product can be treated in isolation from a myriad of other products and the organizational foundations that initially spawned it. These new production modes or production linkages were most conspicuous in (but not exclusive to) the electronics industry (Chen and Ku, 2000). This industry provides the most revealing illustration of how production linkages in Asia are more complex than the trade and investment data describe them.

One of the most striking changes in regional production since the Plaza Agreement has been the rapid shift of much of Northeast Asia's low-end consumer electronics production first to Malaysia and subsequently to Thailand. Most prominent was the massive investment by the Japanese electronics industry. A similar pattern was followed by Taiwanese and, to a lesser extent, Korean electronics investment in Malaysia and Thailand. This large infusion of investment in the electronics industry in Malaysia and Thailand led to the transfer in a mere five years (1996–2000) of much of the low-end, export-oriented consumer electronics assembly industry that had been built up in Japan, Korea and Taiwan since the 1950s. Northeast Asian investment in the ASEAN-4 economies brought a number of changes to the structure of production and exchange in the electronics industry in Asia.

During the late 1980s, the production networks began to spread to Guangdong and Fujian provinces in south China, and a borderless economy encompassing a much larger region with different comparative advantages began to emerge. This sub-region rapidly enlarged due to the complementarities that existed among its economies. It now includes Hong Kong SAR, Macao, Taiwan, and the southern provinces of China like Guangdong, Hainan, Fujian, Zhejiang and Shanghai. Geographically proximate regions possessing different resource endowments tended to develop close trade and investment ties, further intensifying the production networks.[21] As Taiwan moved into high technology industries and Hong Kong SAR moved towards becoming a services economy, China was well placed to receive the 'sunset' industries that were being phased out from both the NIAEs. This reduced the pain of phasing out of these industries in Hong Kong SAR and Taiwan, and to a lesser extent in Korea and Singapore. In the process the sunset industries got a new lease of life through relocation and the pace of industrialization in China quickened. This was China's opportunity to move faster up the industrial value chain into high-technology products.

Early in 2001, the government in Taiwan was considering removing all investment value ceilings on projects intended for the mainland, but closing off certain 'strategic industries' like high-end electronics. Consequently, mutual industrial dependence of the two economies was on the rise (Sender, 2001). Malaysia and Thailand also integrated with the southern part of China by developing close trade and investment links. Together this sub-region of Asia has shown enormous dynamism and, therefore, it is bound to expand in size, level of sophistication, and scope of cooperation. A clarification is necessary here. When the so-called sunset industries were moving from the NIAEs to China, the latter was not the recipient of outmoded technologies. Hong Kong SAR and Taiwan had transferred their entire computer hardware sector to mainland China by the early 1990s, an industry which can hardly be called outmoded. The domestic ICT industry upgraded in textbook fashion, creating a division of labor between manufacturing activities in mainland China on the one hand and Hong Kong SAR and Taiwan on the other (EIU, 2003).

Notwithstanding the outbreak of SARS (Severe Acute Respiratory Syndrome), the GDP and industrial growth of China was having a great deal of impact on the regional and global economies in the early 2000s.[22] With its membership of the World Trade Organization (WTO) since the end of 2001, and the increasing contribution to growth made by its own voracious consumers, the economy now depends far less on the state-owned enterprises (SOEs) for growth. As a result, it is also exerting an unprecedented degree of influence over regional and world trade. Several industrial sectors, including steel, are considered competitive in the global market place. Its imports of iron ore are likely to surpass those of Japan in 2003. According to WTO trade statistics, China accounted for 4.7 percent of world trade in 2002 ($620 billion), up from 2.7 percent in 1995. Rising levels of intra-regional and global trade put severe pressure on China's fast-growing ports. In mid-2003, the southern Chinese city of Shenzhen overtook Kaohsiung in Taiwan to become the world's fifth-largest container port (*The Economist*, 2003b).[23]

Over the last quarter century, two virtuous circles of economic growth operated in East and Southeast Asia and the Asian economies benefited from them immensely. Openness to trade and investment resulted in the first virtuous circle. This can be termed the domestic virtuous circle. The second was a regional virtuous circle, which explains the diffusion of economic growth from one group of dynamic economies to another. The production networks created by Asian firms were an inherent part of the second virtuous circle. Together these virtuous circles reinforced each other leading to brisk real GDP growth in the regional economy. It *prima facie* appeared counterintuitive because increased networking among firms that were themselves competitors, is generally not expected (Borrus et al. 2000). However, it developed as a new trend and is at present successfully operating in Japan, the NIAEs, ASEAN-4 and China. The trade-creating effects of investment are logical in the context of dynamic networking firms. These are the newest trends in the regional economy. The end result is closer integration and increasingly cohesive economic ties and greater regionalization of the Asian economies.[24]

4.   NATURAL TRADING PARTNERS

Asian economies have not only integrated as natural trading partners, the prospects for monetary integration between them are also improving. Two recent studies have concluded that in terms of the economic prerequisites, ASEAN and ASEAN-Plus-Three (APT)[25] are not in a significantly worse position than the EU was a few years prior to the Maastrich Treaty coming into force in 1993 (Bayoumi and Eichengreen, 1997; Bayoumi et al., 2000).[26] However, at the heart of the European Monetary Union (EMU) project was the political commitment to acquiesce to the concept of weakening, or even losing, sovereignty. Without it, deepening of economic integration was not feasible. If the Asian economies intend to emulate the EMU in any shape or size, a firm political commitment is indispensable. The new system must not be viewed merely as a pegged exchange rate arrangement for Asia. Bayoumi et al. (2000) believe that without a pre-determined terminal point to anchor market expectations, the stability of an 'Asian EMU' is open to doubt. However, common basket pegs for the members of APT are well within the realms of possibility.

Debate over whether ASEAN economies have natural tendencies to form an RIA or none at all raged during the 1990s, with noted scholars taking polemical stands. As the debate progressed, the 'natural trading partners' hypothesis became popular in regional trade and integration literature.[27] Using data series until 1989, Meltzer (1991) and Frankel (1991) examined bloc formation, and voted against the natural trading partner hypothesis. They concluded that Asia had a low capacity for bloc formation because the countries are not natural trading partners. Frankel (1991) posited that intra-regional trade in Asia was rising only because economies in the region were growing faster than the rest of the world and not because of any growing bias towards intra-regional trade.

The debate has not been resolved as other analysts disagreed. They believed that the issue of natural trading partners is crucial because to the extent that trade blocs are created between countries that already trade disproportionately with each other, the risk of large amounts of trade diversion is reduced. If the prospective members of an RIA are already major trading partners, integration or RIA formation would reinforce natural trading patterns, not artificially divert them. Their disagreement in inferences was not surprising because these analysts were following different methodologies to arrive at contradictory conclusions. Both Winters (1999) and Schiff and Winters (2003) questioned the fundamental concept of natural trading partners. A la Winters, the term 'natural trading partner' can only be used for the assessment of an RIA if we equate 'natural' with 'desirable', and for an RIA it is difficult to make a direct assessment of its 'desirability'. It is, therefore, better not to use the term 'natural trading partners' except to mean *without any policy inducement or institutional stimulus*. It is difficult to disagree with this stand.

Regional trade data compiled and tabulated by Lee and Roland-Holst (1998) revealed that if the scope of Asian trade is expanded from intra-regional to APEC, one notices that for all large Asian trading economies, APEC countries accounted for two-thirds to three-quarters of their total trade by the mid-1990s. Of particular interest is Japan, which has significantly diversified its trade towards the APEC group since 1980, moving from 51.6 percent to 70.4 percent of its total trade to this country group. They pointed out that as regards the individual countries, the US was the largest non-Asian trade partner for the large exporting Asian economies. Given the size of the

US economy, that is to be expected. As a rule of thumb, the US represents one-quarter to one-half of the APEC trade for the Asian economies. So was Asia emerging as the third trading bloc on the global economic scenario? This kind of RIA formation is poorly explained by mainstream economics.

It bears repeating that according to standard trade theory, the best RIA is the whole globe. That is, global welfare is maximized when either the number of trading blocs is one, or each bloc is very large (see Chapter 2). In the former case, there is free trade by definition, while in the latter the optimal tariff is nearly zero so that once again the result is free trade. However, theory does not always provide a good guide to the formation of sub-global RIAs. A standard approach to analysing RIA formation has been to estimate the importance of intra-regional trade flows. This approach is based on the argument, made earlier, that the welfare gains for countries joining an RIA are likely to be greater the higher the percentage of intra-regional trade. Thus, it can be argued that if intra-regional trade flows are high or increasing, rational or welfare-maximizing countries would try to form a trading bloc. In case of Asia, intra-trade has remained around 50 percent for almost a decade now (refer to section 3.2 for the statistical data). Also, this occurred in a market-driven manner, without institutional initiatives. Asian economies – particularly the East and Southeast Asian economies, along with China – could justifiably be considered natural trading partners.

5.   IMPACT OF OTHER RIAs ON THE ASIA-PACIFIC ECONOMIES

As noted in Chapter 3, section 3, the total number of RIAs notified to WTO stood at 250 in March 2002 (WTO, 2002a). According to the 2002 *Annual Report* of the WTO, 159 agreements were still in force in 2001. Trade and investment diversion would cause the Asia-Pacific economies to lose out on some of their export markets and FDI due to the presence of such a large number of RIAs in the global economy. Several scholars have devoted themselves to the issue of impact. In an extensive study, Frankel and Wei (1997) provided a comprehensive survey of various empirical studies done to calculate the effect of major RIAs on the Asian economies.[28] Studies of the Canada–US Free Trade Area (CUSFTA) show a decline in trade with third countries in general (Cox and Harris, 1992; Braga, et al., 1994). If anything, the developing Asian economies have more to lose from NAFTA because their labor-intensive manufactured products will lose some of the Canadian and US markets to Mexico. Noland (1994) estimated that NAFTA could divert trade from Korea, which could amount to 1 percent to 3 percent of total Korean exports. Similar trade diversions would be experienced by the other

NIAEs. A large part (almost two-thirds) of this estimated impact would be in the textiles, spinning and weaving sectors where Multifiber Arrangement (MFA) quotas were applicable. Hufbauer and Schott (1994) estimated that NAFTA could divert from Korea and Taiwan, manufactured exports worth $300 million annually that previously went to the US. According to them, machinery and transport equipment sectors would suffer the largest loss of export markets. These authors also found that the range of estimates for effects on Southeast and South Asia were similar. They estimated that Southeast and South Asian developing economies, excluding Korea and Taiwan, would lose $350 million in manufactured exports. Again, machinery and transport equipment sectors would be the hardest hit sectors. The other two sectors that would be most adversely affected were clothing and consumer goods. Exports of primary products from these countries would also be adversely affected, to the extent of $100 million.

Safadi and Yeats (1993) examined the effects of NAFTA on South Asian economies alone and inferred that trade diversion effects would be concentrated in their textiles and apparel sectors. Although industrialized countries pledged under the Uruguay Round to phase out their textile quotas, the schedule has such a backlog that NAFTA could make a big difference to textiles trade of South Asian economies (Das, 2000b). These estimates of impact are not trivial, but are not particularly large either. Part of the reason was that US tariffs were low to begin with. They were slightly lower against some Mexican goods than against imports from other industrial economies under the Generalized System of Preferences. Safadi and Yeats posited that this was the reason that the scope for both trade creation and trade diversion in the US market was small.

The US and other industrial economies have had low tariff barriers. Not the same can be said about NTBs and administrative protection measures like anti-dumping duties.[29] Exports from Canada and Mexico to US do not face many non-tariff barriers, although they are not out of reach for anti-dumping actions. This has turned out to be an important benefit of an RIA. However, NTBs do adversely affect Asian exports to the US. This mode of trade diversion does seem to be a valid concern of the Asian economies. Another similar snag is created by the rules of origin (ROO). They can be interpreted in such a manner as to divert Asian vehicle exports intended for the US. It would benefit Mexican exporters at the expense of those from Asia. There are distinct possibilities of trade diversion. Rapid growth in Mexico–US trade since 1993 seemed consistent with these concerns.

FDI is another concern of the Asian economies because both CUSFTA and NAFTA include provisions to promote investment within the RIA. It is logical to assume that this could cause diversion of investment from Asian economies to Mexico. Although this was a general concern of the Asian economies, portfolio investment was considered especially vulnerable because it is fungible and mobile. McCleery (1993) argued that investment diversion is a more serious effect of NAFTA than trade diversion. According to him it would have a more serious adverse impact over the Asian economies. He calculated that Indonesia would lose 4 to 5 percent of FDI to NAFTA, which would cause a 2.2 percent decline in GDP. The corresponding figures for other countries: Malaysia would lose 5 to 7 percent causing a 1.4 percent decline in GDP; Singapore 2 to 3 percent of FDI, which would lead to a 1.3 percent GDP decline; for Thailand the loss would be 4 to 5 percent, leading to a 1.0 percent decline in GDP. These numbers seem to be biased upwards. Other Asian economies, according to McCleery (1993), would be affected less than these ASEAN countries. Kreinen (1998) predicted that a significant amount of FDI might be diverted from ASEAN economies to Mexico in the following sectors: food, chemicals, textiles, metals, transport equipment, and electronics. US FDI in Mexico started growing rapidly in 1993. In the future, as its economy liberalizes further and becomes more productive, Mexico might start attracting Japanese investment as well.[30]

As a hemisphere-wide Free Trade Area of the Americas (FTAA) was proposed in 1994 during the Miami Summit of Latin American countries, Hufbauer and Schott (1994) estimated its impact. For each major commodity group they calculated how much of the increased US imports from Latin America would divert trade from other trading partners. Their estimates indicated $7.3 billion worth of diverted exports from the NIAEs annually by 2002. They concluded that this was equal to 2.6 percent of the NIAEs' exports to the US market in that year. They also subdivided trade diversion in various sectors and found that textiles and apparel would be affected most with almost 40 percent of the diversion. The leather and leather products category was the next affected sector, followed by primary metals and sporting goods. As for the South Asian economies, they similarly found that this country group would suffer large trade diversions in the textiles and apparel sectors as well as food products sectors. Their estimates of total diversion were substantial. They estimated it at $3.2 billion, or 2.8 percent of the projected exports to the US market.

Studies of trade creation and trade diversion effects of EU formation found that trade creation is five to seven times larger than trade diversion (Kreinen, 1982). With regard to the impact of SEM on the Asian economies, studies show that Australia, New Zealand and NIAEs would gain from it, while Japan would experience diversion of its skill-intensive exports to the EU. Even in the 1980s, and especially after 1992, the Japanese vehicle industry was particularly hit by the spread of import quotas from France and Italy to the other EU members. Both Anderson (1993) and Gundlach et al. (1993) concluded that Japanese exports of photocopiers, electric scales, electric typewriters, and semiconductors have also been affected due to ROO interpretation of the EU. As opposed to this they found that primary commodity exports of the Asian economies would not be diverted. This was essentially because the EU economies neither produce them nor have any close substitutes. In 1995, the EU was enlarged to include some of the former members of the European Free Trade Area (EFTA), namely Austria, Finland and Sweden. This should have affected the skill-intensive exports of Japan, although no empirical estimates are presently available. This is not likely to be the situation with the 2004 enlargement of the EU. Labor-intensive exporters of Asia would naturally suffer as a result and their labor-intensive exports would be diverted to the 10 new members joining the EU.

6. THE GRAVITY MODEL

For studies related to regional trade or regional integration, the gravity model can be a successful empirical tool. In a direct and simple application it relates volume of trade between two countries positively to their incomes and negatively to transaction costs. Thus, economic size (GDP, population, land area) and transaction costs (geographic distance between the two countries, and cultural dissimilarities) are treated as the two most important factors explaining bilateral trade flows in this model. It is called the gravity model because it is analogous to gravitational attraction between two masses in physics (Bergstrand, 1985). Lee and Roland-Holst (1998) specify the basic resulting equation as follows.

$$T_{ij} = \beta_o \, Y_i^{\beta_1} \, Y_j^{\beta_2} \, d_{ij}^{\beta_3} \, A_{ij}^{\beta_4} \, e^{\beta_5 D_{ij}} \, u_{ij}$$

where T_{ij} is the bilateral trade flow from country i to country j, Y_i and Y_j are the exporting and importing countries' gross domestic products, and d_{ij} is the geographical or economic distance between the two countries. D_{ij} is an array of dummy variables such as those for preferential trading arrangements, A_{ij} is an array of other factors that could either facilitate or impede trade between i and j, and U_{ij} is a log-normally distributed error term with $E(\log U_{ij}) = 0$. The per capita income variable is generally included in A_{ij}.[31]

The popularity of the gravity model is relatively recent. Bayoumi and Eichengreen (1995) call the gravity model 'the workhorse for empirical studies of the pattern of trade'. Its empirical robustness made it much used for investigations of the geographical pattern of trade. During the 1960s and 1970s trade flows were estimated with it but it was criticized because it has a weak theoretical foundation. Tinbergen (1962), Poyhonen (1963) and Linneman (1996) provided initial specifications and estimates of the determinants of trade flows and Aitken (1973) applied it to RIAs. After Anderson (1979) provided a rigorous economic justification, its use expanded again.[32] With a revival of interest among the economists in economics and geography, the gravity model has again become popular. Bergstrand (1985) and Deardroff (1997) have provided partial theoretical foundations for the gravity equation, although none of the models generate exactly the equation generally used in empirical work.

Trade statistics confirm that the magnitude of intra-trade within the following three regional groupings, namely, the EU, Asia-Pacific and North America, has been disproportionately high. One plausible explanation behind this apparent bias towards intra-regional trade in these three country groups is geographical proximity among the countries. The immediate consequence of geographical proximity is reduction in transport costs, short delivery time, less interest payable on export credits and low spoilage. Both Krugman (1991a) were of the opinion that the disproportionate intra-trade in the above-named three country groups is largely due to proximity, and the other traits associated with it. They are wedded to the concept that proximity promotes trade. Krugman (1991b) goes further and argues that the three trading blocs are welfare enhancing natural groupings. This logically means that there are some 'unnatural' trade groupings where partners are not close but far apart. He provided the example of the United Kingdom and members of the Common-wealth as an 'unnatural' trading arrangement. The argument supporting this hypothesis is that because of little or no distance between trading partners, intra-continental RIAs are likely to be more trade creating than trade diverting.

Using the gravity model, Solonga and Winters (1999) examined the impact of nine RIAs, namely, the Andean Community, AFTA, CACM, EU, EFTA, the Gulf Co-operation Council (GCC), LAIA,[33] MERCOSUR and NAFTA. Using non-fuel imports and exports data for 58 countries, they compared the before-and-after scenario of the trade patterns of these nine RIAs. The central variables of the gravity model – the volume of GDP of countries i and j, the area of these countries, and the absolute distance between i and j – were found to have the expected sign and were all significant at 1 percent. Trade was found to increase with the level of GDP of the importer and exporter and decrease with the size and distance. The variables reflecting population of importer and exporter countries were positive and almost always significant. The degree of remoteness of the importer country from its suppliers had the expected positive sign and was always significant. The estimated parameters for 'common land borders' were not significant in any year of the sample, reflecting probably some colinearity with the parameter for remoteness. Their results are interesting and show that for all the RIAs involving Latin American countries (CACM, LAIA, and Andean Community) the intra-trade coefficients were positive and statistically significant for the whole sample.

However, their results were far from uniformly positive and statistically significant. For NAFTA, the result was positive but never significant, while for the GCC it was positive but significant for only a certain number of years. The coefficients for the intra-bloc trade were negative for the EU, EFTA and AFTA, although they were not statistically significant.

Again, Frankel and Wei (1997) provided extensive examinations of possible RIAs in Asia-Pacific. They also considered a sequence of 'nested country groupings' in Asia, like ASEAN, East Asia, and South Asia and the whole of Asia. In their gravity model exercise, they measured the log of distance between two major cities – usually the capital cities – of the respective countries for their empirical model. They also added a dummy 'adjacent' variable to indicate when two countries shared a common border. In another similar study, Frankel et al. (1994) tried to test with a more thorough measure of distance that took into account land, and sea routes. The results of both the studies tended to be similar. Frankel and Wei (1997) took GNP in product form because it is empirically well established in bilateral trade regressions and can be justified by the modern theory of trade under imperfect competition. Countries a priori choose larger countries to trade with because they offer a greater variety of goods to choose from than smaller countries. Also common language tends to facilitate trade by enhancing exporters' and importers' understanding of each others' cultures, commercial and legal systems, which have a great deal of influence on trade. To capture these effects Frankel and Wei (1997) included dummy variables that took the value of one if the country pair in question had a favorable impact on trade due to these effects, and zero if they did not. They used ordinary least square (OLS) regression, which tests effects of each independent variable while holding constant the effects of the others. They used the United Nations trade matrix and the International Monetary Fund's *Direction of Trade Statistics* for data and employed the panel regression technique that allows for year-specific intercepts.

The inferences of Frankel and Wei (1997) may be summarized as follows. As posited by the gravity model, geography matters. Distance has an economically and statistically large effect on trade. As distance increased by 1 percent, trade declined by 0.5 percent. The 'adjacency' dummy showed that two countries with a common land border have a larger volume of trade than two otherwise identical countries. Another important conclusion was that common language or past colonial connections facilitated trade; it brought in 50 percent more trade than otherwise.

As regards the degree of integration within Asia, two ASEAN countries were found to have 600 percent more trade than two otherwise identical economies. As Singapore is an entrêpot trade center, its imports and exports are usually more than 100 percent of GDP. It was possible that the apparent intra-ASEAN bias was partly or wholly a reflection of the extreme openness of Singapore. A Singapore dummy was added to examine this. The coefficient of the ASEAN dummy was reduced somewhat but remained quantitatively large and statistically significant. This suggested that Singapore's extreme openness did not explain all of the apparent inward bias among the AEAN countries. It was also found that all East and Southeast Asian countries tended to concentrate their trade with each other, and that the tendencies of the ASEAN economies were not unique in this regard. As expected, two Chinese-speaking countries appeared to trade an estimated four and half times as much as other similarly situated countries. Chinese business practices, culture and Chinese language business terminology raises the possibility that the influence of the Chinese diaspora was a dominant source of East Asian intra-regional trade.

A noteworthy point here is that China–Taiwan trade does not appear in the statistics because official statistics deny it takes place. However, this trade is large and rapidly growing, and routed through Hong Kong SAR. Thus, this trade was counted twice in HK data and may have exaggerated the estimate of the influence of the Chinese variable. This double counting in trade was corrected, and the gravity estimates rerun with trade among the so-called Greater Chinas. The independent Chinese language effect was no longer found to be significantly stronger than other linguistic links around the globe. Frankel (1997) reported that the two South Asian economies in the sample, India and Pakistan, were negatively impacted by their historical animosity. Their trade was found to be 70 percent less than two otherwise identical countries. Over all, the assertion of Krugman (1991b) that proximity promotes trade stands up. The gravity equation estimated convincingly that distance is a very important determinant of trade. South Asia has proved to be an exception, apparently because historical enmity reduced trade between India and Pakistan.

Thus, a good number of empirical studies, using the gravity model, are now available. They point toward two broad conclusions. First, East and Southeast Asian economies clearly show certain inward bias among themselves. Second, even after controlling for a special Asia effect, East and Southeast Asian economies en masse appear to trade more among themselves than one would expect based on their economic and geographic characteristics. Adding the Hong Kong SAR and Singapore dummies does not change the qualitative feature of the picture.

7.   FORMAL REGIONALISM IN ASIA-PACIFIC

Notwithstanding the high level of market-driven intra-trade, historically the

Asia-Pacific economies did not display as much enthusiasm for RIA formation as those in Europe and Latin America. Even at the beginning of the twenty-first century, formal regional trading arrangements are neither numerous nor have gone very far in Asia. The first wave of regionalism, of the 1960s, almost passed the region by. The genesis of regionalism can be traced back to a proposal for a regional economic grouping to counter the creation of the EEC, as it began to unfold after the signing of the Treaty of Rome. Kiyoshi Kojima (1968) is credited with positing the concept of the first ever regional organization for Asia, which he named the Organization for Pacific Trade and Development (OPTAD).[34] Kojima also introduced the concept of a Pacific Free Trade Area (PAFTA). Under the aegis of OPTAD, a series of annual conferences was organized on Asia-Pacific trade and developmental issues, beginning with the first in Tokyo in 1968. Under the general direction of Kojima this debating forum remained active.

The Pacific Economic Co-operation Conference (PECC) was born in September 1980 and was the expression of the next wave of regionalism. It was a product of the Canberra seminar on the Pacific Community. In 1992, the PECC membership consisted of Australia, Brunei Darussalam, Canada, Chile, China, Hong Kong SAR, Indonesia, Japan, Malaysia, Mexico, New Zealand, Peru, the Philippines, Russia, Singapore, Taiwan, Thailand, the US and the Pacific island nations. OPTAD became an institutional member of the PECC. Both China and Taiwan were admitted to full participation of PECC in 1986, which became the new reality of Asia-Pacific regionalism in the 1980s.

Other than regional cooperation and integration, there are several areas in Asia where sub-regional cooperation began taking place. This new type of localized economic cooperation began to appear towards the end of the 1980s. Autonomous sub-regional blocs began to develop. While there were differences, two common features of these regional groupings were the participation of two or more countries, and the inclusion of only parts of certain countries. The groupings were given various names but the term 'growth triangle' gradually emerged as a popularly accepted generic term. These growth triangles were the outcome of a complex interplay of key factors, including massive flows of FDI, outward-oriented development strategies, differences in factor costs and factor endowments, and the need for each country to have an element of balanced spatial development.

Although these groupings are still relatively new, given the likely continued existence of these key factors, growth triangles have probably established their place within the region. The following sub-regions are presently operational: (1) the Southern China Growth Triangle, which includes the Fujian province of China, Hong Kong SAR and Taiwan, (2) the Johor–Singapore–Riau Growth Triangle, (3) the Tumen River Area in Northeast Asia, which comprises China, Japan, the two Koreas, and Eastern Russia, and (4) the East Asian Growth Area, which comprises Brunei Darussalam, Indonesia, Malaysia and the Philippines. There are two other smaller growth triangles, namely: (1) the Indonesia, Malaysia, Singapore Growth Triangle and (2) the Indonesia, Malaysia and Thailand Growth Triangle.

In their most basic form these growth triangles exploited complementarities between geographically contiguous areas of different Asian countries to gain a competitive edge in export promotion. To be effective, they required close cooperation between the private and public sectors of each of the countries involved. As a rule of thumb, the private sector provides the capital for investment, and the public sector provides infrastructure development, fiscal incentives, and a favorable administrative framework. Interest in forming growth triangles was heightened during the 1990s by the success of the southern part of China (discussed in section 3.3), in achieving high rates of growth through economic cooperation with neighboring economies.

At the beginning of the twenty-first century, proclivity towards regionalism in Asia ostensibly began to strengthen. Led by Singapore, the political leadership in Asia grew increasingly inclined towards it. There were fervent calls to take advantage of new opportunities and meet unprecedented economic challenges. To this end, it was felt that Asian economics needed to work in a proactive manner towards regionalism (McNulty, 2001). As the latest advances in information and communications technology were revolutionizing work, business, economies and lifestyle, it became more important to regionally integrate Asian economies. In several high-technology sectors including ICT, resources of a large geographical area can be integrated for the benefit of the region. A large pool of talented Asian professionals propel the industrial economies. By encouraging further regional integration in terms of investment and trade, Asia can create synergy, which in turn would retain its talented professionals.

Although there are not many RIAs in the Asia-Pacific region, there is a good deal of intra-trade. As given in section 3.2, the 2001 value of intra-regional trade was $722 billion, which was 48.2 percent of the total Asian merchandise trade. The existing RIAs or RIA-like arrangements do show an impressive variety in the range of these agreements. In chronological order, they include Australia–New Zealand Closer Economic Relations (ANZ-CER or only CER) agreement, ASEAN Free Trade Area (AFTA), the APEC forum, and SAARC Preferential Trade Area (SAPTA).[35] The history, motivation and objectives of these RIAs vary widely. Of these, only CER and AFTA can be treated as integrated RIAs. Of the other RIAs or RIA-like arrangements, some are formal, others are not. Some are successful, others are there only in name and merely work towards facilitating trade. Some are more than a decade old, while others are little more than a concept.

7.1 Australia–New Zealand Closer Economic Relations

Australia and New Zealand were known for their long-standing deep-rooted commitment to protectionist policies. Until the 1970s, they had the highest average levels of protection for their import-competing manufacturing industries in the OECD countries. Economists cited them as examples of slow-growing countries with high levels of protection and an inability to adjust to changes. In 1965, Australia and New Zealand agreed on the establishment of a free trade area. This was the first formal RIA in the Asia-Pacific region. Technically a CER (which is the same as ANZ-CER) is a free trade area (FTA) and each country retains independence in its trade policies with the non-members.

During the 1980s and 1990s, the two economies pursued sets of trade policies which shared many elements and represented a style of trade policy that is distinctive. The common elements included an accelerated unilateral reduction in barriers to trade with other nations, and a sharp movement away from NTBs, particularly from quantative restrictions (QRs). The earlier agreement was superseded by the new 1983 CER agreement, which was intended to reinforce the CER and accelerate its movement toward regional trade and investment liberalization. The provisions of the agreements were substantially widened and deepened. However, the 'negative list' still covered some 40 percent of trans-Tasman trade in manufactured goods. All border restrictions were to be ended within twelve years. Tariffs were to be phased out by 1988, performance-based export incentives by 1987, and QRs and tariff quotas by 1995. In reality, these targets were met by July 1990, some five years ahead of schedule. In addition, anti-dumping measures (ADMs) between the trans-Tasman partners ceased from the same date.

A comprehensive review of the CER was undertaken in 1988, in which the two partner governments *inter alia* addressed the issue of domestic production subsidies. This issue had caused a great deal of acrimonious discussion in the mid-1980s. In 1988, the two partners of the CER decided that industry assistance should be avoided where it would have a distortive impact over trans-Tasman competition (BIE, 1995). Australia's Export Facilitation Scheme for passenger motor vehicles was originally excluded from this arrangement, but the exclusion was later withdrawn. During the late 1980s, there was a change in the mindset of the policy makers. Both Australia and New Zealand became fairly aggressive trade reformers. Building on the achievements of free trade in goods, the two governments raised their sights to the more ambitious objective of creating a single trans-Tasman market. An important condition for the creation of a 'single market' is the removal of administrative and the so-called 'behind-the-border' impediments to trade and investment flows. The process of removing these impediments is called 'trade facilitation', to distinguish it from the removal of traditional trade barriers, described as 'liberalization'. For the purpose of trade facilitation, the CER employed measures like liberalization and integration of purchasing procedures, harmonization of standards and conformance procedures, harmonization of some aspects of business law, and streamlining and harmonization of customs procedures (BIE, 1995). Further facilitation measures continued to be introduced, with a notable addition being the agreement on food standards in 1996.

A Protocol on Services was concluded in 1988, providing for MFN and national treatment for services providers in both the countries, albeit with some exceptions. The 'negative' list of services excluded from free trade was limited. This approach was more transparent than the 'positive' list approach recommended by the General Agreement on Trade in Services (GATS). However, there are some frictions remaining in the CER over liberalization of some services sectors and investment regulations in Australia. A review of this agreement was carried out in 1992. It led to several modifications, including the commitment to harmonize business law and competition policy between the two members of the CER.[36]

With the passage of time, the CER went on expanding the scope of its activities. Since 1992, it has enjoyed a smooth and uncontroversial progress towards a single market because of the unilateral liberalization and deregulation that has occurred in Australia and New Zealand. The common system of government, law and customs and a shared language have obviously been important. The CER agreement contains provisions on the application of countervailing measures, subsidies and government procurement. Anti-dumping provisions do not apply to trade between Australia and New Zealand. This is an important innovative step taken by the CER and has attracted international attention. Any 'unfair trade' claims are treated according to national competition laws in the country where the complaint occurs. Disputes are settled by consultation. An important feature of this progress is that it was achieved with simple rules. There is no administrative organization or secretariat to supervise the CER agreement. Lloyd (1997) described CER as the 'most clean and most outwardly open of all the RIAs approved under the GATT'. Lloyd also considers CER among the regional trading arrangements second only to the EU, particularly in its bringing down of trade barriers and introduction of trade facilitation measures.

Another notable feature of the CER is that it has been achieved by strong unilateral movements towards free trade and deregulation in both the partner economies. It exemplifies 'open regionalism' because regional liberalization in CER has progressed with liberalization vis-à-vis countries outside the CER.

The other region, perhaps the only other, regional trading arrangement in the world that achieved substantial regional liberalization along with substantial unilateral liberalization is ASEAN.

As the CER is an RIA of an advanced variety, it needs to be judged by standards of a highly developed regional arrangement like the EU or NAFTA. Intra-CER trade is a small share of each partner's total trade. Although Australia is New Zealand's largest trading partner, in 1990s its share of New Zealand's exports ranged between 18 and 21 percent, with its share of New Zealand's imports only slightly higher at 20 to 22 percent. The only aberration was 1996 when the share of New Zealand's imports shot up to 24 percent. As opposed to this, New Zealand's share in Australia's trade has remained even lower. During the 1990s, New Zealand accounted for 4 to 5 percent of Australia's imports and 5 to 7 percent of its exports (Scollay, 2000). In addition, the growth in the share of intra-CER trade of the two countries total trade has not been dramatic. The significance of intra-trade in CER rises markedly when trade in manufactured goods is taken into account. Manufactures dominate the intra-trade of Australia and New Zealand, which is completely unlike their pattern of exports to the rest of the world. Another interesting feature is that while Australia is a net importer from the rest of the world as a whole in each of 13 major categories of manufactured goods, it is a net exporter to New Zealand in all but three of those categories (Scollay, 2000).

McMillan (1993) and Scollay (1994) inferred that significant reduction in external barriers against third countries have accompanied the elimination of barriers between the two partner economies of the CER. This is a welfare enhancing condition. It has been noted above that substantial unilateral trade liberalization took place in Australia and New Zealand, while they eliminated trade barriers between each other. The efficiency improvements brought about in the manufacturing sector through unilateral trade liberalization helped to ensure that the manufactured goods trade – stimulated by CER – would also be primarily welfare enhancing.

Using the gravity model for the CER, Frankel (1997) reported it as being highly significant statistically. It had a slightly upward trend, reaching 1.7 in 1970. Empirical tests show that the antipodean pair trades 5.5 times as much as an otherwise similar pair of countries. The openness term shows that trade by Australia and New Zealand with other partners is consistently low. However, the openness term has no discernible impact on the bloc coefficient. In the future, further rationalization in the trans-Tasman marketplace would not only integrate the two partner economies closer, it would help them in making the profound adjustments that would be required by the APEC vision of free trade and investment in the Asia-Pacific region.

7.2 ASEAN Free Trade Area

The second RIA in the Asia-Pacific region was related to the ASEAN countries. In August 1967, ASEAN was established between five Southeast Asian economies, namely, Indonesia, Malaysia, the Philippines, Singapore and Thailand. As the earlier regional initiatives among developing economies were not known for their success, ASEAN restricted its scope to cooperation on strategic and political issues. Its objectives were to promote peace and stability. It needs to be emphasized that ASEAN was not born as a sub-regional economic organization. Brunei Darussalam joined ASEAN in 1984. The four members that joined later were Vietnam in 1995, Laos and Myanmar in 1998 and Cambodia in 1999, bringing the membership to 10 Southeast Asian economies. Strengthening trade and economic linkages did not come into it until 1977, when the founding five members of ASEAN put into force an Agreement on ASEAN Preferential Trading Arrangement (APTA).[37] This APTA granted 10 to 15 percent margins of preferences on 71 commodities and industrial products. A stronger free trade proposal had fallen through during the APTA negotiations.

The APTA was weak and inconsequential, as the most important sectors were exempted from the system of preferences that the members were supposed to grant to each other. The product-by-product nature of negotiations, non-genuine offers of preferences, high domestic content requirements, and the limited nature of preferences themselves rendered the PTA rather ineffective. It had little impact over trade between ASEAN countries. In an infamous example, Indonesia removed mutual trade barriers on the imports of snow shovels. Over the 1985–87 period, the ASEAN leaders agreed to expand the list of sectors covered by the APTA and also to increase the margin of preferences. However, until the end of the 1980s the fraction of goods eligible for regional preferences was still only of the order of 3 percent of the total number of goods traded. Thus, ASEAN had little success on the economic integration front. Between 1967 and 1992, it remained more or less a political organization.

In January 1991, the ASEAN countries agreed to upgrade the APTA and establish an ASEAN Free Trade Area. The proposal was made by Thailand and accepted by all the members a year later during the fourth ASEAN Summit meeting in Singapore in January 1992. AFTA came into force in 1992, which breathed a new lease of life into ASEAN. The original goal of AFTA was to reduce tariff rates on intra-ASEAN trade to between zero and 5 percent within 15 years beginning January 1993. The principal instrument for adopting this objective was the common effective preferential tariff (CEPT) plan.

The CEPT plan divided goods into two categories: (1) the fast-track goods whose tariffs would be reduced to 0 to 5 percent within 7 to 10 years depending upon whether the initial tariff was below or above 20 percent, and (2) the normal-track goods on which tariffs would be reduced more slowly and in two stages. Subsequently, during the 1993 and 1994 ASEAN summit meetings the rate of planned tariff liberalization was accelerated and other changes were adopted, whereby 11 000 tariff items – which included 20 percent of total tariff lines – were to reduce tariffs by January 1994. Members decided that the fast-track tariff lines would be liberalized by 2000 and normal-track tariff reductions would be achieved by the year 2003 instead of 2008. Vietnam, which joined ASEAN in 1995 and AFTA in 1996, was granted a ten-year implementation period ending 2006. By 1999, AFTA had 10 members.

AFTA can indeed make a useful contribution to trade and investment in the region. However, it became obvious that CEPT had serious limitations. First, it emphasized tariffs, which became less important relative to regulatory NTBs as impediments to trade in the ASEAN countries. Second, CEPT also focused on merchandise trade, which had been declining in importance relative to trade in services and investment. Third, most analysts considered the CEPT timetable to be slow. The justification given was that it would give business enterprises time to adjust and restructure. Besides, the AFTA economies had not overcome all their miscellaneous disagreements. More important, the CEPT agenda still covered less than half of intra-ASEAN merchandise trade. Broadening CEPT to give a wider coverage of intra-ASEAN trade was vitally important.

The CEPT scheme was based on four lists: the inclusion list (IL), the temporary exclusion list (TEL), the sensitive list (SL) and the general exception list (GEL). These four lists were the instruments that were to determine the pace and scope of liberalization of the trade regime of the ten member economies. The trade products on which tariff reduction was to be taken up immediately were included in the first list, IL. By 2003, all the products on the IL were to have tariffs in the range of 0 to 5 percent. The products on the TEL were not subject to tariff reduction initially, but all of them were to be moved to IL in 2000 in five equal installments beginning in 1995. Import tariffs on these products were to be slashed to a 0 to 5 percent range by 2003. The SL comprised unprocessed agricultural products, which were to be phased into IL between 2001 and 2003. Their tariffs were to be slashed to the 0 to 5 percent range by 2010. The last GEL was based on Article XX of the GATT-1994, therefore, items on this list were excluded from tariff reductions for reasons of national security, protection of public morals, protection of human, animal and plant life and health, and the protection of articles of artistic, historic and archaeological value.

A noteworthy feature of the CEPT is that participating economies were required to trade concessions on a product-by-product basis. To be eligible for concession under the CEPT, a trade item had to meet three conditions. First, it had to be on the IL of both the importing and exporting economies. Second, the product in question needed a tariff of 20 percent or below. Third, it had to satisfy the local content requirement of 40 percent. In addition, after the tariff concessions were applied to a product, all the NTBs on that product had to be eliminated in five years.

At the time of creation of ASEAN, most member economies had only just embarked on their industrialization programs and lacked confidence to let their tariff barriers and NTBs down. They now developed a great deal of confidence, thanks to rapid outward-oriented industrial development. Many member economies have succeeded in learning about global trade regulations and negotiations. By the early 2000s, five of the ten ASEAN economies (namely, Indonesia, Malaysia, the Philippines, Singapore and Thailand) had acquired the status of emerging-market economies.[38] Brunei Darussalam is an oil-rich kingdom.

The members of AFTA have now become ambitious about regional integration and before notable progress in intra-trade expansion was made, they began considering harmonization of standards and policy integration related issues. AFTA has also begun addressing trade facilitation issues. To that end, the ASEAN Consultative Committee on Standards and Quality was established to work on harmonization of standards, testing and accreditation of laboratories, conformity assessment, and technical information. A Consultative Forum on FDI met in 1993, and there were plans to hold macroeconomic consultations. However, the trade facilitation agenda was slow to get off the ground. To make things worse, it was overtaken by that of the APEC forum. Disagreements among members have persisted. During the October 2000 meeting of the ASEAN, Malaysia scuttled the timetable for lowering tariff barriers. There was a possibility of a chain reaction whereby other members could decide to keep tariffs on favored local industries (AWSJ, 2000). In 2001, the intra-AFTA exports were $90 billion and intra-AFTA imports were $70 billion.[39]

The gravity model for AFTA provided evidence for the fact that the ASEAN bloc shows highly significant openness (Frankel and Wei, 1997). The dummy for the ASEAN was found to be extraordinarily large and statistically significant. Interpreted literally, two ASEAN economies trade 600 percent more than two otherwise identical economies. As Singapore plays an entrepôt role, its exports and imports are larger than its GDP. Therefore, the extreme openness of Singapore can be reflected in the intra-ASEAN bias. To examine this, a Singapore dummy was added, which was found to have a positive and significant coefficient. The coefficient on the ASEAN dummy was reduced but it still remained quantitatively large and statistically significant. Thus, one can infer that Singapore's extreme openness did not explain all the inward bias among the ASEAN countries and that – notwithstanding the plethora of problems and delays – it is likely that the ASEAN economies have a tendency to expand their trade with each other.

7.3 Asia Pacific Economic Co-operation Forum

The idea of creating a multilateral forum to enhance economic cooperation among Asia and Pacific economies was launched by Australian Prime Minister Bob Hawke in 1989. The concept was nurtured jointly by Australia and Japan. The genesis of APEC lies in the specific circumstances of the late 1980s. The EU was promising to strengthen its customs union and advancing towards its Single Market Programme, Canada and the US were negotiating extension of their free-trade area, CUSFTA, to form NAFTA, and the Uruguay Round was seemingly stumbling. Asian economies were apprehensive of being left out of the move towards RIAs in a period when failure of the multilateral trading system was a very real threat. For its part, Australia was concerned about being left out of an Asian regional body which was being suggested by Malaysia.

APEC had a fairly humble beginning and was initially greeted with marked skepticism. The basic objectives were economic cooperation and consultation. Although APEC was born as a regional arrangement of sorts, it had adopted the difficult, if somewhat paradoxical, mission of combating preferential regionalism. Accordingly, members explored various ways in which regionalism can be *open*. As noted above, this kind of *open regionalism* was pioneered by the CER.

APEC started with meetings between foreign and finance/economic ministers and with several relatively small projects. However, since then it has grown in scope and prominence, and achieved a more significant status with the agreement to hold annual summit meetings of heads of state. The first such meeting took place in 1993 on Blake Island in Seattle. APEC had twelve members at the time of launching. Five of them were industrial economies (Australia, Canada, Japan, New Zealand, and the US), six ASEAN members (Indonesia, Malaysia, the Philippines, Singapore, Thailand and Brunei Darussalam) and the Republic of Korea. Between 1989 and 1994, six more countries (China, Hong Kong and Taiwan in 1991 and Mexico, Papua New Guinea and Chile in 1994) joined APEC, increasing membership to 18. A three-year membership moratorium was adopted in 1996. As soon as it ended, Peru, Russia and Vietnam were admitted, bringing its membership to 21.

The criterion for inclusion was that the aspiring member must be on the Pacific Ocean, have close economic relations with existing members and accept the goal of trade liberalization, at the latest, by 2020. Although membership has now been closed for the next ten years, APEC represents the most significant and diverse group of countries ever assembled. Spanning both sides of the Pacific Ocean and incorporating two trade super powers – the US and Japan – APEC embraces 40 percent of the global population in 2000, 54 percent of global GDP, and 42 percent of world trade. In 2001, the value of intra-regional exports of APEC was $1938 billion and intra-regional imports $2076 billion, both substantially (almost a third) higher than those for the EU.[40]

Notwithstanding the creation of the APEC secretariat in Singapore and an Eminent Persons' Group, APEC continues to remain a rather loose consultative forum or an informal body, which was in keeping with the original objectives behind its creation. This was the condition for continued participation of ASEAN economies in APEC. In the early 1990s, it was criticized by scholars for being a mere 'talking shop' (Pomfret, 1995). Initially the members of ASEAN were hesitant about joining APEC because they were apprehensive of being overshadowed by a larger group that included large industrial economies. However, they have since adopted the APEC cause as their own. Joining APEC was partly responsible for up-gradation of APTA to AFTA. An important development of the early 1990s was that Australia became more actively involved in the Asian economies and economic diplomacy.

The nature, structure, formation and operating process of APEC were fundamentally different from that of the EU or NAFTA. In some respects APRC is an antithesis of the EU – for instance, its informality and loose structure. These differences originated from the three principal driving forces behind the creation of APEC. First, the Asian economies had an idiosyncratic process of post-war growth and integration. As explained above, this was the market-led process of economic integration. Second, many of the regional economies had enormous stakes in the global trading system. Their diversity notwithstanding, dynamic Asian economies were more firmly committed to the multilateral trading system under the aegis of the GATT than the other developing economies. They saw several tangible benefits in the GATT system. They benefited from the lowering of tariff barriers under various rounds of MTNs under the aegis of the GATT. Several of them also benefited from the 'special and differential treatment' which was provided to them under Part IV of the Articles of Agreement of the GATT. Consequently, these economies enjoyed considerable scope for domestic policy autonomy.

The chairmanship rotates to a different member country every year. Member countries submit ideas and proposals to the chair for consideration during the next annual meeting. The member countries consider this process a definite strength of the APEC forum. It eliminates the possibility of dominance by one member and the final agenda can be the amalgam of the best proposals submitted by the members. A consensus is needed for decision-making. This operational style was adopted from the ASEAN. The members also agreed to alternate annual meetings between ASEAN and non-ASEAN countries, elevating the importance of ASEAN in the APEC forum (Sakakibara and Yamakawa, 2003).

While Asian economies remained avid supporters of the multilateral trading system, they eyed regionalism in other parts of the globe with suspicion. They were neither totally convinced of the advantages nor were they passionately in favour of forming a formal RIA (Lawrence, 1996). They saw RIAs as unnecessary dependence on large economies. Developing Asian economies did not depend on the Japanese market to the degree Mexico or Canada depended on the US market. The political logic that primarily brought the EU economies together in the form of an inward-looking RIA, did not exist for the Asian economies. Unlike the Europeans, few Asians nurtured the dream of eventually becoming a United States of Asia. Historical, cultural and economic differences among the Asian economies are much too large to support such regional arrangements. The distribution of political power in Asia was, and continues to be, highly skewed. The economic prowess of Japan or geo-political power of China would dominate the region for a long time to come. In the context of APEC, the US would be the most powerful country both economically and geo-politically.

These considerations were important in shaping the major initiative for regional arrangements in the Asia-Pacific region. Therefore, APEC was neither conceived as an RIA nor did it have a treaty underpinning its trade liberalization plan. Funabashi (1995) accused APEC of being 'four adjectives in search of a noun'. This criticism was unfair because APEC members had agreed to form a 'community'. They were also clear on their definition of a community. It was neither intended to be a community of quasi-federal arrangement like the EU, nor was it to establish a large organization. Also, for the foreseeable future it was not to be a common market or a customs union. It was instead decided that the APEC forum would promote trade and investment through a mix of policies that deal with trade liberalization, trade facilitation and economic cooperation. Trade facilitation included initiatives in streamlining standards, improving customs procedures, coordinating competition policies, and dispute mediation. Economic cooperation included development assistance and cooperation on projects in human resources, infrastructure, energy, and the environment. Trade facilitation related research work done under the aegis of APEC is widely considered pioneering and respectable, including by the WTO (Moore, 2000).

APEC has gradually progressed ahead of its initial objectives, organized better and got structured, starting with areas where members were in agreement. A significant time point for APEC was 1993, when the US hosted the first Economic Leaders' Meeting in Seattle and proposed that APEC should aim at creating an Asia-Pacific economic community, something on the lines of an Asia-Pacific EU. Since then, APEC has made meaningful progress in trade liberalization and facilitation. In 1994, during the sixth ministerial and leaders' meeting, the ambitious Bogor (Indonesia) declaration was adopted by members, with specified targets for trade liberalization in the region. The 18 participating leaders declared their intention of turning the APEC forum into a zone of free trade and investment. The targets included trade liberalization by 2010 for the five industrial economies and by 2020 by the rest of the APEC members. The guidelines for implementing the Bogor plan were embodied in the Osaka Action Agenda adopted in 1995, during the seventh ministerial and leaders' meeting. They were further refined in 1996 at the eighth ministerial and leaders' meeting during the formulation of the Manila Action Plan (Yamazawa, 1998; Yamazawa, 2000).

The Bogor commitment presented both risks and opportunities. The principal benefit could be in achieving improved market access that goes beyond that feasible under the WTO regulations. The size of APEC has important political consequences. The GATT or the WTO never laid down an entire schedule to achieve global free trade at a single moment. When members of APEC committed themselves to free trade as a long-term goal, they are likely to concentrate on making progress toward free trade in small steps. This would create momentum towards reduction in trade barriers, beginning with sectors having the least political resistance. This in turn could push the global trading system towards free trade. Besides, after the creation of NAFTA, many Asian economies were concerned about being shut out of the large NAFTA market, but since both Canada and Mexico are part of APEC, an APEC-wide free trade area would not let that happen. Likewise, some Asian economies were apprehensive that the US might lose interest in the Asia-Pacific region, but again the APEC initiatives would help keep the US involved in the region. As opposed to these plausible benefits, the risk lay in promising too much and in the process losing credibility (Lawrence, 1996).

There are two noteworthy features of APEC. Unlike other free trade agreements, the achievement of Bogor targets has so far been based on (1) individual or national action plans, rather than on rigid target application to all member states, and (2) concessions in terms of lowering of trade and non-trade barriers have been extended to all the non-member trading partners. This is based on the principle of *open regionalism*, noted above.[41] This strategy runs in contrast to the closed regionalism of the 1950s and the 1960s. Misperceptions exist regarding the term 'open regionalism' because few attempts have been made to define the term systematically. Some economists found it an oxymoron. The argument went as follows: if an arrangement is open, how can it be confined to a region.

Two noteworthy attempts were made to define open regionalism: one by the Eminent Persons Group (APEC, 1994) and the other by the Council of Economic Advisors (CEA) to the US President in 1995. The two definitions are similar. The CEA definition goes as follows:

> Open regionalism refers to plurilateral agreements that are non-exclusive and open to new members to join. It requires first that plurilateral initiatives be fully consistent with Article XXIV of the GATT, which prohibits an increase in average external barriers. Beyond that, it requires that plurilateral agreements not constrain members from pursuing additional liberalization either with non-members on a reciprocal basis or unilaterally. Because member countries are able to choose their external tariffs unilaterally, open agreements are less likely to develop into competing bargaining blocs. Finally, open regionalism implies that plurilateral agreements both allow and encourage non-members to join.[42]

APEC formally espoused open regionalism at its Osaka meeting in 1995 and the Osaka Action Agenda was premised on the voluntary nature of the APEC process, an essential corollary to the idea of open regionalism (APEC, 1995a). APEC took the stand that liberalization can only be achieved through voluntary actions of individual members. As the economic development levels of the members were diverse, it was believed that having one set of rules for all members would not be effective. This thinking is in direct opposition to the stand taken by the WTO, which is wedded to the principle of 'single undertaking' and binding of tariffs.[43]

Thus viewed, one of the most important criteria of open regionalism is the freedom available to member countries to liberalize further unilaterally or with non-members on a reciprocal basis. It should be noted that in a customs union, individual members are not permitted to lower their tariffs. Common external tariff of a customs union cannot be lowered unless all members agree to it. Under open regionalism, policy commitments are voluntary and are not legally binding. When adopted, this strategy of voluntary liberalization was considered without precedent. Its comprehensive coverage requires not only the reduction of tariffs and NTBs and elimination of barriers on trade in services, but also harmonization of rules and standards and other facilitation measures. The last named ones are not attempted until a country group is attempting to form an economic union. During the APEC meeting in Manila, all the 18 members announced their individual action plans (IAPs) and launched into implementation of IAPs in January 1997. These features of APEC are viewed by some scholars as positive and likely to lead, albeit with some modifications, to significant progress towards the Bogor targets (Petri, 1997). However, others disagree and view these features as impediments to serious liberalization and negotiations. The earlier apprehension regarding the APEC forum persists in some quarters and some analysts still believed that with such characteristics APEC might well be reduced to little more than a 'chat forum' (Flamm and Lincoln, 1998).

As the immediate agenda of APEC includes trade liberalization, trade facilitation and economic cooperation, monetary and macroeconomic cooperation and development and technical cooperation projects were launched under the sponsorship of APEC. Many of these projects and policy measures came from the agenda for deeper integration and could be implemented in a shorter timescale than the establishment of a formal RIA. Thus, APEC could be more successful in achieving deeper integration in some areas than in achieving shallow integration. Several of these issues were promoted with great enthusiasm by the Pacific Business Forum (PBF), which was formed after the 1993 summit in Seattle. The PBF includes business representatives from throughout the APEC region. The business leaders also presented a vision document that *inter alia* included calls for rapid liberalization of trade, an investment code for the APEC region, facilitation of customs procedures, the establishment of a business-person visa, and establishment of a small and medium enterprise foundation.

If the members of APEC go beyond tariffs and NTBs dismantling and consider agreements on domestic practices that reinforce market forces, trade with and entry of non-members would become easier, which in turn would have trade creation rather than trade diversion effects. For instance, harmonized regulations, more efficient customs procedures, or increased regulatory transparency would automatically help both insiders and outsiders in the APEC forum. This would also impart new meaning to *open regionalism*. In many Asian economies interest in liberalization and deregulation has grown. Some countries might find it easier to undertake these measures if they were part of a regional agreement.

APEC declarations and statements recognized the superiority of the global trading system, led by the WTO, and emphasized that regional trade liberalization should be implemented within the framework of the WTO. After the conclusion of the Uruguay Round, an APEC ministerial declaration recognized the primacy of the WTO and the need to strengthen the multilateral trading system (APEC, 1995b). After 1996, APEC changed its stance and called for cooperation on trade liberalization at the regional and multilateral levels. At this stage, APEC appeared more inclined towards its regional identity and was even eager to emphasize its differences from the WTO. In the Vancouver declaration, ministers noted that 'regional and multilateral trade and investment initiatives complement and support each other' (APEC, 1997).

The gravity model was run for APEC trade flows for APEC members until 1992 (Frankel and Wei, 1997). Results reveal that of all the possible implicit trade blocs in the Asia-Pacific region the one that shows the strongest intra-regional bias is the APEC group that includes the US as its member. This regression exercise found that two APEC members trade 200 percent more than two otherwise identical economies. Controlling for an APEC effect left the coefficient on the East Asia bloc greatly reduced; it became marginally significant at the 10 percent level. This suggested that East and Southeast Asian economies, although they trade a lot among themselves, did not trade substantially more than other APEC countries. Even after controlling for an APEC effect, there was a pan-Asia bloc effect that exhibited a strong inward bias.

Of late, regionalization moves through APEC have been losing their momentum and APEC has become near-moribund, if not an 'ailing regional organization'. One of the concerns at the 2000 Summit of APEC leaders[44] was backsliding on agreements made during earlier APEC meetings. As the APEC agreement on achieving free trade and investment by 2010 and 2020 was non-binding and voluntary, this agenda fizzled, faltered and completely collapsed in the wake of the Asian crisis. The IAPs were facing serious problems. In the absence of credible advances towards the target of free trade and investment, some APEC members are turning towards sub-regional arrangements to reach these goals (discussed below). In an assessment of three key areas carried out in 2000, the private sector APEC Business Advisory Council found that the IAPs in many cases contained incomplete information about how members intend to fulfill their commitments.

Culpability for APEC's stagnation rests with the two largest economies, Japan and the US. They have shown little leadership, so desperately needed by APEC. The US policy makers allowed global liberalization to stall as they lost control of domestic policy by pandering to special interests. Japan blocked attempts to pursue a sectoral approach to liberalization within APEC (Wain, 2000). Partly out of frustration with APEC, members were increasingly pursuing alternative institutional arrangements to achieve their priority economic objective. They took the form of sub-regional trade and financial pacts, discussed at length below. These initiatives primarily took place within East Asia and the Pacific but included some trans-Pacific members of APEC as well. An immediate scrutiny of the progress and achievements of the organization is warranted to ensure that the proliferating sub-regional arrangements do not eventually serve to fragment the APEC initiative.

7.4   The Indian Ocean Rim and SAPTA

The Indian Ocean rim or region (IOR) is a large geographical area of the globe comprising sub-regions like Southeast Asia, the South Asian sub-continent, West Asia, North and East Africa, South Africa, and Indian Ocean island economies. The total number of IOR economies adds up to 47 littoral and land-locked countries. A large majority of these economies are not only small in terms of GDP but are also small traders. There are comparatively large economies in this group, like India, but they have a history of adopting an inward-looking strategy, and not giving it up until quite late in the day, and then not abandoning it completely. Economic activity in many of these countries was dominated by public sector activity for a long time. FDI was traditionally considered irrelevant and by using a high tariff wall, government licenses and various NTB mechanisms, trade was discouraged. This was one of the many reasons why their real long-term growth rates were disappointingly low and they fell behind in accumulating capital and technological know-how, which *inter alia* led to a high incremental capital output ratio in their industrial sector, developed a high-cost industrial structure and accumulated large foreign debt.

The generalization holds that the IOR economies were not particularly impressed by the Washington consensus. Although a country like India was able to achieve something close to economic self-sufficiency, it was at the cost of a low long-term growth rate and a high level of absolute poverty. Although India is a part of the IOR economies, it failed to learn from the dynamic economies in the Eastern part of the IOR. Its growth potential was under-achieved by a wide margin because of its autarkic policies. Although South Africa could have taken the East Asian route to success, apartheid and the periods of trade and investment embargoes forced it into a policy regime of self-dependence.

The quarter century between 1960 and 1985 were neither conducive to brisk GDP growth nor establishment of economic linkages in the IOR. A quantum jump was visible in the policy regime after the launch of the Uruguay Round in 1986. Some of these countries slowly began to unilaterally liberalize their economies, and started turning their policy regimes towards outward-orientation. Trade, transfer of technology and labor mobility among the IOR economies began. In the 1990s, many IOR countries made some discernible progress towards trade liberalization as well as reduction of tariff, NTBs and excessive government interference in the economy. Some of the common strands in policy changes included macroeconomic stability through fiscal and monetary policies, currency depreciations to ensure realistic exchange rates, attempts to create an investor-friendly macroeconomic environment, removal of exchange rate controls to gain outward-orientation, and improving efficiency in resource allocation through privatization and deregulation of prices. Although this transformation was not easy, movement of policy regimes in the IOR towards liberalization provided some impetus to the expansion of trade, including intra-regional trade. This process was slow to begin with and needed to stay the course. Whatever policy transformation took place in the IOR economies was more institution-driven than market-driven.

With the ongoing process of economic reforms in major IOR economies like India and South Africa, the market forces are likely to become more effective in the future, that is, if these economies stay the course. If policy liberalization and market forces coalesce, there is a potential for the formation of an Indian Ocean Rim Grouping (IORG) in the future.

The South Asian Association for Regional Cooperation (SAARC) is a sub-set of IORG. It was formed in 1985 as a political consultation entity. Its membership comprised seven south Asian nations, namely, Bangladesh, Bhutan, India, the Maldives, Nepal, Pakistan, and Sri Lanka. A good deal of strategic rivalry exists between these seven nations. Any economic dimension of the organization was an afterthought. In April 1993, members of the SAARC concluded a trade agreement, which did not become operational until December 1995. The initiative to form a preferential trade area (PTA) was taken by Sri Lanka. They have cautiously formed what is called the SAARC Preferential Trade Area (SAPTA). It is the first stage of a regional integrative arrangement (see Chapter 1, section 6). So far this PTA has not made a great deal of progress. Forming SAPTA did not lead to an increase in intra-regional trade. For some years during the late 1990s, the recorded trade even declined in absolute terms. Interestingly, a great deal of trade between these seven South Asian countries is unofficial and unrecorded, suggesting possibilities of forming a successful RIA. A large amount of unrecorded trade between the seven members of SAPTA is a unique characteristic, not to be found in any other RIA. Two of the larger members of SAPTA, India and Pakistan, have had not-so-cordial political and economic relations, which limits the possibility of intra-trade expansion.

Results of gravity model show SAPTA so far is a non-block (Frankel, 1997; Frankel and Wei, 1997). Estimates show that recorded trade between India and Pakistan is 70 percent lower than two otherwise identical economies. From the sub-regional economic perspective this conclusion is a bit ironic because several studies have established that SAARC countries can benefit enormously by cooperating economically and promoting regional trade (Srinivasan and Canonero, 1993, 1995). These studies used a more stylized model, although along the lines of the gravity model. Their equation was identical to a gravity equation, but they broke it down by commodity. They added explicit measures of tariffs to the gravity equation, and used those coefficients to infer the effect of various changes in trading arrangements. For all countries in the region, the most important effects came in the textile fibers sector (particularly textile yarn and clothing) and in manufactures. They inferred that if SAARC becomes an active RIA, it would substantially expand trade for the smaller countries of the sub-region. After regional integration, Bangladesh's estimated new trade within the sub-region would be 21 percent of GNP, more than double the level of total trade for that period. Nepal's new trade was estimated to be even larger, 56 percent of GNP, almost three times the erstwhile level. For these countries, the benefits of regional integration are likely to be large, partly because their base levels of trade were small. For the two large sub-regional economies, India and Pakistan, SAARC would have a small trade-creating effect.

7.5   ASEAN-Plus-Three

The newest idea in regional integration in Asia is the ASEAN-Plus-Three (APT) grouping. A consensus regarding the creation of the APT between ASEAN and its three north Asian partners (China, Korea and Japan) was reached in 1996, during the Asia Europe Meeting (ASEM). The de facto grouping that emerged was further cemented by the regional initiatives to combat the Asian economic crisis during the 1997 Kuala Lumpur ASEAN summit.

The Asian crisis lent urgency to the APT grouping. Asian governments were disappointed by the solutions applied to resolve the crisis by the International Monetary Fund (IMF) and western governments. Regional governments, therefore, turned to creating homegrown solutions to their economic and financial problems that might arise in the future. Failure to reform the global financial architecture gave an impetus to greater collaboration in the monetary and economic areas among the APT countries (FT, 2000). The APT group held its first summit in 1998 and created an 'East Asia Vision Group' (EAVG) to guide its work. Since then, APT leaders have met annually and their commitment to regionalism increased academically, bureaucratically and culturally. Institutionalization increased the pace of APT activities. For instance, meetings of various APT fora like the e-APT Working Group, the APT Young Leaders, and the APT Labor Ministers, were continuously organized. Since 1998, the APT has also begun holding regular meetings of its finance ministers.

The EAVG comprised eminent scholars from the member countries and undertook research on the APT and regional integration. Plans for an APT Secretariat in Kuala Lumpur were being discussed in 2002. There were three principal reasons behind the rapid progress in the APT activities. The first was a spurt in global regionalism during the 1990s, and second was the keen desire to avert future occurrences of a 1997-like contagion in the region. Risk of a contagion is a serious downside of globalization. It has made closer economic cooperation and integration imperative among the APT economies. The third reason was China's rise as a regional economic power of significance. China's trade with the members of ASEAN has increased rapidly since 1977 when it stood at $925 million, to $94 billion in 2002. For the ASEAN economies, China is both a large market and a strong competitor in third-country markets.

In 1999, EAVG published a study on the *East Asia Economic Co-operation System*, which focused on nurturing and furthering APT integration. The EAVG report contained a proposal to further liberalize regional trade and create an East Asia Free Trade Area (EAFTA) as well as liberalization of trade well ahead of the Bogor target set by the APEC forum. While emphasizing that the regional integration arrangement should be consistent with WTO arrangements so as to reinforce the multilateral trading system, the EAVG report recommended the establishment of preferential treatment for the least-developed countries (LDCs) in the region. It also recommended that the Framework Agreement on an ASEAN Investment Area be expanded to include all of East Asia.

Several integration plans between the APT economies have also been under discussion and negotiations. For instance, a free trade agreement involving ASEAN and South Korea has been considered, and this would revitalize trade and increase investment and competitiveness of the APT economies. The ASEAN Free Trade Area has some way to go before becoming an effective means of strengthening the region's competitive economic position on the global market. Also, intra-ASEAN trade volume is not high relative to ASEAN's total global trade volume (section 7.2). It is believed by the APT member countries that AFTA can be an effective regional trading arrangement when linked with Northeast Asia through bilateral arrangements (i.e., ASEAN–China, ASEAN–Japan and ASEAN–Korea), or within the context of a comprehensive APT. The next logical stage of regional integration could well be ASEAN forming a linkage with Australia and New Zealand.

Even before the formal launching of APT, this group of 13 Asian economies has become the most active RIA outside Europe, and has more sophisticated machinery than NAFTA (*The Economist*, 2000b). The reverse of the coin is that the grouping is still at an early stage and has not integrated with the three new northern partners. The APT is proceeding more rapidly on financial issues than on trade. The Asian crisis of 1997–98 is responsible for this emphasis. Members of this group, in the Chang Mai Declaration (1999), announced a region-wide system of currency swaps to help them deal with any future Asian crises. This facility has been created for the APT economies, although no formal institution has been created. This plan is similar to the one drawn up by the Group of Ten (G-10) industrial nations in the early 1960s, when they faced the first global monetary hiccups of the post-war era. The Bretton Woods institutions expressed strong support for the Chiang Mai initiative which entailed expanded financial cooperation. They considered it a complement to the IMF's own financial assistance for the Asian economies (Kohler, 2001).

Sub-regional financial structures are also evolving. ASEAN has created a surveillance mechanism to try to anticipate and head off any future crises, using sophisticated early-warning indicators. The northeast Asian economies agreed to jointly keeping an eye on short-term capital movements in their own economies and in the vicinity. There has been much talk of common currency baskets and joint intervention arrangements to replace both the discredited dollar pegs of the pre-Asian crisis era and the costly free floats imposed by it. Japan has actively promoted the establishment of a network of currency swaps to protect Asian economies against speculative attacks, which plagued the Asian economies during the crisis period (FT, 2000).

Although the Japanese proposal of an Asian Monetary Fund (AMF) was rejected out of hand in 1998, it began to re-evolve in the later half of 2000. China was initially critical of the original AMF proposal, but changed its stance and strongly supported the initiative in 2000. Hong Kong SAR and the Philippines have proposed an Asian currency unit (acu), patterned along the lines of the euro. These were far-reaching concepts, which would take years to materialize. However, a couple of years ago they would have not even been seriously considered by any of the group members. The APT is emerging as a credible economic initiative. Whether it would be a force to reckon with will only be evident in the medium-term.

8.   'NEW AGE' BILATERAL INITIATIVES

During 2000, there was a new fervor for bilateral and plurilateral free trade agreements. As tariffs have declined worldwide, the focus of FTAs shifted toward other issues, including rules governing FDI, e-commerce regulations, trade in services, as well as trade facilitation issues like harmonization of technical standards, sanitary and phytosanitary regulations, technical barriers to trade and streamlining of customs procedures.

Australia, Canada, Chile, Japan, South Korea, Mexico, New Zealand, Singapore and the US rushed to sew up a web of bilateral free trade deals. After the debacle of the WTO Ministerial Conference in Seattle in 1999, popularity of bilateral FTAs suddenly increased. At the end of 2003, over 40 bilateral trade agreements were either formally proposed, or being negotiated or were signed. Interest in the bilateral agreements was due to the concern regarding the spread of regionalism in Europe and Latin America. Economies in other parts of the globe apprehended that their trade would be adversely affected if they failed to negotiate parallel agreements. In some Asian economies, particularly in Korea and Japan, pressure for negotiating bilateral agreements came from the private sector. *Keidanren* (the Japanese Federation of Economic and Business Organizations) noted that while European and US exported to Mexico at zero tariff rates, Japanese exports faced an average duty of 16 percent. The timing of such a large number of bilateral agreements in

Asia-Pacific can be explained by the slow progress and disappointing outcomes of trade and investment liberalization under the aegis of both AFTA and APEC. In addition, members of AFTA wanted to exclude several crucial areas of trade from the liberalization program (Ravenhill, 2003; WTO, 2003a). Historically, Australia, Japan and New Zealand were strong supporters of multilateralism and the MFN principle. However, that was in the past and now they do not seem to have anything against RIAs or even bilateral trade agreements. Japan relied completely on the multilateral system in the past, but it is also actively pursuing preferential trade agreements with Korea, Mexico and Singapore. Japan and Korea expected to use their bilateral trade agreements later on as a bridge to other free trade constellations.

The other two Asian economies, which traditionally relied on a multilateral trading system and were negotiating preferential trade agreements, were New Zealand and Singapore. The two economies signed a bilateral accord forming a 'Closer Economic Partnership' or CEP on 14 November 2000.[45] The two partners have characterized the accord as a prototype for other bilateral agreements. The provisions of the CEP accord include free trade in goods, clear rules of origin, a ban on exports subsidies, an open and positive stance on investment, free trade in services (which is to be phased in over ten years), harmonization of professional qualifications and technical standards and access to all government procurement in the other country. This is the newest paradigm in RIA and is called the 'new age' bilateral FTA. Going forward, the new age FTAs also envision collaboration in intellectual property rights, education and training, media and broadcasting and tourism.

In November 2000, Singapore and the US agreed to negotiate a free trade agreement (de Jonquieres, 2000). Singapore also took the initiative in exploring the possibilities of new age bilateral trade deals with Canada and Korea. The CEP agreements, noted in the preceding paragraph, had a demonstration effect. Early in 2001, New Zealand was trying to negotiate CEP deals with Chile and the US, and Australia was negotiating a similar deal with the US. AFTA had also begun exploring a linkage with the ANZ-CER. A northeast Asia free trade area was under study in 2002; when created it would link China, Japan and Korea. If it did come about, it is likely to merge with AFTA, covering the whole of East and Southeast Asia. In January 2001, the Philippines began discussing, but not negotiating, the possibilities of a CEP agreement with the US and Thailand with Korea.

There are several reasons why the new age bilateral trade pacts and financial initiatives have sprung to action at the outset of the twenty-first century. The first and the most important factor is the Asian financial crisis, which mauled virtually the entire region. The crisis-affected Asian economies realized that they received inadequate bilateral support and multilateral assistance. As noted earlier, a good deal of disappointment persisted among Asian policy makers on this count. Second, the debacle at Seattle and resistance to starting the next WTO round of MTNs caused a great deal of concern to Asian economic policy makers. They grew anxious about their globalized economic sectors like telecommunications, banking and finance, information technology, agriculture and national airlines. They hoped that narrow bilateral trade pacts might supplement multilateral arrangements. Expectation regarding bilateral trade pacts correcting regional ills may not be correct, because it would take much more than bilateral agreements to resolve these problems (Bhatia, 2000). Third, the inspiration provided by European integration and the Single European Market was always one of the factors. Fourth, the regional political and economic leadership felt let down by the poor quality of leadership provided by the US and the EU in the global economic arena (Areddy, 2000; *The Economist*, 2000b). Fifth, impatience with the slow progress or virtual impasse in APEC and ASEAN was another cogent motivation behind the rush into bilateral free trade agreements. Some of these perceptions may not be correct, but Asia seems to have decided that it does not want to be in thrall to Washington or the West. It is neither rejecting the multilateral institutions, nor opting out of the international capital markets. It would continue to participate in the globalization of trade and investment. However, it seems that Asian economies have planned to work within the global economic framework, but be a more independent third pillar of it.

Not all the recent initiatives are likely to reach worthwhile fruition, but what matters is the changing mindset in Asia. Asian economies, in particular Japan, have become less eager to submit unconditionally to global US leadership in economic and financial affairs. Japan's motivation behind regional initiatives was partly defensive. It was apprehensive that development of the euro might eventually push the world into a two-currency bloc, squeezing the yen out of the global currency markets. If that led Japan to play a more effective and constructive role of its own in Asia, it was a healthy development for the region. Being the largest regional economy, and the second largest global economy, Japan is aptly suited to play a long-term lead role in Asia and contribute to regional economic and financial stability.

8.1   'New Age' Bilateral FTA: Japan and Singapore

A desirability and feasibility study of a Japan–Singapore FTA was underway during 1999 and 2000 (JSG, 2000a; JSG 2000b).[46] The principal objective of this bilateral FTA was to (1) liberalize trade further by reduction of tariffs and elimination of NTBs, (2) liberalize trade in services, and (3) adopt trade facilitation measures like mutual recognition of national standards, stream-lining of customs procedures, and establishment of an 'exemplary framework for FDI'. The two prospective partners also envisaged collaboration on issues like intellectual property rights, education and training, media and broadcasting, and promoting mutual tourism. This bilateral 'new age' FTA is considered a pioneering one and was being closely watched by the other large trading economies in the Asia-Pacific region.[47] Closely on the heels of the Joint Study Group between Japan and Singapore, another identical study group was set up to study the feasibility of a Japan–Korea bilateral FTA (KIEP, 2000).

Hertel et al. (2002) calculated Japan's total merchandise trade bias towards Korea, Singapore and the rest of the world. They used this method to capture the determinants of export shares, taking into account the size, the openness and product composition of the importing markets. The bias component offers a kind of proxy for the transaction costs that an FTA is intended to lower. The higher the bias, the more attractive the export destination the partner economy would be relative to the rest of the world. They found that over the preceding three decades attractiveness of exporting from Japan to South Korea and Singapore has been cut into half. Likewise, export bias from Korea and Singapore towards Japan has also been falling steadily. While trading costs between Japan and these two regional economics has fallen significantly over the last three decades, they fell more between Japan and its other trading partners.

The Japan–Singapore FTA aims at eliminating bilateral tariffs. Food and agricultural products are exported from Singapore to Japan by *entrepôt* exporters. These are sensitive products and given the high tariffs on them when imported from other destinations, the incentive for trans-shipment through Singapore is likely to be high when the FTA comes into force. The prospects of enforcement costs associated with rules of origin in the FTA are likely to be high. Therefore, it is likely that agriculture would be finally left out of this FTA, or perhaps included after a long delay. Textiles and apparel and leather goods also face non-negligible tariffs in Japan. Under the FTA, substantial expansion in the export of these products would take place.

The trade relationship in terms of products is highly skewed. Japanese exports to Singapore are highly concentrated in machinery and equipment sectors, followed by business and financial services, petrochemicals, mineral products and other extractive manufactures, in that order. Similarly, Singapore's exports to Japan are highly concentrated in financial services, followed by machinery and equipment sectors, petrochemicals and mineral products, in that order. Bilateral trade between the two economies is based on a great deal of intra-industry trade in machinery and equipment sectors, which is likely to receive a substantial impetus under the FTA.

Another objective of a Japan–Singapore FTA is trade facilitation by lowering customs clearance costs, so that bilateral costs of trade could be lowered. The two study group reports (JSG, 2000a, 2000b) cited a United Nations Conference on Trade and Development (UNCTAD) study that concluded that customs paperwork and procedure costs add up to 7 percent of global value added in international trade, which may be correct on an average but seems high for Japan–Singapore trade. However, in a period of increased regional cooperation and vertical production integration in industries, small increases in trade costs have a good deal of negative impact over intra-industry trade. Any trade cost on this count, which is higher than 1 to 2 percent, would amount to a substantial barrier to trade, akin to industrial tariffs. Therefore, the Joint Study Group proposed reduction in customs clearance costs through the implementation of the Electronic Trade Documentation Exchange System (ETDES). It was believed that ETDES would not only increase the pace of customs clearance but also quicken the exchange of documents. An electronically harmonized customs system would reduce the time and cost of paperwork, processing and shipment. While Singapore presently uses ETDES, Japan needs to install it.

Using a dynamic GTAP (Global Trade Analysis Project) model for the proposed FTA, Hertel et al. (2002) concluded that the impact of this bilateral FTA on investment, capital accumulation and economic growth would be significant. This conclusion applies more to Singapore than to Japan. In addition, they concluded that global benefits were to be substantial. They were quantified at \$9.5 billion per year by 2020. As regards the distribution of gains between the two FTA partners, 70 percent are likely to be captured by Japan because a greater part of the FTA related reforms would be undertaken by Japan. This study found that there is a strong probability of trade diversion, leading to losses to the several non-participating regions of the world.

8.2　Bilateral FTA between Singapore and the United States

The United States and Singapore have successfully finalized a Free Trade Agreement that will result in greater trade liberalization between the two countries. The US is Singapore's second largest market. The Agreement, which was signed on 6 May 2003 in Washington DC, was approved by the US House of Representatives on 25 July 2003 and by the Senate on 1 August 2003. Ambitious and comprehensive, the Singapore–United States Free Trade Area (SUSFTA) covers trade in goods and services and is 'consistent with Article XXIV of GATT 1994 and Article V of GATS'.[48] Both the partners have agreed to go much above their WTO commitments. It will also be NAFTA-plus in a number of areas, including the protection of intellectual property, the inclusion of e-commerce and ICT services, together with advanced rules of origin and customs cooperation. As the first free trade agreement to be concluded between the US and an Asian country, the SUSFTA will cement the already strong economic ties between Singapore and the US. It will also serve as a catalyst towards deeper US economic engagement in the region and spur other ASEAN-wide FTAs.

The principal objective of the trade liberalization efforts involves the reduction and eventual elimination of tariff for merchandise goods. In the SUSFTA, up to 92 percent of Singapore's exports to the US[49] and 100 percent of US exports to Singapore would enjoy the preferential tariff treatment once the FTA goes into force. In addition, Singapore companies will also benefit from the waiver of the 0.21 percent Merchandise Processing Fee (approximately $30 million) and the Vessel Repair Duty (approximately $4 million a year) in the SUSFTA. However, it should be noted that both countries already have very liberal trade policies. Singapore has virtually zero tariffs (except for beer, stout, samshoo and medicated samshoo) and the US has an average tariff rate of 0 percent to 5 percent on merchandise goods.

With such low levels of protection, the degree of tariff reduction cannot be significant.[50] Therefore, the impact of trade liberalization in merchandise goods alone between these two open economies is likely to be modest. In contrast to this, liberalization of trade in services is expected to benefit both the economies substantially because the services sector is the largest in both the economies and its contribution to GDP is 65 percent or more. Therefore, improved access in the services sector is sure to benefit the two partner economies in terms of improvement in productivity and competitiveness.

In an aggressive burst of purposeful activity Singapore completed bilateral FTAs with New Zealand in November 2000, the European Free Trade Association in January 2003 and Australia in July 2003. (At present, EFTA comprises Iceland, Liechtenstein and Switzerland.)

9. CONCLUSIONS AND SUMMARY

Notwithstanding the fact that the approximately half of the trade is intra-regional, the Asia-Pacific region was late in adopting regionalism in its institutional form. Several sub-groups of Asian economies grew highly successful by following export-led or trade-induced growth. These sub-groups included NIAEs, followed by the ASEAN-4 and subsequently China. The market expansion and regional integration that took place in Asia was both vertical and horizontal. First the NIAEs and then the other emerging-market economies of Asia developed tiers of complex trade and manufacturing hierarchies. This occurred in association with the large flows of intra-regional investment into Southeast Asia and China. Over the preceding quarter century, Japan, Taiwan and Korea provided massive amounts of FDI to Southeast

Asian economies and China, and in the process increased their commitments in these markets.

Intra-trade in Asia has been well developed since the beginning of the twentieth century. During the early decades, it was close to half the total trade in Asia, which was dominated by Japan's colonial pattern of economic relations. After 1931, the Japanese colonial pattern of trade gave way to building independent industrial capacity outside Japan, essentially in China, Korea and Taiwan. This kind of economic relationship between Japan and other Asian economies led to significant intra-regional investment as well as development of regional transportation and communications infrastructure networks. Over the post-war period, development of Asian production networks supported mutually reinforcing trade and investment. The result was the creation of complex regional economic ties among these economies as well as trade dependencies. The increasing trade dependence of Asia is clearly reflected in a simple measure, namely, intra-regional trade as a share of total trade of the region.

During the 1970s, a triangular production relationship had developed between Japan, the NIAEs and the US, bringing the former two sets of economies closer together. Japan supplied the necessary components and technology to the NIAEs, which in turn produced and competitively marketed industrial products to the US market. After the Plaza Accord in 1985, the currency value configuration changed. The dollar had reached a high against the yen in early 1985, which intensified imports from East and Southeast Asia into the US market, and Japan was able to maintain its exports even as its production costs were rising vis-à-vis its Asian rivals. Changes in currency value configuration and economic complementaries buttressed this trend. Gradually the production locus shifted from firms to networks of regional production. Asian economies were pioneers in this respect. Production networks soon became a significant force driving the process of economic integration in East and Southeast Asia as well as that of globalization. During the late 1980s, the production networks began to spread to Guangdong and Fujian provinces in south China, and a borderless economy encompassing a much larger region with different comparative advantages began to emerge.

Although there is some disagreement regarding the concept of natural trading partners, Asian economies have not only integrated as natural trading partners, but the prospects for monetary integration among them are also improving. Evidence is available to show that trade and investment diversion due to formation of RIAs around the globe would cause the Asia-Pacific economies to lose out on some of their export markets and FDI. Also, a good number of empirical studies, using the gravity model, lead towards two broad conclusions. First, East and Southeast Asian economies clearly show a certain inward bias among themselves. Second, even after controlling for a special

Asia effect, East and Southeast Asian economies en masse appear to trade more among themselves than one would expect based on their economic and geographic characteristics.

Asian-Pacific economies did not display as much enthusiasm for RIAs as those in the EU and Latin America, nor did formal regional trading arrangements that *were* entered into, go very far. Despite this general trend in regional cooperation and integration, there are several areas in Asia where sub-regional cooperation is taking place. These regional cooperation endeavors have been christened the 'growth triangles'. In their most basic form they exploit complementarities between geographically contiguous areas of different Asian countries to gain a competitive edge in export promotion. To be effective, they require close cooperation between the private and public sectors of each of the countries involved.

At beginning of the twenty-first century, proclivity towards regionalism in Asia began to strengthen. Led by Singapore, political leadership in Asia grew increasingly inclined towards it. There were fervent calls to take advantage of new opportunities and meet unprecedented economic challenges. To this end, it was felt that Asian economies needed to work in a proactive manner towards regionalism. Although there are not many RIAs in the Asia-Pacific region, the existing ones do show an impressive variety in their range. In a chronological order, they include Australia–New Zealand Closer Economic Relations (ANZ-CER or only CER) agreement, ASEAN Free Trade Area (AFTA), APEC, and SAARC Preferential Trade Area (SAPTA). The history, motivation and objectives of these RIAs vary widely. Of these, only CER and AFTA can be treated as integrated RIAs. Of the others, some are formal, others are not. Some are successful, others are there only in name and merely facilitate trade. Some are more than a decade old, while others are little more than a concept. During 2000, there was a new fervor of New Age bilateral FTAs in Asia. The Japan–Singapore FTA is considered a pioneer, while a Singapore–China FTA is being prepared.

NOTES

1. Unless otherwise specified, 'Asian' in this chapter implies East and Southeast Asian economies, while 'Asia-Pacific' means Asia plus Oceania.
2. Based on real GDP growth and other usual indicators of economic performance during the last three decades, the East and Southeast Asian economies and the People's Republic of China (or China) are widely regarded as the dynamic economies of Asia. Economists tend to separate 'dynamic' Asia from the rest of Asia.
3. Hong Kong SAR, South Korea, Singapore and Taiwan.
4. Namely, Indonesia, Malaysia, the Philippines, and Thailand.
5. The source of GDP growth statistics is IMF (2003), Table 1.1.
6. The source of these are the trade statistics published on the WTO website. Refer to *International Trade Statistics 2002*, at http://www.wto.org/english/res_e/statis_e/statis_e.htm.

7. Reported in the *Annual Report 2002*, of the World Trade Organization. See Appendix Table II.1, p.22.
8. Although Macao should be added to this definition of Greater China, conventionally it is not.
9. Refer to Chapter 4 of 'Regional Integration in East Asia: Challenges and Opportunities' by E. Sakakibara, and S. Yamakawa, Part II, Keio University, Tokyo, June (2003) p.5.
10. For greater details regarding the achievement of stability, please refer to Ikenberry (2000), WTO (1995) and WTO (1999).
11. The five crisis-affected Asian economies were Korea, Indonesia, Malaysia, the Philippines and Thailand.
12. The eleven member central banks or monetary authorities are those from Indonesia, Korea, Malaysia, Mongolia, Myanmar, Nepal, the Philippines, Singapore, Sri Lanka, Taiwan, and Thailand.
13. The central banks and monetary authorities that participated in EMEAP were those from Australia, China, Hong Kong SAR, Indonesia, Japan, South Korea, Malaysia, New Zealand, Philippines, Singapore, and Thailand.
14. The ASEAN-Plus-Three grouping comprises the members of ASEAN, China, South Korea and Japan.
15. On 22 September 1895, the Group of Five (G-5) finance ministers and central bankers met at the Plaza Hotel in New York to accord recognition to the view that 'recent shift in fundamental economic conditions ... together with policy commitments for the future' had to be fully reflected in foreign exchange markets. The communiqué declared that in the international economic milieu 'some further orderly appreciation of the main non-dollar currencies is desirable' and that an exchange rate policy should play a role in place of laissez faire. The accord communiqué called for the appreciation of the yen and the deutsche mark, instead of the depreciation of the dollar. The Plaza communiqué had a substantial short-term impact over the foreign exchange markets and the dollar went into a steep decline, while the yen and deutsche mark began to appreciate, the former sharply (Das, 1993).
16. Chapter 4 in Das (1996) presents a detailed account of the new division of labor and development of regional and sub-regional production networks in Asia.
17. The World Trade Organization, *Trade Statistics*, Table III.3, July 2003.
18. Refer to Table 2.1, in Frankel, 1997, p.22.
19. For a detailed account of international production networks in Asia, please refer to Borrus et al. (2000).
20. Flying geese hypothesis implies a more developed economy aiding and stimulating economic growth in the less developed ones, which in turn aids and stimulates growth in the even less developed economies, in the process making a functional chain of leader-follower economies. Generally there will be one leader economy and several follower ones at various strata of economic development, providing an imagery of flying geese. Asian economic development, according to Akamatsu (1961) followed this paradigm, where the Japanese economy was the lead economy, followed by the NIAEs as the second tier economies, and further down the line came the ASEAN-4 and China. The so-called flying geese paradigm remained an accepted paradigm of Asian growth for decades.
21. Intra-regional production networks in East and Southeast Asia have been studied by Hansen (2001); OECD (2002); Fukasaku and Kimura (2002) and Sakakibara and Yamakawa (2003).
22. China's real GDP growth rate for 2003 was estimated at 9.5 percent (*The Economist*, 2003b).
23. The rapidly growing export value and volume in China is reflected in its fast expanding ports. In addition to Shenzhen, the Chinese city of Shanghai, which in 2002 overtook Kaohsiung as the world's fourth-largest port (after Hong Kong SAR, Singapore and South Korea's Pusan), saw traffic rise by almost 40 percent during 2002-03. Thanks to a surge in exports from southern China, throughput at Hong Kong SAR's container terminals is soaring. Traffic at the Kwai Chung terminal, for instance, was up by 25 percent in the first half of 2003 compared with the same period in 2002, according to the Port and Maritime Board of Hong Kong SAR (*The Economist,* 2003b).

24. Refer to Das, 1996. Chapters 4 and 5 deal with this issue at great length and also provide relevant statistical data.
25. The three of 'Plus Three' are China, Japan and South Korea.
26. As noted in Chapter 1, note 11, the Agreement on a Treaty on the European Union with a timetable for Economic and Monetary Union was signed on 10 December 1991. The Maastrich Treaty came into force on 1 November 1993, and with that the EEC became the EU.
27. The expression 'natural trading partner' originated in Lipsey's (1960) famous survey.
28. This section has benefited from the Frankel and Wei (1997) survey.
29. Non-tariff barriers include para-tariff measures, price control measures, financial measures, monopolistic measures, and technical measures.
30. Results of these empirical studies are presented here in a cursory manner. Researchers dealing with this issue are advised to consult the detailed survey in Frankel and Wei (1997). It is acknowledged that this section draws heavily on it.
31. For more details about the gravity model refer to Lee and Roland-Holst (1998).
32. Other attempts were made to provide a theoretical foundation for the gravity model but they lacked a compelling economic justification. Anderson (1979) derived a reduced-form gravity equation from a general equilibrium model incorporating the properties of expenditure systems.
33. LAIA stands for Latin American Integration Agreement. Its former name was LAFTA or the Latin American Free-Trade Area. This is a case of dual membership in that all the members of the Andean Group and MERCOSUR are also the members of LAIA or LAFTA.
34. It should be clarified that if the Australia–New Zealand Closer Economic Relations (ANZ-CER) is considered part of the Asian regional scenario, the CER is three years older than OPTAD. The CER was agreed between the two economies in Oceania in 1965.
35. The acronym SAARC stands for South Asian Association for Regional Co-operation.
36. For an in-depth study of the characteristics and growth pattern of CER, readers are referred to BIE (1995).
37. This agreement was signed in Manila, the Philippines, on 24 February 1977.
38. This is according to the IMF definition of the emerging-market economies.
39. The World Trade Organization, *Trade Statistics*, Table 19, July 2003.
40. The World Trade Organization, *Trade Statistics*, Table 19, July 2003.
41. It needs to be explained and clarified. The Eminent Persons Group report (APEC, 1994) has the following to say about open regionalism: 'We recommend that APEC advocate the maximum extent of further unilateral liberalization by all member economies'.
    'A number of economies in the Asia-Pacific region, especially those with relatively high levels of protection, have unilaterally reduced their barriers to both trade and investment to a significant degree over the past decade. Indeed, such initiatives have been a major element in expanding trade, investment and growth in the region – both for the economies undertaking the liberalization and for their partners. We believe that unilateral liberalization is not only virtuous per se but that it tends to feed on itself via positive demonstration effects. Individual economies are encouraged to liberalize when they see their trading partners doing so. They are in fact often impelled to do so, fearing that a more liberal neighbor may become a more formidable competitor in trade terms and a more attractive site for foreign investment.'
42. Plurilateral agreement implies an agreement between three or more members.
43. Tariff binding is defined as commitment not to increase a rate of duty beyond any agreed level. Once a rate of duty is bound, it may not be raised without compensating the affected trading partners. Tariff binding is enshrined in Article II of GATT-1994.
44. The 2000 Summit of APEC took place in Bandar Seri Begawan, Brunei Darussalam, 12–13 November 2000.
45. The CEP accord between New Zealand and Singapore was signed after 15 months of negotiations. It came in force on 1 January 2001.
46. The term 'new age' was first used by the joint study group report, namely, *Japan–Singapore Economic Agreement for a New Age Partnership*. Tokyo and Singapore. Ministry of Foreign Affairs, Japan, and Ministry of Foreign Affairs, Singapore.

47. It should, however, be pointed out that this was not the first ever bilateral RIA. In 1985, an FTA was signed between Israel and the US, which was the first bilateral FTA between an industrial and emerging market economy. The agreement envisaged full reciprocal treatment between the two partners, with some concessions to Israel. It was granted permission to impose extra protection for its infant industries against imports from the US. The scope of infant industry protection was limited to those industries that were set up after the FTA was signed. The period of infant industry protection was also limited to two years. This RTA has been adjudged a successfully functioning arrangement between the two partners.
48. Refer to Article 1.1, Paragraph 1, of the Articles of Agreement.
49. The rest of the tariff lines are to be eliminated within eight years.
50. Although the extent of tariff reduction may be modest in percentage terms, the amount of tariff saving in absolute level terms would be substantial given the high volume of trade (approximately $35 billion) between Singapore and the US.

6. Regionalism in the Western Hemisphere

1. THE GLOBALISM AND REGIONALISM DICHOTOMY

During the preceding quarter century, the dual forces of globalism and regionalism have been affecting the economies of Latin America. In a striking contrast to Asia, regional integration initiatives have long been part of the landscape here. They flourished in the early post-war era, but then lost momentum. In the mid-1980s, a new wave of regional integration began. It could be considered the resurgence of regionalism in Latin America, which coincided with the global phenomenon of 'new regionalism'. The strong post-war preference of the United States for multilateralism, as opposed to regionalism, is well recorded. A tectonic shift in US strategy towards regional trading blocs took place in 1985, when President Ronald Reagan instructed the office of the United States Trade Representative, Department of Commerce, to explore just how crucial regional and bilateral agreements were for global trade liberalization. This development had far-reaching repercussions.

During this period, regional economies began reducing tariff barriers unilaterally. By the late 1990s, average tariff rates came down to 12 percent, from 40 percent in the mid-1980s. The regional economies were active participants in the Uruguay Round and by the end of the 1990s all of them had become members of the World Trade Organization (WTO). Along with these global measures, 22 regional trade agreements were entered into force in Latin America between 1990 and 2001, or old ones were renegotiated.[1] Upgrading and revision of several past accords, which had lost momentum, was also undertaken during this period. Some of these agreements, like CARICOM (Caribbean Community and Common Market, see section 9.3), updated their founding treaty in order to establish the legal basis for moving towards a single market in the short term.[2]

The growth of globalism and regionalism in Latin America during this period progressed *pari passu* with brisk growth in global trade until the Asian crisis in mid-1997. Intra-regional trade also expanded from 13 percent of the total in 1990 to 20 percent in 2000. This was due to a decade-long trend according to which intra-regional trade grew at almost twice the rate of exports to markets outside the region (IDB, 2002a). Annual average increase in merchandise exports for the 1990s was 8.4 percent in terms of volume, which was only surpassed by China and a few other Asian economies. The onward march of globalization made the policy mandarins in the region reevaluate their development strategy. Their conscious objective was to realign it with the ongoing globalization, and be well integrated with the global economy. They were aware that globalization, managed well, has enormous welfare implications (Das, 2003b). To meet this challenge, they strongly supported a liberalized trade regime. Proactive endeavors were made to strengthen economic ties with the North American economies and the European Union. Liberalization of trade policy did improve trade performance in the region, as the trade statistics show. However, this dynamism on the trade front was not reflected in real GDP growth rate in the region. In particular, the smaller economies of the region continued to face the additional difficulties because of their size including a lack of scale economies, higher unit costs of production and unfavorable competitive position in most industries (ECLAC, 2002).

2. THE GENESIS OF REGIONALISM IN LATIN AMERICA

Regional integration initiatives in the Southern Hemisphere date back to the independence of the region. Thus, regionalism is Latin America has a much longer history than that in Asia and other parts of the globe. The original objective behind making regional or sub-regional trading blocs was political, but in the post-World War II era the principal motivating factors changed. Economic development became the prime objective driving the formation of regional trading blocs. During the 1950s, before the Treaty of Rome was signed (1957), there were frequent public debates on the need to create regional blocs like a Latin American Common Market. After a decade of deliberations and debates, followed by negotiations, the Latin American Free Trade Area (LAFTA)[3] was launched in 1960. Countries of the southern cone and Mexico were its constituent members. The five-member Central American Common Market (CACM)[4] was also launched in 1960, followed by the Andean Group (AG) in 1969.[5] These three regional trading blocs, in particular the CACM, enjoyed some measure of initial success. Of the three, CACM and AG were contiguous sub-regional country groupings. However, by the mid-1970s, they began experiencing serious difficulties and fell into complete disarray in the early 1980s.

When these trading blocs were formed, developing economies, including Latin American ones, were strongly under the influence of the old strategy of 'export pessimism' propounded by Ragner Nurkse and Raul Prebisch. This was the conventional wisdom of the mid-twentieth century and had wide acceptance in the developing world. The regional trading blocs of this period were formulated with the express purpose of underpinning the on-going public-sector-led import-substituting industrialization endeavors in the Latin American economies. Built into the export pessimism strategy was skepticism regarding the private sector as well as presence of foreign firms. It was believed that foreign firms would create a dependence on them in the developing Latin American economies, in turn undermining domestic economic development. It was firmly believed by the erstwhile policy makers that the road to industrialization goes through import-substitution. For this strategy to succeed, maintaining high or very high tariff levels was a necessary condition. It was common to have effective protection rates of 150 percent to 200 percent in the Latin American economies during this period.

The principal policy planks of the ISI strategy were economic and industrial planning, creating large public sector enterprises and large-scale government intervention in the markets, so much so that the market forces were completely stifled. This was a dirigiste regime. Policy makers were of the opinion that regional trading blocs fit well into the ISI regime because it would allow elimination of intra-regional trade barriers while maintaining a high level of external protection. Therefore, it was expected that regional integration agreements (RIAs) would enable the constituent members to plan for the entire regional or sub-regional markets, which would cover all the member economies. The hope was that this strategy would step up the pace of regional industrialization and lead to rapid real GDP growth.

Intra-regional liberalization was based on a complex mix of multiple positive lists, coupled with more complex arrangements of 'special and differential treatment' for the less developed members of the RIA. However, contrary to the initial hopes, the creation of European Economic Community style bureaucracies and sectoral industrial planning choked private sector development in the Latin American economies. Trade liberalization endeavors at the national level did not succeed under the ISI regime. Effective liberalization was limited and intra-regional trade was even more so. These regional accords were highly bureaucratized and, therefore, procedure and paperwork oriented. Many of their agreements could never be implemented and remained merely on paper, which in turn was filed away by the large bureaucracies.

3. IMPACT OF THE 1982 CRISIS

The 1982 debt crisis, which started in Mexico, was not only a serious blow to the economies in Latin America but also affected several large regional economies in an adverse manner.[6] The crisis also had global financial repercussions and drove the global financial system to the brink of a precipice. The regional economies suffered from a deep balance-of-payments induced recession, which in turn was followed by a contraction in trade, including intra-regional trade. Imports of the Latin American economies suffered a serious contraction in the post-crisis period, which again included intra-regional imports. As they were the counterpart of intra-regional exports, recession in these economies resulted in the collapse of intra-regional trade. The regional economies, both small and large, were gripped with an economic paralysis. Consequently, many of the weakened regional trading agreements (RTAs) collapsed, or were close to collapsing. Devlin and Estevadeordal (2001) called the 1982 crisis 'a death blow for regional integration'. Most observers believed that the economies in Latin America would not have any penchant for regional integration in the near future.

As alluded to in the preceding section, economies in Latin America, like those in South Asia, had a history of following autarkic policies. The post-1982 crisis environment evolved in a different manner. The new growth strategy turned out to be an antithesis of the popular import-substituting industrialization strategy of the past. It was based on liberalization, deregulation, privatization, outward-orientation, correct relative prices, a market-friendly policy ambience, relinquishment of 'statist' strategy[7] and acceptance of the 'Washington consensus', as propounded by John Williamson.[8] In conjunction with macroeconomic and political reforms that were undertaken after the crisis, there was serious trade liberalization in a majority of the Latin American economies. Tariff barriers were reduced and rationalized and non-tariff barriers were used less frequently. Large regional economies dramatically slashed their tariff rates. For instance, average tariffs in Argentina were around 30 percent in 1989, 51 percent in Brazil and over 100 percent in Uruguay. These rates were reduced under the unilateral reforms undertaken in 1991 when the Treaty of Asuncion was signed. Common external tariffs in 1995 were down to 10.7 percent (Laird, 1995; see also Estevadeordal et al., 2002a).

4. THE ERA OF RESURGENCE IN REGIONAL INTEGRATION

Much to the surprise of many observers, new initiatives to form RIAs began to appear in the latter half of the 1980s. Given the backround of debt crisis of 1982, such initiatives were not expected at this point in time. Most analysts believed that the Latin American economies would be more busy in bringing in some semblance of order to their domestic economies than launching new regional trade initiatives. A strong second wave of regionalism materialized in the global economy during the 1990s and early 2000s. It provided an impetus to regionalism in Latin America as well. The *causae causantes* for adopting regionalism for these economies was that they believed that it provided them with a policy tool to participate in the increasingly integrated global economy (see section 1). There was substantial evidence for the policy makers to observe that successful countries tended to deploy policies that proactively harnessed the forces of globalization for economic growth and development, while those countries that distanced themselves from these forces were lagging behind.

It was due to these endeavors that since the mid-1980s, various economies and sub-regions in Latin America experienced a quickened pace of integration among themselves as well as with the global economy. The measures adopted for liberalization in the area of trade were swift and extensive.[9] Economies became increasingly open, therefore traded components of output and consumption as a share of GDP rose steadily. This was the tangible result of a concerted liberalization endeavor in the region (Markusen and Diniz, 2003). Integration brought local goods and services face-to-face with those from different regional and global economies. Many firms and economies in the region lost their traditional markets and product specializations to new regional and global firms. Many firms that had been shortsightedly serving their local markets were undercut by the more competitive imports, both from within the region and without. Under these circumstances economies or regions found attracting and retaining capital a difficult proposition. In the new dynamic scenario, fresh investment could no longer be taken for granted.

Adoption of neo-liberal strategy, ongoing regionalization and globalization has resulted in markedly intensified competition among the Latin American economies and sub-regions over the last two decades. Competition for markets has also intensified between Latin America and the other regions of the globe. The emerging *mise-en-scène* made the local firms examine their product lines, cost structures, and the export potential of their products. The competition offered by imported regional goods and services forced them to worry about their present and future markets. They were forced to reevaluate their comparative advantage, exploit it if they could, or find new market niches if they did not have comparative advantage in their product lines (Castells, 1999; Conti and Graciara, 2000).

The Latin American economies treated RIA formation as one of the tools for trade policy liberalization (see Chapter 2, section 2). The RIAs represented a third tier of trade policy reform, which aims to complement and reinforce the unilateral (the first tier) and multilateral (the second tier) liberalization undertaken as part of the structural reform programs that had been underway since the mid-1980s. Multilateral organizations like the International Monetary Fund (IMF), the World Bank and the GATT-WTO system contributed significantly to this liberalization and reform process. The RIAs became an integral part of it and were instrumental in promoting and anchoring liberalization and reform endeavours (Stiglitz, 2002).

The impact of the neo-liberal strategies was visible in the regional trade, which has expanded substantially over the last two decades. Exports soared from $92 billion to 406 billion over the 1980-2000 period, while imports rose from $93 billion to $418 billion. The performance of Mexico has been outstanding in this respect, where exports leaped from $16 billion to $180 billion over this period. Increases in trade volumes resulted in small increases in current account deficits, which was normal. However, the Latin American economies also suffered from large capital account deficits. The two principal causal factors were the large stocks of international debt and remittances serving the external asset holdings from foreign direct investment (FDI). Between 1980 and 2000, the level of international debt in Latin America rose from $205 billion to $740 billion, heavily increasing the pressure on the balance of payments of the regional economies. During the 1980s, the real GDP growth in Latin America was weak at 1.2 percent per annum, which did not even keep pace with the population growth. During the 1990s, it improved to 3.2 percent, but in per capita terms it was again merely 1.2 percent. Regional disparities were a traditional economic malaise in the region, which still persists (Markusen and Diniz, 2003).

In the early years of the twenty-first century, the regional dimension of trade became a more important part of the domestic policy than ever in the past. Brisk growth of trade in the 1990s between the partner economies of RIAs raised the level of interdependence among them. But a number of RIAs in Latin America encountered problems due to instability in global capital inflows, macroeconomic instability, and backsliding on regional commiments. The contagion effect – economic and financial problems of neighbors effecting the home economy – added to the problems of the individual Latin American economies as well as the RIAs (Das, 2003a). Apparently, the easy stage of regional integration is now over. The sub-regions will need renewed political leadership and commitment and a redoubling of efforts if they are to achieve their objectives regarding deepening of present RIAs.

The Latin American Free Trade Association lost momentum, and a successor was created in 1980 – the Latin American Integration Association (LAIA or ALADI in Spanish)[10] and it was christened Economic Complementary Agreement (ECA or ACE in Spanish). The failures and problems of the 1960s had taught many indelible lessons, which in turn benefited the launching of LAIA. It eschewed the grand but somewhat contradictory objectives and schemes of the 1960s. LAIA focused on a limited number of achievable goals. It confined itself to market access through exchange of partial or full trade preferences on specific product lines. LAIA also adopted regulations on the application of safeguard clauses, rules of origin (ROO), and the like.

A watered-down ACE agreement in the four Southern Cone economies resulted in the signing of the Treaty of Asuncion in 1991 to launch MERCOSUR in 1995.[11] Negotiations continued for the next five years and MERCOSUR did indeed come into force in 1995. It was formed by a contiguous sub-regional group of economies and was planned as a customs union, with ambitions for a higher level of integration. Future plans are to evolve as a common market. Subsequently, it incorporated Bolivia and Chile as associate free trade area members.

As set out in section 2, the Andean Pact (AP) was born with an ambition to be a customs union. The 1988 Protocol of Quito called for amendments to the Andean Group's (AG's) founding treaty. Its institutional structure was also revised in 1988. During the early 1990s, a free trade area (FTA) was formed between the AG countries. Subsequently, an imperfect customs union was formed among three of them, namely, Colombia, Ecuador and Venezuela. In December 1996, they changed their name to the Andean Community (AC or CAN in Spanish) (see section 9.1). As stated in section 2, the CACM was launched in 1960. It was revived and relaunched in 1993 with the same objectives as the AC.

The first ACE agreements were being negotiated and launched in the late 1980s and early 1990s in Latin America. As alluded to in section 1, the shift in the US strategy toward regionalism dated back to 1985. In May 1986, Canada and the US launched their free trade area negotiations. This was a highly significant development because both of these economies had historically shown a marked preference for multilateral trade as opposed to regional trade. Their philosophical opposition to regionalism was well known and they pointedly eschewed regional arrangements of any ilk. In the post-war period, the US was the pioneer of both free trade and multilateral trade, and considered regional trading arrangements as an anathema to the expansion of multilateralism. It was demonstrated by the US enthusiasm and support for the creation of the International Trade Organization and, failing that, for the General Agreement on Tariffs and Trade (GATT).

The progress in negotiations was swift. By October 1987, the 20-chapter Canada–United States Free Trade Agreement (CUSFTA) was finalized. It was signed in 1988 and came into effect on 1 January 1989. The CUSFTA included a schedule for the elimination of all tariffs on trade between Canada and the United States by 1 January 1998. It established a mutually beneficial framework for the fair and predictable treatment of investors and included rules governing trade in services. The CUSFTA established the necessary institutional provisions to provide for the joint management of the agreement and to avoid and settle any dispute respecting the interpretation or application of any element of the agreement. Its dispute settlement mechanism promotes fairness, predictability and security by giving each partner an equal voice in resolving problems through ready access to objective arbitration panels. The CUSFTA established a dispute settlement mechanism that guaranteed the impartial application of each partner's anti-dumping and countervailing duty laws. Binational arbitration panels can review final determinations of dumping or subsidies. The implementation of the CUSFTA generated some transitional employment losses in some sectors, but this was accompanied by employment gains in others. The economies of both countries became more integrated. Canadian exports to the United States have increased, especially in goods such as telecommunications equipment. The same applies to trade in services, particularly in financial services and consulting. There is now much more US investment in Canada and vice versa.

CUSFTA emerged as a different kind of FTA from the run of the mill FTAs negotiated during this period. When Canada and the US launched their free trade negotiations, it transformed the landscape of international trade negotiations, and influenced thinking of the policy mandarins about regionalism. As alluded to in the preceding paragraph, the negotiators had a large number of agenda issues, many more than mere market access and tariffs and non-tariff barriers. The negotiations extended to the so-called 'new issues' like trade in services, regulations on foreign investment, government procurement, intellectual property rights, trade facilitation and the like. There was little consensus on these issues at the multilateral level in the GATT, therefore the US objective was to first pursue a bilateral trade agreement on these 'new issues' of the period. It was hoped that once this was achieved, it would influence the conduct of future multilateral negotiations. The CUSFTA succeeded in achieving this objective. Not only was a model for negotiations established in a range of new areas but new approaches for negotiations were proposed in some of the old areas, like ROO and dispute settlement. The CUSFTA is considered a watershed point in regional negotiations essentially because in this case two countries moved from the usual market access issues to areas which were traditionally considered part of sovereign policy of countries (Devlin and Estevadeordal, 2001; Estevadeordal et al., 2002a).

The CUSFTA accord became a pioneer by bringing the 'new issues' into the fold of an FTA. It is known for breaking away from the well-beaten track of regional negotiations as well as for being pragmatic and innovative. The CUSFTA subsequently became the prototype for launching the North American Free Trade Area (NAFTA).

5. POST-URUGUAY ROUND DEVELOPMENTS IN REGIONALISM

After the completion of the Uruguay Round in 1994, a new generation of RIAs covered Latin America. NAFTA was launched in the same year (see section 6 below). The negotiations for MERCOSUR, as alluded to above, were in the final stages in 1994. An initiative for the most ambitious regional agreement in the region was taken in December 1994 by the Clinton Administration during the Miami Summit. This was called the Free Trade Area of the Americas (FTAA), comprising 34 prospective member countries of North and South America and the Caribbean. Several ministerial meetings have taken place since then (see section 9.4). Formal launch of negotiations took place in 2001. In the Seventh Ministerial Meeting held in November 2002 in Quito, Ecuador, members decided that FTAA should enter into force by December 2005.

This scenario highlights the recent dynamism in regional integration activities in Latin America. Economies and RIAs in this region also participated in extra-regional trading blocs. The Asia Pacific Economic Co-operation (APEC) forum is a good illustration. Mexico became an APEC member in 1993 and Chile the next year. Peru had to wait until 1998 because APEC had declared a three-year moratorium on membership. The APEC announced its so-called Bogor initiative in 1994, the year FTAA negotiations began.[12] According to this initiative, the 21 members of APEC agreed 'to free and open trade and investment in Asia-Pacific' by 2010 for the industrialized economy members and 2020 for the developing members. The other extra-regional trading block that has attracted the attention of the Latin American economies and RIAs was the European Union (EU). At the end of 1995, the EU signed an economic co-operation agreement with MERCOSUR, while a Framework Co-operation Agreement with Chile followed shortly after, in June 1996. The most noteworthy agreement in this regard is the free trade one that Mexico signed with the EU in 1999. It is far-reaching in its significance, and covers economic and political cooperation between the two. In April 2000, the EU, MERCOSUR and Chile launched negotiations for Association Agreement (Estevadeordal, 2002).[13]

For the purpose of preferentially reducing tariff barriers, the older method in Latin America was to negotiate and fix tariffs below the MFN rates. This was normally done only for select sectors and product lines. However, in the 1990s, most RTAs, including the bilateral agreements, followed the NAFTA pattern of preferential tariff reduction. This pattern encourages tariff phase-out programs that were swifter than any in the past and had almost universal product coverage. Each program followed a pre-specified timetable, according to which some tariffs were eliminated right away, while other were dismantled over a period of ten years. For sensitive product lines, ad hoc time lengths were negotiated, while some products or sectors were kept outside the liberalization program. The negotiations generally began with taking the base tariff rates into account, which were usually the MFN tariff rates. The phase-out negotiations and planning began from this.[14]

As set out in section 1, both trade in general and intra-regional trade expanded significantly in the 1990s, but the early 2000s were not so buoyant in this regard. In 2001 and 2002, total exports from Latin America fell. In 2002, they declined by 3 percent. Stagnation in global economic growth in 2001 and 2002 adversely affected Latin American exports. Import demand in the EU, Japan and the US was depressed. Intra-regional trade declined in 2001 and 2002 in the region, it fell sharply by 12 percent in 2002. This was the end of a decade-long trend in which it had grown at more than twice the rate of exports to the extra-regional markets. As regards the sub-regions, during 2002, the sharpest decline in trade was recorded in the MERCOSUR economies. Intra-MERCOSUR exports accounted for only 11 percent of total exports, down from 20 percent in 2000. Intra-Andean Community trade grew by 2 percent in 2002, with 12 percent of the trade being intra-Andean Community in 2002. Intra-CACM trade grew by only 1 percent in 2002, following a growth of 12 percent in 2001 (IDB, 2002a).

6.   NAFTA MADE HISTORY

NAFTA was not only innovative but also historic from several perspectives. The CUSFTA which was regarded as highly imaginative and innovative, was the prototype used for crafting the NAFTA accord. Five years to the day after the CUSFTA was implemented, an expanded free trade area was created with the implementation of NAFTA, which included Mexico. It came into effect on 1 January 1994 and created the largest FTA in the world, covering at the time, some 360 million people and nearly $500 billion in yearly trade and investment. NAFTA maintained the tariff elimination schedule established by the CUSFTA for the bilateral trade between Canada and the United States. Both countries negotiated separate bilateral schedules with Mexico for the elimination of tariffs. However, the three member countries agreed to abolish tariffs and non-tariff barriers completely by 2009. NAFTA had an enormous demonstration effect in Latin America. In fact, it is said to have had a 'domino effect'.

NAFTA set out rules in areas such as investment, services, intellectual property, government procurement, competition policy and temporary entry of business persons. To promote the effective enforcement of each country's labor and environmental laws and regulations, separate agreements were negotiated. The North American Agreement on Labor Cooperation was designed to facilitate greater co-operation between Canada, the United States and Mexico in this area.

The North American Agreement on Environmental Cooperation allows each party to choose the level of environmental protection it considers appropriate. It makes clear that each country may adopt standards more stringent than international standards, but prohibits the lowering of environmental standards to attract investment.

NAFTA was considered historic because for the first time a developing economy was joining hands with two matured and industrialized economic partners. It was the first such reciprocal agreement. Until this point, Mexico was a beneficiary of the Generalized System of Preferences of Canada and the US. As it became a NAFTA partner, its obligations became the same as those of the two industrialized economies. The launching of NAFTA is widely considered a watershed in the economic relations between Canada and the US on the one hand and Latin America and the Caribbean on the other (Ocampo, 2003). It not only set a new precedent but also gave a boost to the debates on the creation of a hemispheric FTA.

After 1994, NAFTA became a prototype for the other agreements in the Americas. Many of the agreements in Latin America that flatteringly imitated it, followed a similar or the same structure and scope as well as treating asymmetries in the identical manner to NAFTA. For instance, the Chile–Mexico and Chile–Canada agreements were based exactly on the innovative NAFTA model, as were the new bilateral FTAs between Chile and Mexico on the one side and countries throughout Latin America on the other. These FTAs began in the traditional manner, emphasizing the market-access-in-trade-in-goods approach, but increasingly acquiring NAFTA-like characteristics. After the launching of NAFTA, many sub-regional accords began to pursue a deep integration strategy involving larger commitments in terms of loss of commercial sovereignty than one finds in a common or garden variety of FTA.

During the latter half of the 1990s, two economies became the trade hub of the hemisphere by signing numerous FTAs. Estevadeordal (2002) has provided complete lists and details of these agreements. One, Mexico, was the first country to finalize three NAFTA-like agreements bilaterally with Colombia, Costa Rica, and Venezuela in 1994. The Group-of-Three (or G-3) Agreement was signed under the Enabling Clause of the GATT between Colombia, Mexico, and Venezuela. Another agreement on the NAFTA model was signed by Mexico with Bolivia. All these agreements came into force in early 1995. Mexico did not lose this momentum and persisted in its endeavors to negotiate similar free trade agreements with Nicaragua in 1997 and the Northern Triangle countries in 2000. It had earlier concluded a free trade agreement with Chile, in 1991, which was upgraded and deepened in 1998 and made into a NAFTA-style agreement.

Chile was another Latin American economy which acquired a reputation for building up strong trade and economic ties with other regional economies on a bilateral basis. Its free trade agreement with Mexico was wide in scope and coverage, and was further upgraded and deepened. It went on negotiating similar agreements with Venezuela (1992), Colombia (1993), and Ecuador (1994). Chile's 1996 agreement with MERCOSUR was deeper and wider in scope and of a more sophisticated variety than the ones negotiated thus far. The same observation can be made about Chile's 1998 free trade agreement with Peru. The most significant and broadest expansion in the free trade agreements signed by Chile took place when it finalized a NAFTA-like agreement with Canada. Chile's 1999 accord with the countries of the Central American Common Market was also based on the NAFTA model. In 2002, Chile started negotiating a NAFTA-like accord with the US. When concluded, it will add to the ever-growing list of North–South free trade agreements in the Latin American region. When these new agreements were being launched, some of the older accords like the AC and CACM were busy carrying out gradual institutional and policy reforms.

The EU–Mexico accord of 1999, noted in section 5, was also based on the NAFTA model. The influence exerted by NAFTA was still strong in 2001 when MERCOSUR was negotiating to create an FTA with the AC. Extending this FTA across the Atlantic to the EU was also on the cards. Also in 2001, Chile was negotiating an FTA with South Korea, and the EU and Costa Rica had completed an FTA with Canada. Negotiations for the large FTAA were progressing and were at an advanced stage for completion and launch in 2005. These negotiations were also benefiting from the much-admired NAFTA prototype.

7. NEW REGIONALISM IN LATIN AMERICA

With the adoption of broad-based structural reforms and trade liberalization in the latter half of the 1980s and 1990s, 'new regionalism' was adopted by the regional economies. It has been noted in section 4 that a three-tier liberalization strategy was pursued, which entailed unilateral, multilateral and regional integration. The liberalization and structural reform strategy linked to the new regionalism was reflected in unilateral slashing of tariff barriers, which were drastically reduced between 1985 and 2000, when they were less than 12 percent on average. The average maximum tariffs in Latin America declined from more than 80 percent in the mid-1980s to 40 percent in 2000, with only two economies applying maximum tariffs of up to 100 percent on a small number of product lines. Tariff dispersion also declined, from 30 percent to 9 percent over this period. The highest average rate of tariffs and highest dispersion rate, as measured by the standard deviation, were 15 percent in 2000. However, to avoid creating an erroneous impression, it must also be indicated that there were still several tariff peaks or 'spikes' in the regional economies. Approximately 22 percent of tariff lines were subject to rates above 20 percent.[15]

As for multilateral liberalization, the regional economies were enthusiastic participants in the last GATT round of multilateral trade negotiations, the Uruguay Round (1986–94). Under their commitments to the GATT, the Latin American economies not only dismantled tariff barriers but also made the new levels of market access legally binding. According to the new trade discipline, all the participating economies were required to bind tariffs to a specified maximum. One of the many achievements of the Uruguay Round was the substantial increase in binding of tariffs by the developing economies. They increased from 22 percent before the round to 72 percent after the round. For the economies in transition, this proportion increased from 78 percent to 98 percent.

Thus, regional integration underpinned continued momentum in the domestic liberalization process. The fiscal implications of domestic liberalization were not high because of a history of autarky in Latin America and low absolute levels of trade among the regional economies. Political resistance to liberalization and regional integration was also not entrenched. The reason was that increasing imports generally worked in tandem with rising exports. Therefore, policy makers in Latin America continued to use regional integration as an effective policy instrument for deepening the liberalization. Regional integration-based regulations and peer pressure were conducive to 'locking in' or anchoring liberalization commitments, which under a unilateral policy would be reversible without any difficulty. Many Latin American economies were forced to reverse some their liberal policies during the 1990s and early 2000s when several of them suffered either from a crisis or the contagion effect. Under severe fiscal or balance-of-payments shocks many economies had to raise tariff walls, and revert to protectionism (Devlin and Estevadeordal, 2001).

Adoption of new regionalism also led to rejection of the old 'dependencia' doctrine, with which the Latin America economies were associated in the past. Consequently, they began to attract FDI instead of obstructing it. The old FDI phobia has turned into current appreciation of FDI, recognition of its contribution to the enhancement of competitiveness of domestic industrial sectors, and its benefits in accessing export markets. In a globalizing world economy, there has been an intense competition for global capital among the developing and emerging-market economies. A small number of emerging-market economies have become highly successful at attracting FDI.[16] Creation of regional blocs like MERCOSUR is being deployed as a way of distinguishing economies from competitors for the purpose of attracting FDI. In addition, the new regionalism provided support to trade and investment activities, which in turn is transforming productive sectors in the Latin America economies. There has not only been a strong growth in extra-regional exports, but also product mix has become more diversified than before. The strategy of new regionalism has also indirectly contributed to greater investment in, and production of, differentiated, knowledge-based manufactured goods and expansion of scale economies through increase in intra-regional trade.

The new regionalism-related strategies, coupled with the adoption of market-friendly outward-oriented strategies, enabled Latin America to be better integrated with the global economy and a more active participant in the global fora. Enhanced regional integration has allowed these economies to cooperate and become more effective global players. During the ongoing negotiations for the FTAA, MERCOSUR, the AC and CARICOM all participated as sub-regional blocs, which gave them more clout than if each country had participated individually.

Although unilateral liberalization and the Uruguay Round coalesced to eliminate or slash most of the tariff lines, regional trade is still obstructed and distorted by non-tariff barriers (NTBs) like onerous customs procedures, technical barriers to trade, and trade-related surcharges. Besides, there is evidence of stringent interpretations of the ROO obstructing regional trade flows. Insufficient harmonization or lack of mutual recognition of regulatory frameworks have also restricted full exploitation of the opportunities for the expansion of regional trade. The economic payoff from effectively addressing these issues would indeed be high and would substantially reinforce the returns to tariff liberalization. However, the political economy of dismantling these obstacles is complex, and progress has so far been unimpressive.

New regionalism failed to resolve some of the age-old problems related to regional integration in Latin America. The case in point is the four sub-regional groups (AC, CARICOM, CACM and MERCOSUR), which had formally declared their objective of creating common markets or economic unions. Formation of a customs union (CU) is a necessary first step in this direction, but to the present time none of the four sub-regional groups has come close to being a CU. They have all agreed to the concept of common external tariffs (CETs) but either they are being developed (CACM and CARICOM), or reformulated (AC), or in the case where they have been developed, CETs have serious unilateral gaps and loopholes (MERCOSUR). Historically, economies in Latin America have had a lot of problems with CETs. The new regionalism has not succeeded in bringing about much improvement in the old malaise. The four sub-regional groupings were also permissive regarding individual members striking out on their own to enter into bilateral deals with non-members, creating complexities and problems in the original RIA. Also, none of the sub-regional groupings has a formula or institutional structure for sharing tariff revenues. The imperfect status of the region's customs unions has created precisely the type of costs that an RIA is supposed to eliminate.

One noteworthy common characteristic regarding the scope and depth of regional integration in Latin America is that so far it has not succeeded in liberalization in areas beyond trade in goods. In their articles of agreements, most RIAs were traditionally confined to goods-only trade liberalization. After the adoption of the NAFTA model, many of them assumed second-generation disciplines with their accords extending to trade in services, intellectual property, and investment, but often have done so with only modest depth or content. To be sure, the most advanced in this regard is NAFTA, under which Mexico's trade liberalization has been comprehensive. Greater progress in following the NAFTA paradigm is likely to lead to wider adoption of second-generation discipline in the future.

8. TRADE CREATION AND ECONOMIC TRANSFORMATION

Indubitably some trade diversion is inherent in any regional integration initiative. What matters in this regard is the net effect. Empirical evidence is available to show that on balance the new wave of regional integration in Latin America has created trade (IDB, 2002b). Trade diversion has been contained in most cases due to regional integration endeavors working in tandem with substantial trade liberalization for the non-member economies – which is part of the so-called 'open regionalism' strategy. It should also be pointed out that not all trade diversion reduces welfare, as in the case when it improves the terms of trade or dynamically evolves into increased international competitiveness.

The other measure of the success of an RIA is the growth of regional trade. As set out above, the majority of RIAs have effectively promoted and reinforced unilateral liberalization, which in turn has allowed neighboring markets to discover each other, particularly in the four sub-regional country groupings (AC, CARICOM, CACM and MERCOSUR). Regional agreements and the awareness they created in the private sector of the member economies have also sparked significant trade growth between distant and hitherto unfamiliar markets. The Chile–Mexico free trade area is an excellent illustration of this kind of awareness and trade expansion.

As regards the present commodity component of intra-regional trade, it is skewed markedly towards higher value-added manufactures vis-à-vis extra-regional trade. In the last two decades it has demonstrated a significant increase in specialization through intra-industry exchange. One can rationally conclude that intra-regional trade is contributing to export diversification in a region. Its traditional focus was on commodity exports. Mexico's participation in NAFTA is again a good example, demonstrating that Mexico's export structure has evolved from petroleum to machinery. This was a direct consequence of the gradual integration of Mexican firms into the production network of North American firms.

The microeconomic effect of creation and expansion of regional markets is increased productivity at the level of firms. The regional agreements also have a significant dynamic effect on overall economic activity like inducing competition and augmenting investment, and thereby raising the level of total factor productivity in the system. Empirical estimates suggest that NAFTA has had significant productivity effects in Mexico (IDB, 2002b). As Mexico integrated with two major industrialized partners with different comparative advantages, it allowed Mexico greater gains from trade, relatively more access to FDI, an opportunity for adopting best corporate governance and financial practices, and access to two large and affluent markets. All these benefits were magnified by geographical proximity. Similar empirical research on Brazil suggested that productivity gains were more associated with unilateral liberalization than with creation of MERCOSUR per se (IDB, 2003). This is not surprising, as Brazil is by far the largest economy in MERCOSUR, and regional trade and investment are a relatively small share of that country's total output.

An age-old complaint of the developing economies, including those of Latin America, is that although the eight rounds of multilateral trade negotiation (MTNs) under the aegis of the GATT had a great deal of success to their credit, large industrial economies, which also are the largest traders, have not allowed multilateral liberalization of trade in sectors that are sensitive to competition from developing economies. These sectors are agriculture, processed foods, textiles and apparel, and steel. Although the Uruguay Round Agreement in Agriculture (AA) did promise multilateral liberalization, so far there is little progress in this regard. The same applies to steel in which Argentina, Brazil and some other Latin American countries have discernible comparative advantage. Similarly, the Agreement on Textiles and Clothing (ATC) of the GATT-1994 was aimed at integrating the textiles sector in the mainstream of WTO discipline by 2005. Although phased integration has been going on since 1995, it has not progressed as was envisaged by the authors of the ATC. Countries in Latin America have comparative advantage in these trade sectors. As international trade has to face high levels of protection in these sectors, RIAs can and have served as an instrument of geographically limited trade liberalization in these important sectors of trade.

In addition, owing to distortionary obstacles like tariff peaks, technical barriers to trade and sanitary and phytosanitary measures, export subsidies and domestic agricultural support in the industrialized countries, Latin American economies have failed to exploit their comparative advantage in agricultural products. It is hoped that the ongoing round of MTNs under the WTO, the so-called Doha Round, would work towards liberalizing world markets in agriculture and other areas of exports where these economies have comparative advantage. Also, it is hoped that contingency protection measures that are often applied in several sectors of great interest for the Latin American economies to penalize successful exporters, would be contained by the negotiations during the Doha Round (IDB, 2003). Until the MTNs address and successfully resolve these contentious issues, they need to be addressed and resolved at the level of the RIAs.

As noted in section 7, traditionally, trade in services was not covered by RIAs in Latin America, the NAFTA being the only exception to this generalization. Many of the new RTAs that followed the NAFTA model also included trade in services in their articles of agreement, but in a limited manner. A large part of the liberalization in the services sector took place either unilaterally or multilaterally. For instance, the financial sector has largely liberalized multilaterally, as Latin American economies accepted the provisions of the General Agreement in Trade in Services (GATS). Banks from the industrial economies now have a significant presence in most domestic financial markets in Latin America economies (Das, 2003b). They have become a major source of competition for the domestic banking sectors. Foreign banks are also inducing modernization of the domestic banking services in these economies. For operating at the regional or even sub-regional levels, domestic financial providers would need to adopt financial practices and protocols that exceed what is required by the GATS (IDB, 2003).

9. FORMAL REGIONAL TRADE NETWORK: PRESENT STATUS

At the beginning of the twenty-first century, the principal concerns of an RIA are integration and market access, strengthening institutional arrangements, development of regional infrastructure, financial integration, and macro-economic and exchange rate coordination. Regional and sub-regional policy makers are also focusing on issues like productivity, FDI, regional disparity and income inequality. The other issues of immediate attention for policy makers are the configuration of sub-regional integration initiatives, the ongoing Doha Round, and North-South initiatives such as the FTAA and interregional agreements with the EU.

The FTAA is looming large over the horizon as well as over all the current RIAs. One intriguing question in this background is how countries will manage the articulation of their FTAA negotiations with their strategically important sub-regional objectives, negotiations with the EU, and the Doha Round negotiations in Geneva, which are scheduled to be completed in January 2005. Second, Latin America presently has a complex network of RIAs. Among the myriad of existing agreements, which ones would have sufficient economic and political relevance to coexist with the FTAA is another debatable point. Third, it is open to question how regional economies would mobilize the capacity and technical skills to effectively participate simultaneously in so many strategically important negotiations and implement their results. All these are questions of monumental proportion for the Latin American economies, because the results of negotiation on all these fronts would effectively regulate the bulk of intra-and extra-regional trade and investment in the short and medium term.

In what follows, I focus on some of the large RIAs, which have a long history in Latin America as well some of the young and inchoate ones. Given the significance of FTAA in the foreseeable future, it is appropriate to present its salient features and details regarding progress in the negotiations so far.

9.1 Andean Community

The Cartagena Agreement was signed in 1969 between the Andean Group of countries and the signatories embarked upon forming a FTA. The program for bringing down tariffs between members was a complicated one. It had different time limits and forms of tariff reductions for different products. Consequently, the progress in trade liberalization remained tardy and inadequate. In 1989, a simplification and streamlining of the tariff reduction program was attempted. This provided for equal participation in tariff slashing from all the members. The new program also provided for the elimination of all other barriers to trade and had high-level political commitment. It was reflected in the pace of implementation, which quickened – Bolivia, Colombia and Venezuela completed their market liberalization for the FTA partners by September 1992 and Ecuador by January 1993. That is when the FTA was officially launched. Each one of these economies maintained their own tariff rates for the rest of the world. As stated in section 4, in December 1996, the name of the Andean Group (AG) was changed to the Andean Community (AC). The 1998 Protocol of Quito called for amendments to the AG's founding treaty. Its institutional structure was also revised in 1998.

Peru reached an agreement with the other members of the Andean FTA in

July 1997 and began liberalizing its trade with the partner economies. The members approved its tariff liberalization schedule in August. The liberalization process was assigned the time limit of 2005. In 1999, this schedule was revised and readjusted and some product groups were prioritized for zero tariffs beginning in 1999. A unique feature of this FTA was that tariffs were removed from all the tradable products in the tariff universe. The list of exceptions, a normal feature of FTAs, did not exist for the Andean FTA. The creation of this FTA was not an end in itself. Since its inception, policy makers knew that it is a means to their future goals of creating a customs union (CU) and further economic integration resulting in a common market.

In the Santa Cruz Declaration of January 2002, the presidents of the Andean Community countries declared their intention to apply common external tariffs (CETs) by December 2003, turning the AC into a CU. In April 2003, the Andean countries reached the final agreement on the adoption of CETs. Bolivia, Colombia, Ecuador and Venezuela signed the agreement, but Peru has not. The AC has set a target for itself to form a common market by 2005.

For harmonizing and streamlining trade procedures and thereby reducing the transaction costs, the AC devised the Common Classification of the Andean Community Member Countries (NANDINA in Spanish). This was to be used for classifying and coding tradable items and is essentially based on the international classification called the Harmonized System, which in turn was devised by the World Customs Organization (WCO). NANDINA has also taken into account the latest text of the Harmonized System introduced by the third amendment of the recommendations of the WCO, which entered into force on 1 January 2002. The AC countries harmonized their customs valuation system so that custom duties can be applied uniformly without introducing distortions in the AC trade.

The AC has its own provisions for determining the rules of origin (ROO) of the traded goods in the sub-region. These provisions specify the conditions products must meet to be considered sub-regional and be eligible for being treated as intra-Andean trade, and benefit from the larger market. For over two decades, trade among the AC countries was governed by the old organization, LAFTA. The ROO for the AC were initially based on those for LAFTA, and were approved in 1987, but subsequently revised in 1991. Rapid advances in sub-regional trade as well as integration and formation of the CU made it necessary to update the ROO and establish more precise criteria of origin. The members felt that the ROO needed to be clarified and the procedure to determine them needed to be simplified. The Andean Community Commission (ACC) undertook this exercise in 1997. Following the current practices regarding the ROO, definitions and criteria of various products were laid down afresh and in a more precise manner than in the past.

9.2   Association of Caribbean States

In a region that has a long history of regional integration endeavors, the Association of Caribbean States (ACS) was a relatively novel endeavor. Building upon their geographical proximities and historical linkages, 25 countries of the Caribbean sub-region tried to join together in an economic, cultural and socially cohesive group in 1992. One of their priorities was to forge an effective and timely response to the challenges and opportunities presented by globalization and progressive liberalization of hemispheric trade relations. In forming the ACS, they were responding to the changes in global and regional economic scenarios. Their first and immediate aim was to strengthen sub-regional cooperation and integration so that an 'enhanced economic space' could be created, which in turn could contribute to more competitive participation of the Caribbean region in the regional and international marketplaces.

The second major objective was to facilitate active and cocoordinated participation by the Caribbean region in various multilateral fora. As individually these Caribbean states are small, it was hoped that together they could make their presence felt on the global stage. Adoption of common positions in the multilateral fora was an important objective behind the establishment of the ACS and was clearly laid down in its Preamble. The decision to establish the ACS was taken at the Conference of Heads of Government of the Caribbean Community at its Special Meeting in Port of Spain, Trinidad and Tobago, in October 1992. The Convention Establishing the ACS was signed on 24 July 1994 in Cartagena de Indias, Colombia.[17]

A Special Committee on Trade Development and External Economic Relations was set up to foster cooperation and integration by uniting the efforts of ACS member states and associate members to build and consolidate an enhanced economic space for trade and investment in the Greater Caribbean region. Special and differential treatment (SDT) has been an important issue for this group of small island economies. Therefore, the Committee's work included studies on the possible measures that could be taken to implement SDT in an efficacious manner so that the members of the ACS could reap its benefits.

The small ACS economies have a great deal of intra-trade potential. The population of ACS is 242 million, which is almost half of the total population of the Latin American and Caribbean (LAC) region. The size of the combined GDP of ACS is $938 billion, which is again almost half of the total GDP of the LAC region. Trade volume of the ACS accounts for 68 percent of the LAC total, but only 7 percent of the ACS trade is with the other ACS member countries. Therefore, the principle focus of the ACS action plan is cooperation in the areas of trade, transport and sustainable tourism. The member states see the three activities as inextricably linked in the sub-region.

9.3 Caribbean Community and Common Market

As opposed to the ACS, the Caribbean Community and Common Market (CARICOM) has a long history and was the result of a long drawn-out effort towards regional integration. It was born with the establishment of the British West Indies Federation in 1958, which was a Federation of ten Caribbean island states. Plans for forming a CU existed at that time but in reality little emphasis was placed on the economic aspect of the Federation. No movement towards economic integration was made, not even toward forming an FTA. Four years later, in 1962 the Federation collapsed, but that is widely regarded as the real beginning of the CARICOM. Dissolution of the Federation had a shock value and the sub-regional politicians embarked on serious endeavors for sub-regional economic integration.

To this end, the first heads of the government conference took place in 1963, followed by a series of conferences between the leaders of the Commonwealth Caribbean countries as well as heads of government meetings.[18] In July 1965, talks between the premiers of Barbados and British Guiana and the Chief Minister of Antigua on the possible establishment of an FTA in the Caribbean resulted in the announcement of definite plans to establish one. In December 1965, the heads of government of Antigua, Barbados and British Guiana (now Guyana) signed an Agreement at Dickenson Bay, Antigua, to set up the Caribbean Free Trade Association (CARIFTA). As the ultimate objective was cooperation among all the Commonwealth Caribbean territories, the actual launch of the CARIFTA was delayed on purpose in order to allow the rest of the region, Trinidad and Tobago and Jamaica and all the Windward and Leeward islands, to become members of the newly formed FTA.

The Heads of Government Conference in 1967 produced several tangible results. For instance, the Commonwealth Caribbean Regional Secretariat was established in May 1968, in Georgetown, Guyana, and the Caribbean Development Bank was set up in October 1969 in Bridgetown, Barbados. In 1972, the political leadership of twelve Caribbean countries decided to transform CARIFTA into a Common Market and establish the Caribbean Community of which the Common Market was to be an integral part. The next year the decision to establish the Caribbean Community came into fruition. A draft of the legal instruments was prepared for the consideration of the heads of government, which was subsequently signed by 11 members of CARIFTA. The only exceptions in this case were Antigua and Montserrat.

The Georgetown Accord among the then four independent countries:

Barbados, Guyana, Jamaica and Trinidad and Tobago provided for the signature of the Caribbean Community Treaty on 4 July 1973, which came into effect in August 1973. The Georgetown Accord also provided for the membership of the other eight territories, namely, Antigua, British Honduras, Dominica, Grenada, Saint Lucia, Montserrat, St. Kitts and Nevis, Anguilla and St. Vincent. They signed the Accord to become full members of the Caribbean Community by 1 May 1974. The CARICOM was established by the Treaty of Chaguaramas, which was signed by Barbados, Jamaica, Guyana and Trinidad and Tobago and came into effect on 1 August 1973. Subsequently, the other eight Caribbean territories joined CARICOM. The Bahamas became the thirteenth member state of the Caribbean Community in July 1983, and Suriname the fourteenth in July 1995.

Since its inception, CARICOM has concentrated on promoting the integration of the member economies as well as giving impetus to intra-trade. Coordination of foreign policy was also added to its list of priorities. Some of the principal issues currently on the regional agenda include: restructuring of sub-regional organs and institutions as well as analysis of the impact of NAFTA on the existing arrangements such as the Caribbean–Canada Trade Agreement (CARIBCAN) and the Caribbean Basin Initiative (CBI).

The Eighth CARICOM Heads of Government Meeting was held in 1987, when the Prime Minister of Barbados presented the concept establishing a representative institution, which would bring together the people of the sub-region through their chosen representatives, with the express objective of promoting the regional trade and development process. In 1989, at the tenth such conference in Grenada and Barbados, a discussion paper outlining a proposal for a sub-regional institution was circulated. In March 1990, agreement was reached on a draft inter-governmental agreement providing for the establishment of the proposed Institution. Haiti became a member state of the Caribbean Community on 3 July 2002, bringing the membership of CARICOM to 15 island member states.[19]

At the time of writing, CARICOM was trying to strengthen relations with the wider LAC region through the establishment of trade and economic agreements with Venezuela, Colombia, the other Caribbean states, and the ACS and deepening the integration process in the Community through the formation of a single market and economy. The next natural move, in the foreseeable future, for the CARICOM economies would be harmonization of standards and economic policies.

9.4 Free Trade Area of the Americas

The concept to unite the economies of North and South Americas into a single FTA was announced at the Summit of the Americas, which was held in

December 1994, in Miami. The heads of state and government of the 34 democracies in the region agreed to collaborate to form an FTAA, in which barriers to trade and investment would be progressively eliminated, and to complete negotiations for the agreement by 2005.[20] When launched, it would be the largest FTA in the world, with a population of 800 million and GDP of $11 trillion. Although the objective is to form an FTA, this is not essentially an exercise in shallow regionalism. It is intended to be a broad FTA, reflecting a consensus to negotiate a wide and diverse range of issues. Reciprocal commitments in areas like trade in services, intellectual property rights, environmental protection, trade facilitation as well as investment and competition policies, the so-called 'Singapore issues' are a part of the agenda. The Singapore issues have not been part of the multilateral discipline under the WTO. The FTAA also aims at improving the WTO rules and discipline 'whenever possible and appropriate'.

The US government has shown a high degree of political commitment to the concept of the FTAA. US trade with the hemispheric partners was around $800 billion in 2002. This included computers, grain, movies, aircraft, music, software, sports equipment, semiconductors, and cars. Although high tariffs, arbitrary customs and non-transparent port procedures, and a myriad of other barriers impeded this large trade volume, it supported economic growth and created millions of jobs throughout the two continents. By liberalizing trade regimes and streamlining procedures for such a large volume of trade under an FTA, the partner economies can reasonably expect to substantially gain in welfare terms.

The notion of an FTAA was partly inspired by the success of European integration. While integration has had a large impact on European trade and incomes, one might argue that the Americas offer an even greater potential for trade creation and for using integration as a competitive force to drive economic development in Latin America. However, there is a potential snag in this argument. The Americas may well suffer greater economic divergence as a result of integration than did Europe. The reason is that the initial asymmetries in size and income levels in the Americas are much larger than they were in Europe at the time of the signing of the Treaty of Rome.

An ambitious project like the FTAA is an historic opportunity. When it comes into force, it would provide an opportunity for Canadian and US firms to compete in a larger market arena under the discipline provided by an FTA. Conversely, the FTAA would counter the protectionist tendency of firms in Canada and the US in those sectors in which comparative advantage is slipping. Once the FTAA is launched, this production in these sectors may easily move to the emerging-market or developing economies of Latin America. For their part, firms in the Latin American economies are attracted by the improved access to the large US and Canadian markets. For them, this is one of the principal attractions of hemispheric trade liberalization. The relative significance of the US and Canadian markets in terms of each Latin American economy's trade varies widely throughout the region. Even in economies where trade with the US and Canada is relatively less significant, this large market may constitute an important destination for manufactures. Improved market access for these economies may in turn mean an opportunity to diversify their base of exportable products. Furthermore, elimination of barriers in trade in agricultural commodities and removal of subsidies are expected to provide substantial gains to the Latin American exporters. A computable general equilibrium exercise supported this outcome of the FTAA (Monteagudo and Watanaki, 2002). Trade expansion is certain to promote sustainable development and industrialization of the Latin American economies. As the constituent economies of the FTAA include developing, emerging-market and industrial economies at varying levels of per capita incomes, economic development and institutional maturity, economic theory suggests that the possibility of welfare gains in the FTAA would be enormous.

Beyond these plausible traditional benefits, the FTAA would be functional in attracting FDI to the emerging-market and developing Latin American economies. This may be particularly beneficial to smaller economies willing to participate actively in international outsourcing. In addition, the FTAA may go a long way in disciplining the use of contingency protection measures, like countervailing (CV) duties and anti-dumping measures (ADMs) in the Americas, which creates unjust trade barriers and distortions. These barriers have affected important export sectors in the region, namely, Argentine and Brazilian steel, flowers from Colombia, grapes and salmon from Chile and crude oil and steel from Venezuela – this list is far from exhaustive.

As the FTAA would have a large number of member countries at varying levels of income and growth, asymmetry can logically became an onerous problem. Therefore, the NAFTA approach was adopted to address this issue, which included transitional measures that allow for differential treatment of constituent member economies. These measures were developed after long-drawn out negotiations with Mexico. A flexible approach was being taken and specific transitory and negotiated provisions were being made to address the issue of asymmetry in the FTAA. The alternative course could be to give members exemptions from general rules and disciplines, which was eschewed. A flexible view of the rules of origin and varying schedule of tariff elimination were part of the strategy to deal with the existing asymmetry in the Americas (Lopez-Cordova, 2001).

For the purpose of launching the FTAA, four ministerial meetings took place during the preparatory phase in which all the 34 ministers responsible for trade participated. At their fourth meeting in San José, Costa Rica, in March 1998, ministers recommended to their heads of state and government, the initiation of negotiations for determining the structure, general principles and objectives to guide the negotiations to create the FTAA. On the basis of the San José Declaration, the negotiations were formally launched in April 1998, at the Second Summit of the Americas in Santiago, Chile. The leaders agreed that the FTAA negotiating process be transparent and take into account the differences in the levels of development and size of the economies in the Americas, in order to facilitate full participation by all countries.

The fifth Ministerial meeting – the first since negotiations were formally initiated – took place in Toronto in November 1999. At this meeting, ministers instructed the negotiating groups to prepare a draft text of their respective chapters, to be presented at the sixth ministerial meeting in Buenos Aires in April 2001. Groups responsible for market access issues were directed to discuss the modalities and procedures for negotiations in their respective areas. Ministers also approved several business facilitation measures, designed to facilitate commercial exchange in Latin America, particularly in the area of customs procedures.

At the sixth ministerial meeting, held in Buenos Aires, and at the Third Summit of the Americas held in Quebec City in April 2001, a number of key decisions were made regarding the FTAA negotiations. Ministers received a draft text of the FTAA Agreement from the negotiating groups. In an unprecedented move designed to increase the transparency of the process, the ministers recommended to their heads of state and government to make this text publicly available. The draft FTAA agreement was made available to the public in all four official languages on 3 July 2001. Ministers also highlighted the need to foster dialogue with civil society, and the summaries of the second round of civil society submissions in response to the open invitation were agreed to be placed on the FTAA website. Ministers reiterated the importance of the provision of technical assistance to smaller economies to facilitate full participation by all member countries in the FTAA. Deadlines were fixed for the conclusion and implementation of the FTAA Agreement. Negotiations are to be concluded no later than January 2005. Entry into force will be sought as soon as possible thereafter, but no later than December 2005.

As instructed by the ministers responsible for trade, recommendations on methods and modalities for negotiations were submitted by 1 April 2002, and market access negotiations were initiated on 15 May 2002. Principles and guidelines for these negotiations are set out in the *Document on Methods and Modalities for Negotiations*. A second version of the draft FTAA Agreement was prepared during this third negotiating phase, which ended in October 2002 at the Seventh Ministerial Meeting, in Ecuador.

A number of agreed principles guide the FTAA negotiations. These include, among others: (1) that decisions will be taken by consensus; (2) that negotiations will be conducted in a transparent manner; (3) that the FTAA will

Regionalism in global trade

be consistent with WTO rules and discipline, and should improve upon these rules and discipline wherever possible and appropriate; (4) the FTAA will be a single undertaking (it is known as the 'nothing is agreed until all is agreed' principle); (5) the FTAA can coexist with bilateral and sub-regional agreements and countries may negotiate and accept the obligations of the FTAA individually or as members of a sub-regional integration group; and (6) especial attention will be given to the needs of the smaller economies.

As regards the structure and organization of the negotiations, they were also carried out under an agreed structure that was member-driven and ensured broad geographical participation. The chairmanship of the entire process, the site of the negotiations themselves, as well as the chairs and vice-chairs of the various negotiating groups and other committees and groups, all rotate among participating countries. Chairmanship of the negotiations rotates every 18 months, or at the conclusion of each ministerial meeting. The following countries have been designated to serve as chair of the FTAA process for successive periods: Canada; Argentina; Ecuador; as well as Brazil and the United States (jointly).

The ministers responsible for trade exercise the ultimate oversight and management of the negotiations. They meet every 18 months and, since the negotiations were launched, do so in the country which is holding the FTAA chairmanship. The vice ministers responsible for trade, who act as members of the Trade Negotiations Committee (TNC), have a central role in managing the FTAA negotiations. The TNC guides the work of the negotiating groups and other committees and groups and decides on the overall architecture of the agreement and institutional issues. The TNC is also responsible for ensuring the full participation of all the countries in the FTAA process and ensuring transparency in the negotiations. The TNC also oversees the administrative secretariat and implementation of business facilitation measures. The Committee meets as required and no less than twice a year at rotating sites throughout the hemisphere.

Nine FTAA negotiating groups, which have specific mandates from the ministers and the TNC, are responsible for negotiating text in their subject areas. They were established for market access; investment; services; government procurement; dispute settlement; agriculture; intellectual property rights; subsidies, antidumping and countervailing duties; and competition policy. The negotiating groups meet regularly throughout the year.

Three committees and groups address horizontal issues related to the negotiations. A Consultative Group on Smaller Economies follows the progress in the negotiations with a regard to the concerns and interests of the smaller economies and makes recommendations to the TNC. The group has sought to determine the needs of smaller economies for trade-related technical assistance in their participation in the FTAA and to disseminate information about sources of such technical assistance. These databases have been made available through the FTAA website homepage. In addition to these databases, the Tripartite Committee manages the Trade Education Database, which is 'an inventory of training opportunities available in FTAA-relevant areas of trade policy and negotiation for both government officials and the private sector in the region in order to facilitate access to technical assistance' as mandated by ministers at the Toronto ministerial meeting.

As transparency in negotiations has remained a great concern, Ministers created the Committee of Government Representatives on the Participation of Civil Society, with an objective of broadening public understanding, participation and support for the FTAA. The purpose of this committee is to facilitate the input of the business community, labor, environmental, academic groups, and others who wish to present their views on the issues under negotiation and on trade matters in a constructive manner. The FTAA is the first major trade negotiation where such a group has been established at the outset of the negotiations.

A unique feature of the FTAA negotiations is the involvement of civil society in the planning process. During the first phase of negotiations, the FTAA Committee of Government Representatives on the Participation of Civil Society issued its initial 'Open Invitation to Civil Society'. This called on the interested parties to share their views on the FTAA formulation process in a constructive manner. The submissions were studied by the Committee of Government Representatives on the Participation of Civil Society, who forwarded executive summaries of these positions to ministers, and prepared a report outlining the range of views received in response to the open invitation. At the Toronto ministerial meeting, ministers received this report and requested that the committee 'obtain ongoing input from Civil Society on trade matters relevant to the FTAA'. A second open invitation was issued after the Toronto ministerial meeting, and the committee was again asked to summarize the range of views and forward this to the ministers. The committee's second report, including the executive summaries of the submissions received by civil society groups, was made publicly available on the FTAA website after the Buenos Aires ministerial meeting, at which the Ministers urged 'civil society to continue to make its contributions in a constructive manner on trade-related issues of relevance to the FTAA'. The Open Invitation to Civil Society was again extended permanently.

Another unique feature of the FTAA formulation process is the Joint Government–Private Sector Committee of Experts on Electronic Commerce, established to study how to broaden the benefits to be derived from the electronic marketplace in the hemisphere, and how to deal with this cross-cutting issue within the negotiations. An ad hoc group of experts was established to report to the TNC on the implementation of the customs-related business facilitation measures agreed upon in Toronto. These measures, which do not require legislative approval but can be implemented administratively, are designed to facilitate commercial exchange within the Americas, and indeed benefit all traders. The transparency-related measures and initiatives to increase the flow of information about trade and trade-related issues among the countries of the Americas, are disseminated through the FTAA homepage.

The Tripartite Committee, which consists of the Inter-American Development Bank (IDB), the Organization of American States (OAS) and the United Nations Economic Commission for Latin America and the Caribbean (ECLAC) provides analytical, technical and financial support to the process and maintains the official FTAA website.[21] The individual tripartite institutions also provide technical assistance related to FTAA issues, particularly for the smaller economies of the hemisphere.

As regard institutional developments, the FTAA Administrative Secretariat, located at the same site as the meetings of the negotiating groups, provides administrative and logistical support to the negotiations. It keeps the official archives of the negotiations, and provides translation and interpretation services. The secretariat is funded by a combination of local resources and the tripartite committee institutions. Venues of the negotiations has been established on a rotating basis.

An important potential benefit of the FTAA is that it can serve as an anchor for reform and liberalization endeavors for the developing member economies. In addition, it can provide credibility to national and regional commitments and energizes structural change through trade and investment expansion. During the period of economic distress, the industrialized partner provides an umbrella to the developing economy partner. The on-going FTAA negotiations have begun to favorably affect the economic ambience of Latin America. NAFTA provided this type of umbrella to Mexico during the crisis of 1994–95. The FTAA and comprehensive agreements with the EU raise the prospects of other umbrellas of this kind being extended to the other regional economies.

The launch of the EEC is almost half a century old and would, notwithstanding the dissimilarities, have some parallels and lessons for the FTAA. The trade regimes of the members of FTAA are as restrictive now as those of the EEC economies in the late 1950s. Thus, the internal trade liberalization foreseen in the FTAA is probably about the same magnitude as that of the EEC's original members, with many countries having initial tariffs of around 15 percent. The EEC adopted a common external trade policy and integrated internally. It also liberalized its external trade significantly. It is to be seen whether FTAA members would go the same way. Yet EU experiences probably provide an upper limit on the prospects for trade reorientation following the launch of FTAA. Greater compactness and homogeneity of the

EEC contributed to brisk growth of intra-industry trade, which may not be so rapid in the FTAA. Also, the EEC had been more hostile to internal barriers to trade than the FTAA is likely to be. The EEC eliminated the application of contingent protection measures internally and made little use of the ROO for the purpose of obstructing intra-regional trade. It remains to be seen how FTAA handles these issues (Venables and Winter, 2003).

10. CONCLUSIONS AND SUMMARY

Latin American economies have a longer history of regional integration initiatives than any other developing region. RIAs flourished in the early post-war era, but then they lost momentum. During the mid-1980s, this group of economies began liberalizing unilaterally and a resurgence of regionalism followed. It coincided with the global phenomenon of 'new regionalism'. The US strategy in this regard also underwent a radical transformation in the mid-1980s. Growth of globalism and regionalism in Latin America during this period progressed *pari passu* with brisk growth in global trade until the Asian crisis in mid-1997. This was due to a decade-long trend according to which the intra-regional trade grew at almost twice the rate of exports to markets outside the region.

The first group of RIAs in the region was formed in the 1960s, when the Latin American economies had adhered to the ISI strategy for growth. Therefore, the set of policies pursued included economic and industrial planning, creating large public sector enterprises and large-scale government intervention in the markets, so much so that market forces were completely stifled. Policy makers were of the opinion that regional trading blocs fitted well into the ISI regime because that way intra-regional trade barriers could be eliminated while maintaining a high level of external protection. Many of these regional accords were poorly or never implemented.

The 1982 debt crisis was a serious blow to the economies in Latin America with even the larger regional economies being affected in an adverse manner. Trade in the regions including intra-regional imports, suffered a serious contraction in the post-crisis period. Acute recession in the region resulted in the collapse of intra-regional trade. The regional economies, both small and large, were gripped with an economic paralysis. However, the new growth strategy that evolved turned out to be an antithesis of the popular ISI strategy of the past. It was based on liberalization, deregulation, privatization, outward-orientation, correct relative prices, a market-friendly policy ambience.

New initiatives on launching regional trading blocs began to appear in the latter half of the 1980s. The principal driving forces behind the resurgence included the search for additional policy tools to manage insertion into an increasingly globalized and competitive world economy. Various economies and sub-regions in Latin America experienced a quickening of the pace of integration among themselves as well as with the global economy. The measures adopted for liberalization in the area of trade were swift and extensive. Economies became increasingly open, therefore the traded components of output and consumption as a share of GDP rose steadily. Adoption of neo-liberal strategy, ongoing regionalization and globalization has resulted in markedly intensified competition among the Latin American economies and sub-regions over the last two decades. The Latin American economies treated RIA formation as one of the tools for trade policy liberalization. The RIAs represented a third tier of trade policy reform. The old agreements were renegotiated and new ones were initiated. The principal ones among these were LAIA, CACM, MERCOSUR, AC, and CUSFTA. Of these, CUSFTA emerged as a different kind of FTA from the run of the mill FTAs negotiated during this period. It became a pioneer by bringing the 'new issues' into the fold of an FTA.

After the completion of the Uruguay Round in 1994, a new generation of RIAs covered Latin America. NAFTA was launched in the same year. The negotiations for MERCOSUR were in the final stage in 1994 and an initiative for creating the most ambitious RTA, the FTAA, was taken in December 1994, during the Miami Summit. This scenario highlights the recent dynamism in regional integration activities in Latin America. Economies and RIAs in this region also participated in extra-regional trading blocs. Although regional, intra-regional and intra-sub-regional trade recorded impressive growth during the decade of the 1990s, at least until the onset of the Asian crisis, the early 2000s were lackluster in this regard.

Five years after the implementation of CUSFTA, NAFTA was created which was not only innovative but also historic from several perspectives. CUSFTA, which was regarded as highly imaginative and innovative, was the prototype used for crafting the NAFTA accord. NAFTA had an enormous demonstration effect in Latin America. A network of RIAs that came into being in Latin America adopted the NAFTA model. The NAFTA set out rules in areas such as investment, services, intellectual property, government procurement, competition policy and temporary entry of business persons. To promote the effective enforcement of each country's labor and environmental laws and regulations, separate agreements were negotiated.

The Latin American economies have adopted new regionalism, which entailed unilateral, multilateral and regional integration. The liberalization and structural reform strategy linked to the new regionalism were reflected in unilateral slashing of tariff barriers, which were drastically reduced between 1985 and 2000, when they were less than 12 percent on an average. The average maximum tariffs in Latin America declined from more than

80 percent in the mid-1980s to 40 percent in 2000. However, to avoid creating an erroneous impression, it must also be indicated that there were still several tariff peaks or 'spikes' in the regional economies. Approximately 22 percent of tariff lines were subject to rates above 20 percent. The new regionalism-related strategies, coupled with the adoption of market-friendly outward-oriented strategies, enabled Latin America to be better integrated with the global economy and a more active participant in the global fora. However, new regionalism has so far failed to resolve some of the age-old problems related to regional integration in Latin America.

NOTES

1. These twenty-two agreements were: (1) Caribbean Community and Common Market (CARICOM) (1973), (2) Chile–Mexico (1992), (3) Central American Common Market (CACM), (1961), (4) Chile–Venezuela (1993), (5) North American Free Trade Area (NAFTA) (1994), (6) Colombia–Chile (1994), (7) Southern Cone Common Market (MERCOSUR) (1995), (8) Costa Rica–Mexico (1995), (9) Group of Three or G-3 Agreement between Colombia, Mexico and Venezuela (1995), (10) Bolivia–Mexico (1995), (11) Chile–Ecuador (1995), (12) Andean Community (1969), (13) Chile–MERCOSUR (1996), (14) Canada–Chile (1997), (15) Bolivia–MERCOSUR (1997), (16) Mexico–Nicaragua (1998), (17) Chile–Peru (1998), (18) CACM–Dominican Republic (1999), (19) CARICOM–Dominican Republic, (20) Mexico–European Union (2000), (21) CACM–Chile (2001), (22) Mexico–Northern Triangle (2001); source: (IDB, 2002b).
2. CARICOM revised and up-dated its founding treaty in 2001.
3. The Latin American Free Trade Area was launched in 1960 under Article XXIV of the GATT. In 1980 it was revived as Latin American Integration Association under the Enabling Clause. Its membership includes Mexico, Argentina, Bolivia, Brazil, Chile, Colombia, Ecuador, Paraguay, Peru, Uruguay, and Venezuela.
4. The Central American Common Market was launched in 1960, under Article XXIV of the GATT. It was revived in 1993. Its original membership included El Salvador, Guatemala, Honduras, and Nicaragua. In 1962, Costa Rica also became a member.
5. The Andean Pact or Group was launched in 1969 under the Enabling Clause as a customs union. Its membership was Bolivia, Colombia, Ecuador, Peru, and Venezuela.
6. Mexico declared a moratorium on its international obligations in July 1982, precipitating the Latin American debt crisis.
7. The 'statist' strategy implies intervention of the state in a country's economic activity. This strategy held sway during the 1950s and the 1960s. Subsequently, its failure to achieve any of its objectives made it unpopular. Its popularity began wilting away in the 1970s.
8. For a recent discussion of the Washington consensus refer to *Speeches, Testimony, Papers* by John Williamson. This volume was published by the Institute for International Economics, Washington DC, in 2002. Originally the concept of Washington consensus was published as Chapter 2 of *Latin American Adjustment: How Much Has Happened?*, edited by John Williamson. April 1990, by the same publisher.
9. ECLAC (1994) and Ocampo (2003) provide a detailed account of the liberalization of trade policy regime in Latin American economies during this period.
10. The acronym LAIA stands for Latin American Integration Agreement. The former name of LAIA was LAFTA or the Latin American Free Trade Area, which was notified to the GATT in 1960 under the Article XXIV (refer to section 2). This is a case of dual membership. All the members of the Andean Group and MERCOSUR are also the members of LAIA.

11. MERCOSUR stands for Mercado Comun del Sur or Southern Cone Common Market Agreement. The Southern Cone countries of Argentina, Brazil, Paraguay and Uruguay are members of MERCOSUR.

12. It was called the Bogor initiative because it was announced during the Bogor presidential meeting in November 1994. Bogor is an idyllic holiday resort in Java, Indonesia.

13. During the late 1990s and early 2000s several extra-regional agreements were being negotiated. The tally included: (1) MERCOSUR–EU, (2) Chile–EU, (3) Chile–US, (4) Chile–South Korea, (5) CARICOM–EU (post-Lomé-IV) and (6) APEC–Mexico–Japan.

14. Refer to Estevadeordal (2002) and Estevadeordal et al. (2002a) for detailed accounts of regionalism in Latin America during this period.

15. These statistical data were compiled by Devlin and Estevadeordal (2001).

16. Over the last two decades, China has become the most successful country in attracting FDI.

17. The ACS has 25 Member States and three Associate Members. Eight other non-independent Caribbean countries are eligible for associate membership. The members states are: Antigua and Barbuda, Bahamas, Barbados, Belize, Colombia, Costa Rica, Cuba, Dominica, Dominican Republic, El Salvador, Grenada, Guatemala, Guyana, Haiti, Honduras, Jamaica, Mexico, Nicaragua, Panama, St. Lucia, St. Kitts and Nevis, St. Vincent and the Grenadines, Suriname, Trinidad and Tobago, Venezuela.The Associate Members are: Aruba, France (on behalf of French Guiana, Guadeloupe and Martinique) and the Netherlands Antilles.

18. The heads of the government conference in CARICOM is something akin to the meeting of heads of government in the EU, which is known as the European Council, or simply the Council. Most major decisions are taken in the Council, which holds regular bi-annual meetings.

19. The membership comprises: (1) Antigua and Barbuda, (2) Bahamas, (3) Barbados, (4) Belize, (5) Dominica, (6) Grenada, (7) Guyana, (8) Haiti, (9) Jamaica, (10) Montserrat, (11) St. Kitts-Nevis-Anguilla, (12) St. Lucia, (13) St. Vincent and the Grenadines, (14) Suriname, (15) Trinidad and Tobago. Article 3 of the CARICOM Articles of Agreement recognizes the Bahamas, Barbados, Guyana, Jamaica and Trinidad and Tobago as 'More Developed Countries' and all the others as 'Less Developed Countries'.

20. These 34 democracies are: Antigua and Barbuda, Argentina, Bahamas, Barbados, Belize, Bolivia, Brazil, Canada, Chile, Colombia, Costa Rica, Dominica, Dominican Republic, Ecuador, El Salvador, Grenada, Guatemala, Guyana, Haiti, Honduras, Jamaica, Mexico, Montserrat, Nicaragua, Panama, Paraguay, Peru, St. Lucia, St. Kitts and Nevis, St. Vincent and Grenadines, Suriname, Trinidad and Tobago, Uruguay, the United States of America, and Venezuela.

21. The FTAA has a large and informative website, which is one of the sources of information presented here. For greater details readers are referred to http://www.ftaa-alca.org/View_e.asp.

Bibliography

ADB (Asian Development Bank) (2000), *Asian Development Outlook 2000: Update*, Manila, September.

Aitken, N.D. (1973), 'The effects of the EEC and EFTA on European trade: a temporal cross-section analysis', *American Economic Review*, **63** (4), 881–892.

Akamatsu, K. (1961), 'A theory of unbalanced growth in the world economy', *Weltwirtschaftliches Archiv*, **86** (1), 42–76.

Anderson, J.E. (1979), 'A theoretical foundation for the gravity equation', *American Economic Review*, **69**, 106–116.

Anderson, K. (1993), 'European integration in the 1990s: implications for world trade and for Australia', in D.G. Mayes (ed.), *External Implications of European Integration*, London: Harvester Wheatsheaf, pp.120–148.

Anderson, K. (2001), 'Globalization, WTO and ASEAN', *ASEAN Economic Bulletin*, **18** (1), 12–23.

APEC (Asia Pacific Economic Co-operation), Eminent Persons Group (1994), 'Achieving the APEC vision', second report, Singapore: APEC Secretariat, August.

APEC (Asia Pacific Economic Co-operation) (1995a), *Implementation of the Bogor Declaration*, report, Osaka, November.

APEC (Asia Pacific Economic Co-operation) (1995b), *Joint Statement*, Osaka, November. Available on the Internet at http://www.apecsec.org.sg/virtualib/minismtg.mtgmin95.html

APEC (Asia Pacific Economic Co-operation) (1997), *Joint Statement*, Vancouver. November. Available on the Internet at http://www.apecsec.org.sg/virtualib/minismtg.mtgmin97.html

Areddy, J.T. (2000), 'A new agenda for APEC meeting', *Asian Wall Street Journal*, 6 September, p.4.

Arndt, S. (1969), 'Customs union and theory of tariffs', *American Economic Review*, **59** (1), 108–118.

AWSJ (*Asian Wall Street Journal*) (2000), 'Free trade in trouble: Kuala Lumpur wrecks a consensus within ASEAN', Hong Kong, October 12, p.12.

Bagwell, K. and R.W. Staiger (1993a), 'Multilateral tariff cooperation during the formation of free trade areas', NBER Working Paper No. 4363, National Bureau of Economic Research, Cambridge, MA.

Bagwell, K. and R.W. Staiger (1993b), 'Multilateral tariff cooperation during the formation of customs unions', NBER Working Paper No. 4543, National Bureau of Economic Research, Cambridge, MA.

Bagwell, K. and R.W. Staiger (1999), 'An economic theory of the GATT', *American Economic Review*, **89** (1), 215–248.

Bagwell, K. and R.W. Staiger (2000), 'GATT think', NBER Working Paper No. 8005, National Bureau of Economic Research, Cambridge, MA.

Baun, M.J. (1996), *An Imperfect Union: The Maastricht Treaty and the New Politics of European Union*, Boulder, CO: Westview Press.

Bayoumi, T. and B. Eichengreen (1995), 'Is regionalism simply a diversion? Evidence from the evolution of the EC and EFTA', NBER Working Paper No. 5283, National Bureau of Economic Research, Cambridge, MA.

Bayoumi, T. and B. Eichengreen (1997), 'Optimum currency areas and exchange rate variability: theory and evidence', in B. Cohen (ed.), *Research Frontiers in International Economics*, Princeton, NJ: Princeton University Press, pp.143–184.

Bayoumi, T., B. Eichengreen and P. Mauro (2000), 'On regional monetary arrangements for ASEAN', paper presented at the ADB/CEPII/KIEP Conference on Exchange Rate Arrangements in Asia, in Tokyo, 17–18 December 1999. The paper was revised in May 2000.

Beasley, W.G. (1987), *Japanese Imperialism, 1894–1945*, Oxford: Clarendon Press.

Ben-David, D. (1993), 'Equalizing exchange: trade liberalization and income convergence', *Quarterly Journal of Economics*, **108** (3), 859–887.

Bergstrand, J.H. (1985), 'The gravity equation in international trade: some microeconomic foundations and empirical evidence', *Review of Economics and Statistics*, **67**, 474–481.

Bernard, M. and J. Ravenhill (1995), 'Beyond production cycles and flying geese: regionalization, hierarchy, and industrialization of East Asia', *World Politics*, **47**, January, 171–209.

Bhagwati, J.N. (1997), 'The golden age: from skeptical south to fearful north', *World Economy*, **20** (3), 259–284.

Bhagwati, J. N. and A. Panagaria (1996), *The Economics of Preferential Trade Agreements*, Washington, DC: AEI Press.

Bhatia, M. (2000), 'Free trade two-step', *Asian Wall Street Journal*, 14 November, p.7.

Borrus, M., D. Ernst and S. Haggard (eds) (2000), *International Production Networks in Asia*, London and New York: Routledge.

Braga, C., A. Primo, R. Safadi and A. Yeats (1994), 'NAFTA's implications for East Asian exports', Policy Research Working Paper No. 1351, October, World Bank, Washington, DC.

Breuss, F. (2001), 'Macroeconomic effects of EU enlargement for old and new members', WIFO Working Paper No. 143/2001, Vienna: WIFP.

Brown, D., A.V. Deardroff, S. Djankov and R. Stern (1997), 'An economic assessment of Czechoslovakia, Hungary, and Poland into European Union', in S.W. Black (ed.), *Europe's Economy Looks East: Implications for European Union*, Cambridge: Cambridge University Press, pp.160–192.

BIE (Bureau of Industry and Economics) (1995), *Impact of the CER Trade Agreement: Lessons for Regional Economic Co-operation*, report, Canberra, Australian Government Printing Services.

Campa, J.M. and T.L. Sorenson (1996), 'Are trade blocs conducive to free trade?', *Scandinavian Journal of Economics*, **40** (2), 411–437.

Castells, M. (1999), *A Sociedada em Rede*, São Paulo: Paz e Terera.

Cecchini, P. (1998), *1992, The European Challenge: The Benefits of a Single Market*, report, Aldershot: Wildwood House.

Cernat, L. (2001), 'Assessing regional trade agreements: are South-South RTAs more trade diverting?', Study Series No. 16, Geneva: United Nations Conference on Trade and Development.

Chang, W. and L.A. Winters (2000), 'How regional blocs affect excluded countries: the price effects of MERCOSUR', mimeo, World Bank, Washington, DC.

Chen, T. and Y.H. Ku (2000), 'Globalization of Taiwan's small firms: the role of Southeast Asia and China', paper presented in a symposium on Experiences and Challenges of Economic Development in Southeast and East Asia, Taipei, October.

CID (Center for International Development) (2003), 'Regionalism', Cambridge, MA: Harvard University, available on the Internet at http://www.cid.harvard.edu/cidtrade/issues/regionalism.html, accessed January 31.

Coc, D.T. and E. Helpman (1995), 'International R&D spillovers', *European Economic Review*, **107** (2), 134–149.

Coe. D.T., E. Helpman and A. Hoffmaister (1997), 'North–South R&D spillovers', *Economic Review*, **39** (6), 859–887.

Commonwealth Secretariat/World Bank Joint Task Force Report (2002), *Small States: Meeting Challenges in the Global Economy*, London and Washington DC, April.

Conti, S. and P. Graciara (2000), *Local Development and Competitiveness*, Dordrecht: Kluwer Academic Publishers.

Cox, D. and R. Harris (1992), 'North American free trade and its implications for Canada: results from a CGE model of North American trade', *World Economy*, **15** (1), 31–44.

CSFB (Credit Swiss First Boston) (2000), *Emerging Market Quarterly: Asia Q1:2001*, Hong Kong, 15 December.

Das, Dilip K. (1990), *International Trade Policy*, London: Macmillan.

Das, Dilip K. (1993), *The Yen Appreciation and the International Economy*, London: Macmillan.

Das, Dilip K. (1996), *The Asia-Pacific Economy*, London: Macmillan.

Das, Dilip K. (1998a), 'Trade in financial services and the role of the GATS', *Journal of World Trade*, **2** (6), 79–114.

Das, Dilip K. (1998b), 'Changing comparative advantage and changing composition of Asian exports', *World Economy*, **21** (1), January, 121–140.

Das, Dilip K. (2000a), 'Asian exports: the present predicament', in Dilip K. Das (ed.), *Asian Exports*, Oxford: Oxford University Press, pp.1–24.

Das, Dilip K. (2000b), 'An action agenda for the next WTO round: a post-Seattle perspective', *Journal of World Intellectual Property*, **3** (5), September, 7370–773.

Das, Dilip K. (2000c), 'Debacle at Seattle: the way the cookie crumbled', *Journal of World Trade*, **12** (3), 66–97.

Das, Dilip K. (2001), *Global Trading System at Crossroads: A Post-Seattle Perspective*, London and New York: Routledge.

Das, Dilip K. (2002), 'Global trading system: from Seattle to Doha', *International Journal*, **57** (4), Autumn, 605–623.

Das, Dilip K. (2003a), *Financial Globalization and the Emerging Market Economies*, London and New York: Routledge.

Das, Dilip K. (2003b), *Economic Dimensions of Globalization*, London: Palgrave Macmillan.

Dean, J. (1995), 'The trade policy revolution in developing countries', in *The World Economy: Global Trade Policy*, Geneva: World Trade Organization, pp.173–190.

Dean, J., S. Desai and J. Riedel (1994), 'Trade policy reform in developing countries since 1985', Discussion Paper No. 267, World Bank, Washington DC.

Deardroff, A.V. (1997), 'Determinants of bilateral trade: does gravity work in a classical world?', in J.A. Frankel (ed.), *The Regionalization of the World Economy*, Chicago: University of Chicago Press, pp.131–164.

Deardroff, A.V. and R.M. Stern (1994), 'Multilateral trade negotiations and preferential trading arrangements', in A.V. Deardroff and R.M. Stern (eds), *Analytical and Negotiating Issues in the Global Trading System*, Ann Arbor: University of Michigan Press, pp.27–94.

de Jonquieres, G. (2000), 'Asian ambition', *The Financial Times*, 28 November.

de Serres, A., P. Hoeller and C. de la Maisonneuve (2002), 'The width of the intra-European economic border', Economics Department Paper No. 304, Organization for Economic Co-operation and Development, Paris.

De Melo, J. and A. Panagaria (1992), 'The new regionalism in trade policy', London: Center for Economic Policy Research.

Devlin, R. and A. Estevadeordal (2001), 'What is new in the new regionalism in the Americas?', INTAL-ITD-STA Working Paper No. 6, May, Buenos Aires.

Diao, X., T. Roe and A. Somwaru (1999), 'What is the cause of growth in regional trade: trade liberalization or RTAs', Working Paper No. 99–01, Department of Applied Economics, University of Minnesota.

Drucker, P. (1987), *Frontier of Management*, New York: Harper and Row.

EAVG (East Asia Vision Group) (1999), *East Asia Economic Co-operation System*, Singapore: ASEAN Secretariat.

ECLAC (The Economic Commission for Latin America and the Caribbean) (1994), *Globalization and Development*, Santiago, Chile.

ECLAC (The Economic Commission for Latin America and the Caribbean) (2002), *Globalization and Development*, LC/G.2157. SES.29.3, Santiago, Chile.

The Economist (2000a), 'Asian economies: happy neighbors', 26 August, p.71.

The Economist (2000b), 'Towards a tripartite world', 15 July, pp.20–22.

The Economist (2003a), 'Will there ever be a breakthrough?', available on the Internet at http://www.economist.com/agenda/displaystory.cfm?story_id= 1666372, accessed 28 March.

The Economist (2003b), 'On a roll', available on the Internet at http://www.economist.com/agenda/displaystory.cfm?story_id=1872018, accessed 27 June.

EIU (Economic Intelligence Unit) (2003), *Leaping Dragon, Trailing Tigers? Taiwan, Hong Kong and the Challenge of Mainland China*, London: EIU.

EIU (Economist Intelligence Unit) (2003), *Europe Enlarged: Understanding the Impact*, London: EIU.

Estevadeordal, A. (2002), 'Traditional market access issues in RIAs: an unfinished agenda in the Americas?', paper presented at the conference on The Changing Architecture of the Global Trading System, organized by the World Trade Organization, Geneva, 26 April.

Estevadeordal, A., J. Harris and M. Shearer (2002a), 'Towards trade in the Americas', Washington, DC: Inter-American Development Bank.

Estevadeordal, A., J. Goto and R. Saez (2002b), 'The new regionalism in the Americas: the case of MERCOSUR', INTAL-ITD-STA Working Paper No. 5, April, Buenos Aires.

Ethier, W.J. (1997), *Modern International Economics*, New York: W.W. Norton.

Ethier, W.J. (1998a), 'Regionalism in a multilateral world', *Journal of Political Economy*, **106** (6), December, pp.1214–1245.

Ethier, W.J. (1998b), 'The new regionalism', *Economic Journal*, **108** (3), July, 677–694.

Ethier, W.J. (1999), 'Regionalism in a multilateral world', in J. Pigott and A. Woodland (eds), *International Trade Policy and the Pacific Rim*, Basingstoke: Macmillan, pp.130–163.

Evans, D. (1998), 'Options for regional integration in Southern Africa', IDS Working Paper No. 94, Institute of Development Studies, University of Sussex.

Fernandez, R. (1998), 'Returns to regionalism: an evaluation of nontraditional gains from regional trade agreements', *World Bank Economic Review*, **14** (2), 32–58.

Flamm, K. and E. Lincoln (1998), 'Reinvigorating APEC: how the Pacific trade and investment organization can be salvaged', *International Economy*, January–February, 18–24.

Foroutan, F. (1998), 'Does membership in a regional preferential trade arrangement make a country more or less protectionist?', *World Economy*, **21** (3), May, 305–335.

Frankel, J.A. (1991), 'Is a yen bloc forming in Pacific Asia', in R. O'Brien (ed.), *Finance and International Economy*, Volume 5, Oxford: Oxford University Press, pp.88–102.

Frankel, J.A. (1997), *Regional Trading Blocs in the World Economic System*, Washington, DC: Institute for International Economics.

Frankel, J.A. and S.J. Wei (1996), 'ASEAN in a regional perspective', mimeo, International Monetary Fund, Washington, DC.

Frankel, J.A. and S.J. Wei (1997), 'The new regionalism and Asia: impact and options', in N.P. Rao and A. Panagariya (eds), *The Global Trading System and Developing Asia*, Hong Kong: Oxford University Press, pp.83–135.

Frankel, J., E. Stein and S.J. Wei (1994), 'Trading blocs and the Americas: the natural, the unnatural, and the super-natural', Working Paper No. C 94-034, University of California, Berkeley.

Frankel, J., E. Stein and S.J. Wei (1996), 'Regional trading agreements: natural or supernatural', *American Economic Review*, Papers and Proceedings, **86**, 52–56.

Freund, C. (2003), 'Reciprocity in free trade agreement', Working Paper No. 3061, World Bank, Washington, DC.

FT (*Financial Times*) (2000), 'New balance in Asia', 11 October, p.18.

Fujita, N., P. Krugman and A.J. Venables (1999), *The Spatial Economy: Cities, Regions, and International Trade*, Cambridge, MA: MIT Press.

Fukasaku, K. and F. Kimura (2002), 'Globalization and intra-firm trade: further evidence', in P.J. Lloyd and H.H. Lee (eds), *Frontiers of Research in Intra-Industry Trade*, Basingstoke: Palgrave Macmillan, pp.130–162.

Funabashi, Y. (1995), *Asia-Pacific Fusion: Japan's Role in APEC*, Washington DC: Institute for International Economics.

GATT (General Agreement on Tariffs and Trade) (1994), *The Results of the Uruguay Round of Multilateral Trade Negotiations: the Legal Text*, Geneva: GATT.

Gilbert, J., R. Scollay and B. Bora (2001), *Assessing Regional Trading Arrangements in the Asia-Pacific*, Policy Series No. 15, United Nations Conference on Trade and Development, Geneva.

Greenaway, D. and W.O. Morrissey (1993), 'Structural adjustment and liberalization in developing countries: what lessons have we learned?', *Kyklos*, **24** (2), 241–262.

Grether, J.M. and M. Olarreaga (1998), 'Preferential and non-preferential trade flows in world trade', Staff Working paper No. ERAD-98-10, September, World Trade Organization, Geneva.

Gundlach, E., U. Hiemenz, R. Langhammer, P. Langhammer and P. Nunnenkamp (1993), 'Regional integration in Europe and its impact on developing countries', in K. Ohno (ed.), *Regional Integration and Its Impact on Developing Countries*, Tokyo: Institute of Developing Economies, pp.134–158.

Hamilton, C. and J. Whalley (1996), *The World Trading System after the Uruguay Round*, Washington, DC: Institute for International Economics.

Hansen, G. (2001), 'Should countries promote foreign direct investment?', Discussion Paper Series No. 9, United Nations Conference on Trade and Development, G-24, Geneva.

Harris, R. and D. Cox (1986), 'Quantitative assessment of the economic impact on Canada of sectoral free trade with the United States', *Canadian Journal of Economics*, **19** (2), 377–394.

Hertel, T.W., T. Walmsley and K. Itakura (2002), 'Dynamic effects of the "new age" free trade agreement between Japan and Singapore', research report, Global Trade Analysis Project, Perdue University, West Lafayette, IN.

Heydon, K. (2002), 'RIA market access and regulatory provisions', paper presented at the conference on The Changing Architecture of the Global Trading System, organized by the World Trade Organization, Geneva, 26 April.

Hirschman, A.O. (1958), *The Strategy of Economic Growth*, New Haven, CT: Yale University Press.

Hoekman, B.M. and M.M. Kostecki (2001), *The Political Economy of the World Trading System*, Oxford: Oxford University Press.

Hoekman, B.M., M. Schiff and L.A. Winters (1998), 'Regionalism and development: main message from recent World Bank research', mimeo, World Bank, Washington, DC.

Hufbauer, G. (1994), *Latin America Economic Integration*, Washington, DC: Institute for International Economics.

Hufbauer, G. and J. Schott (1994), 'Regionalism in North America', in K. Ohno (ed.), *Regional Integration and Its Impact on Developing Countries*, Tokyo: Institute of Developing Economies.

IDB (Inter-American Development Bank) (2002a), 'Integration and trade in the Americas', Washington, DC. Available on the Internet at http://www.iadb.org.int/itd/, accessed 22 December 2002.

IDB (Inter-American Development Bank) (2002b), *Integration, Trade and Hemispheric Issues*, Washington, DC: IDB.

IDB (Inter-American Development Bank) (2003), *Beyond Borders: The New Regionalism in Latin America*, Washington, DC: IDB.

Ikenberry, J.G. (2000), 'The political economy of Asia-Pacific regionalism', *East Asian Economic Perspective*, March, 35–61.

IMF (International Monetary Fund) (2003), *World Economic Outlook*, Washington, DC: IMF.

JSG (Joint Study Group) (2000a), *Report on Free Trade Agreement between Japan and Singapore*, Ministry of Foreign Affairs, Japan, and Ministry of Foreign Affairs, Singapore.

JSG (Joint Study Group) (2000b), *Japan-Singapore Economic Agreement for a New Age Partnership*, Ministry of Foreign Affairs, Japan, and Ministry of Foreign Affairs, Singapore.

Keller, W. (1998), 'Are international R&D spillovers trade-related? Analyzing spillovers among randomly matched partners', *European Economic Review*, **42** (8), 1469–1481.

KIEP (Korea Institute for International Economic Policy) (2000), 'Economic effects and policy direction for Korea-Japan FTA', Seoul: KIEP.

Kohler, H. (2001), 'Opening remarks at press conference', Tokyo. Japan National Press Club. Available at http://www.imf.org/external/np/speeches/2001/011201.htm, accessed 12 January.

Kojima, K. (1968), *Pacific Trade and Development*, Tokyo: Japan Economic Research Center.

Kose, M. A. and R. Riezman (1999), 'Understanding the welfare implications of preferential trade agreements', CSGR Working Paper No. 45/99, Centre for the Study of Globalization and Regionalization, University of Warwick.

Kose, M. A. and R. Riezman (2000), 'Small countries and preferential trade agreements: how severe is the innocent bystander problem?', CSGR Working Paper No. 48/00, Centre for the Study of Globalization and Regionalization, University of Warwick.

Kreinen, M. (1982), 'Effect of EC enlargement on trade in manufactures', *Kyklos*, **108** (3), 110–138.

Kreinen, M. (1998), 'Multinationalism, regionalism, and their implications for Asia', paper presented at the Conference on Global Interdependence and Asia-Pacific Cooperation, 8–10 June, Hong Kong.

Krueger, A.O. (1996), 'Free trade agreements versus customs union', NBER Working Paper No. 3476, National Bureau of Economic Research, Cambridge, MA.

Krueger, A.O. (1999), 'Trade creation and trade diversion under NAFTA', NBER Working Paper No. w7429, National Bureau of Economic Research, Cambridge, MA.

Krugman, P. (1991a), 'Is bilateralism bad?', in E. Helpman and A. Razin (eds), *International Trade and Trade Policy*, Cambridge, MA: MIT Press, pp.9–24.

Krugman, P. (1991b), 'The move towards free trade zones', in *Policy Implications of Trade and Currency Zones*, Kansas City: Federal Reserve Bank of Kansas, pp.7–41.

Laird, S. (1995), 'Trade liberalization in Latin America', *Minnesota Journal of Global Trade*, **4** (1), 101–127.

Laird, S. (1997), *Mercosur: Objectives and Achievements*, paper presented at the third annual World Bank Conference on Development in Latin America and the Caribbean, Montevideo, September.

Lamy, P. (2002), 'Facing the challenge of globalization: regional integration or multilateral rules', Buenos Aires. Available on the Internet at http://www.europa.eu.int/comm/trade/speeches_articles/spla99_en.htm, accessed 1 March.

Lawrence, R.Z. (1996), 'Regionalism, multilateralism, and deeper integration', research paper, Washington, DC: Brookings Institution.

Lee, H. and D. Roland-Holst (1998), 'Prelude to the Pacific century: overview of the region', in H. Lee and D. Roland-Holst (eds), *Economic Development and Cooperation in the Pacific Basin*, Cambridge: Cambridge University Press, pp.3–36.

Lejour, A.M., R.A. de Mooij and R. Nahuis (2001), 'EU enlargement: economic implications for countries and industries', CESifo Working Paper No. 585, Center for Economic Studies and Institute for Economic Research, Munich.

Lewis, J.D., S. Robinson and K. Theirfelder (1999), 'After the negotiations: assessing the impact of free trade agreements in Southern Africa', TMD Discussion Paper No. 27, International Food Policy Research Institute, Washington, DC.

Linneman, H. (1996), *An Econometric Study of International Trade Flows*, Amsterdam: North-Holland.

Lipsey, R. (1960), 'The theory of customs unions: a general survey', *Economic Journal*, **10** (2), 498–513.

Lloyd, P.J. (1997), 'The future of trans-Tasman closer economic relations', *Agenda*, **2** (3), 267–280.

Lopez-Cordova, J.E. (2001), 'NAFTA and the Mexican economy: analytical issues and the lessons for the FTAA', Occasional Paper No. 9, Institute for the Integration of Latin America and the Caribbean (INTAL), Buenos Aires, November.

Low, L. (2001), 'Rise of regionalism', available on the Internet at http://www.mti.gov.sg/public/infocentre/pdfFiles/Regionalism.pdf, accessed 15 February 2001.

Machlup, F. (1977), *A History of Thought on Economic Integration*, London: Macmillan.

Markusen, A. and C.C. Diniz (2003), 'The differential competitiveness of Latin American regions: opportunities and constraints', paper presented at a seminar organized by the Inter-American Development Bank on Global and Local: Confronting the Challenges of Regional Development, 22 March, Milan.

Mattoo, A. and C. Fink (2003), 'Regional agreements and trade in services: policy issues', *Journal of Economic Integration* (forthcoming).

McCleery, R. (1993), 'Modeling NAFTA: macroeconomic effects', in K. Ohno (ed.), *Regional Integration and Its Impact on Developing Countries*, Tokyo: Institute of Developing Economies, pp.42–60.

McMillan, J. (1993), 'Does regional integration foster open trade? Economic theory and GATT's Article XXIV', in K. Anderson and R. Blackhurst (eds), *Regional Integration and Global Trading System*, London: Harvester Wheatsheaf, pp.203–241.

McNulty, S. (2001), 'Singapore seeks strength via Asian model of integration', *Financial Times*, 11 January, p.6.

Meade, J.E. (1955), *The Theory of Customs Union*, Amsterdam: North Holland.

Meltzer, A. (1991), 'US leadership and post-war progress', in *Policy Implications of Trade and Currency Zones*, Kansas City: Federal Reserve Bank of Kansas City, pp.237–258.

Michaely, M. (1998), 'Partners to a preferential trade agreement: implications of varying size', *Journal of International Economics*, **46** (1), 73–85.

Midelfart-Knarvik, K-H. and H.G. Overman (2002), 'Delocation and European integration: is structural spending justified?', *Economic Policy*, **35** (2), 321–359.

Midelfart-Knarvik, K-H., H.G. Overman, S. Redding and A.J. Venables (1999), *The Location of Industry in Europe*, London: Centre for Economic Policy Research.

Milner, C. and R. Read (2002), 'Introduction: the GATT Uruguay Round, trade liberalization and the WTO', in C. Milner and R. Read (eds), *Trade*

Liberalization, Competition and the WTO, Cheltenham: UK and Northampton, MA, USA: Edward Elgar, pp.1–22.

Monteagudo, A.S. and Y. Watanaki (2002), 'Asymmetries and cooperation in the free trade areas of the Americas', paper presented at the conference on *Confronting the Challenges of Regional Development in Latin America*, held in Milan, Italy, on 22 March.

Moore, M. (2000), 'Globalizing Regionalism', Press releases. *WTO News*, Geneva. http://www.wto.org/english/news_e/spmm_e/spmm45_e.htm, accessed November 2000.

Mundell, R. (1964), 'Tariff preferences and terms of trade', *Manchester School Economic Social Studies*, **32**, 1–13.

Nagarajan, N. (1998), 'On the evidence for trade diversion in MERCOSUR', *Integration and Trade*, **2** (6), 3–30.

Ng, F. and A. Yeats (2003), 'Major trade trends in Asia', World Bank Policy Research Working Paper 3084, World Bank, Washington, DC.

Noland, M. (1994), 'Asia and the NAFTA', in Y.S. Kim and K.S. Oh (eds), *The US-Korea Economic Partnership*, Aldershot and Brookfield, VT: Ashgate Publishers, 134–148.

Nordstrom, H. (1995), 'Customs unions, regional trading blocs and welfare', in R.E. Baldwin, P. Haaparanta and J. Kinder (eds), *Expanding Membership of European Union*, Cambridge: Cambridge University Press, pp.54–78.

Ocampo, J.A. (2003), 'Asymmetries and co-operation in the Free Trade Area of Americas', paper presented at a seminar organized by the Inter-American Development Bank on Global and Local: Confronting the Challenges of Regional Development in Milan, on 22 March.

OECD (Organization for Economic Co-operation and Development) (2000), *One Year On*, Paris: OECD.

OECD (Organization for Economic Co-operation and Development) (2001), *An Economic Survey of Euro Area*, Paris: OECD.

OECD (Organization for Economic Co-operation and Development) (2002), *Foreign Direct Investment for Development: Maximizing Benefits and Minimizing Costs*, Paris: OECD.

Ohmae, Kenichi (1985), *Triad Power*, MacMillan Free Press.

Page, S. (2000), *Regionalism among Developing Countries*, London: Macmillan.

Panagariya, A. (1998), 'Should East Asia go regional?', in H. Lee, D.W. Roland-Holst (eds), *Economic Development and Cooperation in the Pacific Basin*, Cambridge: Cambridge University Press, pp.119–159.

Panagariya, A. (1999), 'The regional debate: an overview', *World Economy*, **22** (4), 477–511.

Perroni, C. and J. Whally (1996), 'How severe is global retaliation risk under increasing regionalism?', *American Economic Review*, Papers and Proceedings, **86**, 57–61.

Petri, P. (1994), 'The East Asian trading bloc: an analytical history', in R. Garnaut and P. Drysdale (eds), *Asia Pacific Regionalism: Readings in International Economic Relations*, Sydney: Harper Educational Publishers, pp.107–124.

Petri, P. (1997), 'Measuring and comparing progress in APEC', *ASEAN Economic Bulletin*, **14** (1), 44–62.

Pomfret, R. (1995), 'APEC and the lessons of Asian growth', Policy Discussion Paper No. 95/09, Centre for International Economic Studies, University of Adelaide.

Poyhonen, P. (1963), 'A tentative model for the flows of trade between countries', *Weltwirtschatftliches Archiv*, **90** (1), 85–104.

Puga, D. (2002), 'European regional policy in the light of recent location theories', *Journal of Economic Geography*, **2** (4), 372–406.

Ravenhill, J. (2003), 'The move to preferential trade in the western Pacific rim', *Asia-Pacific Issues*, No. 69, June, Honolulu, Hawai'I, East–West Centre.

Riezman, R. (1999), 'Can bilateral trade agreements help induce free trade?', CSGR Working Paper No. 44/99, Centre for the Study of Globalization and Regionalization, University of Warwick.

Roessler, F. (1993), 'The relationship between regional integration agreements and the multilateral trade order', in K. Anderson and R. Blackhurst (eds), *Regional Integration and the Global Trading System*, New York: Harvester Wheatsheaf, pp.180–202.

Rutherford, T.F. and J. Martinez (2000), 'Welfare effects of regional trade integration of Central American and Caribbean nations with NAFTA and MERCOSUR', *World Economy*, June, 799–825.

Sachs, J.D. and A. Warner (1995), 'Economic reform and the process of global integration', *Brookings Papers on Economic Activity*, No. 1. Washington, DC: Brookings Institution, pp.1–118.

Safadi, R. and A. Yeats (1993), 'The North American Free Trade Agreement: its effect on South Asia', *Journal of Asian Economics*, **5** (2), 197–216.

Sager, M.A. (1997), 'Regional trade agreements: their role and the economic impact on trade flows', *The World Economy*, **20** (1), January, 239–273.

Sakakibara, E. and S. Yamakawa (2003), 'Regional integration in East Asia: challenges and opportunities', Part I and Part II, Keio University.

Schiff, M. (1997), 'Small is beautiful: preferential trade agreements and the impact of country size', *Journal of Economic Integration*, **12** (2), 359–387.

Schiff, M. (1999), 'Will the real "natural trading partner" please stand up?', Policy Research Working Paper No. 2161, World Bank, Washington, DC.

Schiff, M. (2001), 'Multilateral trade liberalization, political disintegration, and the choice of free trade agreements versus customs unions', mimeo, World Bank, Washington, DC.

Schiff, M. (2002), 'Regional integration and development in small states', mimeo, World Bank, Washington, DC.

Schiff, M. and L.A. Winters (2003), *Regional Integration and Development*, New York: Oxford University Press.

Schill, M. (1996), *Small is Beautiful*, Working Paper No. 1668, World Bank, Washington, DC.

Schott, J.J. (2002), 'Trade pacts with big powers are essential for developing countries', *Financial Times*, 6 November, p.12.

Scollay, R. (1994), 'Open regionalism and regional trading arrangements', in G. Yen (ed.), *New Directions in Regional Trade Liberalization and Investment Cooperation*, Singapore: Pacific Economic Cooperation Council, pp.120–146.

Scollay, R. (2000), 'CER: future developments', in D. Robertson (ed.), *AFTA-CER: A Way Forward?*, Melbourne: Melbourne Business School, pp.68–90.

Sender, H. (2001), 'China steps up chip production', *Asian Wall Street Journal*, January 10, pp.N1 N2.

Serra Puche, J. (1998), 'Regionalism and the WTO', paper presented at the World Trade Organization Symposium, Geneva, Switzerland, 50 Years: Looking Back, Looking Forward, on 30 April.

Sharer, R. (1999), 'Trade: an engine of growth for Africa', *Finance and Development*, **36** (4), 22–25.

Smith, M. and A.J. Venables (1988), 'Completing the internal market in European Community: some industry simulations', *European Economic Review*, **32** (8), 1501–1525.

Solonga, I. and L. Alan Winters (1999), 'How has regionalism in the 1990s affected trade?', Policy Research Working Paper 2156, World Bank, Washington, DC.

Spinanger, D. (2002), 'RIAs and contingent protection: are anti-dumping measures really an issue?', paper presented at the conference on The Changing Architecture of the Global Trading System, organized by the World Trade Organization on 26 April, in Geneva.

Srinivasan, T.N. and G. Canonero (1993), 'Preferential trading arrangements: estimating the effects on South Asian countries', mimeo, Yale University and the World Bank.

Srinivasan, T.N. and G. Canonero (1995), 'Preferential trading arrangements in South Asia: theory, empirics and policy', mimeo, Yale University and the World Bank.

Stiglitz, J. (2002), *Globalization and its Discontents*, New York: W.W. Norton.

Summers, L.H. (1991), 'Regionalism and the world trading systems', in *Policy Implications of Trade and Currency Zones*, Kansas City: Federal Reserve Bank of Kansas City, pp.295–302.

Suppel, R. (2000), *Emerging Europe's EU Accession: The Economics'*, London: Morgan Guaranty Trust Company.

Tinbergen, J. (1966), *Shaping the World Economy: Suggestions for an International Economic Policy*, New York: Twentieth Century Fund.

Trachtman, J.P. (2003), 'Toward open regionalism? Standardization and regional integration under Article XXIV of the GATT', *Journal of International Economic Law*, **6** (2), 230–256.

Trebilcock, M.J., M.A. Chandler and R. Howse (1990), *Trade and Transitions*, London: Routledge.

UN (United Nations) (2001), *World Economic Situation and Prospects 2001*, New York: UN.

UNCTAD (United Nations Conference on Trade and Development) (2000), *The World Investment Report 2000*, Geneva and New York: UNCTAD.

Vamvakidis, A. (1997), 'International integration and economic growth', PhD dissertation, Department of Economics, Harvard University.

Vamvakidis, A. (1998), 'Regional integration and economic growth', *World Bank Economic Review*, **12** (2), 251–270.

Vamvakidis, A. (1999), 'Regional trade agreements or broad liberalization: which path leads to faster growth?', *IMF Staff Papers*, **46** (1), 42–68.

Vedrine, H. (2000), 'A greater Europe by reform', *Financial Times*, 7 September, p.14.

Venables, A.J. (2002), 'Winners and losers from regional integration agreements'. Available on the Internet at http://econ.lse.ac.uk/staff/ajv/research_material.html#regint, accessed April 2003.

Venables, A.J. (2004), 'Regional integration agreements: a force for convergence or divergence?', *Economic Journal*.

Venables, A.J. and L.A. Winters (2003), 'Economic integration in the Americas: European perspectives', unpublished manuscript, London School of Economics.

Viner, J. (1950), *The Customs Union Issue*, New York: Carnegie Endowment for International Peace.

Wain, B. (2000), 'Asia-Pacific body loses its way', *Asian Wall Street Journal*, 10 November, p.8.

WB (World Bank) (2000), *Trade Blocs*, New York: Oxford University Press.

Whalley, J. (2000), 'Why do countries seek regional trade agreements?', Working Paper No. 5552, National Bureau of Economic Research, Cambridge, MA.

Winters, L.A. (1999), 'Regionalism for developing countries: assessing costs and benefits', in J. Burki, G. Perry and S. Calvo (eds), *Trade: Towards Open Regionalism*, Washington, DC: World Bank, pp.141–185.

Winters, L.A. (2000), 'Regionalism and multilateralism: what do economists have to say?', *DEC Note*, Washington, DC: World Bank.

Wolf, H. (2000), '(Why) do borders matter for trade?', in G. Hess and E. van Wincoop (eds), *International Macroeconomics*, Cambridge: Cambridge University Press, pp.159–186.

World Investment Report (2000), New York and Geneva: United Nations.

WTO (World Trade Organization) (1995), 'Regional and the world trading systems', report, Geneva.

WTO (World Trade Organization) (1998), 'Report of the Committee on Regional Trade Agreements to the General Council', WT/REG/7, Geneva.

WTO (World Trade Organization) (1999), *Annual Report 1999*, Geneva: WTO.

WTO (World Trade Organization) (2001), 'WTO Ministerial Conference: Briefing Notes', Geneva. Available on the Internet at http://www.heva.wto-ministerial.org/english/thewto_e/minist_e/minist01_e/brief_e/brief01.

WTO (World Trade Organization) (2001a), 'Doha Ministerial Communiqué', published by the WTO on 14 November 2001.

WTO (World Trade Organization) (2002a), 'Regional trade integration under transformation', background paper prepared by the Trade Policy Review Division of the WTO for the conference on The Changing Architecture of the Global Trading System, organized by the World Trade Organization on 26 April, Geneva.

WTO (World Trade Organization) (2002b), *Basic Information on Regional Trade Agreements*, WT/REG.W/44, Committee on Regional Trade Agreements, Geneva.

WTO (World Trade Organization) (2002c), *Annual Report 2002*, Geneva: WTO.

WTO (World Trade Organization) (2003),'Trade liberalization statistics', available on the WTO website at http://www.gatt.org/ July 02.

WTO (World Trade Organization) (2003a), 'A changing landscape of RTAs', published by the WTO on 14 November 2001.

Yamazawa, I. (1998), 'Progress towards the Bogor target: a quantitative assessment', report, Pacific Economic Cooperation Council, Japan Committee, Tokyo.

Yamazawa, I. (2000), 'Regional cooperation in a changing global environment: success and failure of East Asia', paper presented at the UNCTAD X, High-Level Round Table on Trade and Development, in Bangkok, 12 February.

Yeats, A. (1998), 'What can be expected from African regional trade agreements? Some empirical evidence', mimeo, World Bank, Washington, DC.

Yi, S.S. (1997), 'Stable coalition structures with externalities', *Games and Economic Behavior*, **20** (1), 201–31.

Zissimos, B. and D. Vines (2000), 'Is WTO's Article XXIV a free trade barrier?', CSGR Working Paper No. 49/00, Centre for the Study of Globalization and Regionalization, University of Warwick, February.

Zoellick, R.B. (2002), 'Falling behind on free trade', *New York Times*, Section 4, 14 April, p.13.

Index